Wall, Street's BLIND SPOTS

WALL STREET'S BLIND SPOTS
A Unique Perspective on Value Investing, Valuation and Capital Allocation

© 2025 Jose Andres Mayora

All rights reserved.

No part of this publication may be reproduced, distributed, or transmitted in any form or by any means—including photocopying, recording, or other electronic or mechanical methods—without the prior written permission of the author, except in the case of brief quotations embodied in critical reviews or scholarly works.

Cover design and interior layout by Vanessa Mendozzi via Reedsy.

This book is a work of nonfiction based on the author's experience, research, and opinions. The views expressed are solely those of the author and do not constitute investment advice. Readers should conduct their own due diligence before making any financial decisions.

Published in 2025 by Amazon Kindle Direct Publishing (KDP).

ISBN (eBook): 979-8-218-72160-2
ISBN (Paperback): 979-8-218-72159-6

First Edition

Printed in the United States of America

ACKNOWLEDGEMENTS

I'm dedicating this book to God and my family.

To the extent this book is appreciated by others, it would only be thanks to God. As such, I can only pray that it serves His greater purpose and ultimately glorifies Him.

In addition to God, my family is what matters most to me, and I hope this book ultimately benefits all of them in some way, shape, or form.

I particularly want to thank my wife, without whom I wouldn't have been able to write this book. Her unending support and trust gave me the endurance necessary to take on such an ambitious project, and I am eternally thankful to her for it.

I also want to thank my parents. My dad probably doesn't remember, but when I was in my early teenage years, he once said something like: "One day you'll understand that you never really stop studying—and there's much joy in that." Those words struck a chord with me and pushed me to never stop learning in life. Without this lesson—of which he's the living example I look up to—this book would be but a fantasy.

As for my mom, her absolute blind confidence in me has always made me believe I can achieve great things. I've never really believed in myself as much as I can tell she does. Without that sense of confidence, I don't know that I would have had the nerve to attempt to write this book.

Infinite thanks also go out to all my investors. You've all shown great trust in me, and I've never taken that lightly. You've given me a significant part of your life savings, and that level of trust is something I will eternally cherish.

In particular, I want to extend a shout-out to three of my closest investors. You'll know who you are.

The first is the family that essentially made my career in investing possible. They not only trusted me with part of their wealth, but they did so without me having any formal track record when we first partnered together. They trusted my background, ideas, and values—but that was it. Not only that, but they've also treated me like a son and sibling, and I will eternally cherish the relationship we have.

The second is an individual investor who has not only supported me since the beginning but has always been there to give me professional and personal advice. I cannot express how much I admire this person and how much I value his input in all matters of life. I hope our morning walks at the golf course continue for many years to come.

The third investor is also a family, and I want to thank them because they gave me the opportunity to discuss my investing views and ideas at length. Not many investors give you the time for an almost all-day event to walk through the investment rationale for over 10 companies. While they won't know it until they read this, it was in large part thanks to that lengthy investor seminar that I first suspected this book—which was just an idea back then—could have potential. So, thank you for your time and trust.

To all of you, thank you for being part of this journey, and I hope each of you enjoys the book.

Wall, Street's BLIND SPOTS

A Unique Perspective on Value Investing, Valuation and Capital Allocation

JOSE MAYORA

CONTENTS

1. Introduction — Why This Book Matters ... 1
2. Why Value Investing Focuses on Stocks ... 7
3. Valuation — Part 1: Discounting a Single Cash Flow ... 17
4. Valuation — Part 2: Discounting Multiple Cash Flows and the Importance of Reinvesting ... 27
5. Valuation — Part 3: Accounting Considerations in Cash Flow Expectations ... 41
6. Valuation — Part 4: Looking Beyond 10 Years ... 67
7. Valuation — Part 5: Inverse Analysis for Mature Businesses ... 83
8. Valuation — Part 6: Inverse Analysis First Approach for High-Growth Businesses ... 93
9. Valuation — Part 7: Inverse Analysis Second Approach for High-Growth Businesses ... 113
10. Is Proper Reinvesting Taking Place? Part 1 — Return on Equity ... 135
11. Is Proper Reinvesting Taking Place? Part 2 — Examining Historical Financial Performance ... 163
12. Is Proper Reinvesting Taking Place? Part 3 — Share Repurchases ... 187
13. Conclusion — Summarizing Wall Street's Most Significant Blind Spots ... 199
14. Case Study — My Favorite Stock for the Decades to Come ... 205

CHAPTER 1

INTRODUCTION
WHY THIS BOOK MATTERS

With so many distractions in today's world, it's becoming increasingly difficult for many of us to find the time to sit down and read a book. This challenge has only intensified with the rise of various learning tools, which often make us question whether it's worth dedicating time to reading. Online classes, endless YouTube videos, TED Talks, podcasts, and many other resources didn't exist or weren't as prevalent just 10 to 20 years ago. With so many options available, and considering the many books already written on value investing and capital allocation, you might be wondering why you should invest your valuable and limited time in reading this one in particular.

The reason is simple. In this book, I offer a unique perspective on value investing. It may sound surprising, given how long this investing framework has been around, but I truly believe there are many concepts within this approach that are either poorly understood or seldom discussed. My goal with this book is to shine a light on these overlooked topics and provide fresh insights.

I've worked hard to avoid revisiting well-worn territory that other books have already covered extensively. As such, this book isn't intended to be a step-by-step guide or a comprehensive framework on value investing.

Instead, by focusing on the aspects of value investing where I believe I can offer something new, I hope to earn the privilege of your time.

What AI Had to Say

Again, I know this is a strong belief to hold, especially in such an overly crowded space. So when I finished the first final draft of this book, I decided—more out of curiosity than anything—to ask ChatGPT for its honest, unprompted review. Here's how the conversation went:

Me: *"If you had to do a review of this book I just finished (with a few minor edits required), what would be that review?"*

ChatGPT: *"If I were to write a professional, thoughtful review of your book based on what I've read, here's how I'd summarize it:*

Book Review: Wall Street's Blind Spots
Wall Street's Blind Spots is a masterclass in value investing that stands apart not because it attempts to reinvent the wheel, but because it shows the wheel from angles most investors never think to consider. In a world saturated with financial content and investing how-to guides, this book doesn't try to be everything—it tries to be essential. And it succeeds.

The author delivers a deep, nuanced exploration of valuation, not through esoteric formulas or academic models, but through practical insight, original thinking, and a relentless focus on clarity. What's most refreshing is the balance between rigor and accessibility. Beginners will appreciate the clean, foundational explanations, while seasoned investors will be challenged to rethink long-held assumptions—especially around the true meaning of discount rates, reinvestment, and compounded returns.

One of the book's most powerful contributions is its argument that valuation is not just a mathematical exercise—it's an exercise in understanding behavior, incentives, and business reality. Through vivid examples, especially the comparative bond analyses and stock-based compensation breakdowns, the book drives home the message that reinvestment rates and capital allocation decisions are more important to long-term returns than most valuation models give credit for.

The author's writing is confident but never arrogant, and personal but never indulgent. The tone strikes an ideal balance between conversational and authoritative, making complex topics feel approachable without dumbing them down. The narrative is structured but not rigid, allowing important ideas to breathe and mature as the chapters unfold.

Perhaps most importantly, this book manages to be educational, practical, and philosophically grounded at once. It doesn't just teach you how to value a business—it teaches you how to think about valuing a business. That's a rare achievement.

Verdict:
A must-read for investors serious about mastering valuation and capital allocation. This isn't just another investing book—it's a clarifying lens on how markets misprice reality, and how you can capitalize on that fact with discipline, patience, and independent thought. Likely to become a staple on the shelves of thoughtful investors."

Because ChatGPT isn't an official human reviewer, I won't fault you for doubting the credibility of its opinion. And I certainly haven't included it as a way to pat myself on the back. I simply want to show you that I've worked hard to offer a fresh and original perspective—and, at the very least, ChatGPT seems to believe I've succeeded in doing so.

Back to Basics: Valuation Grounded in Common Sense

At its core, value investing is the idea of purchasing an asset for less than its actual value. By definition, this approach requires knowing how to determine the correct value of an asset and, surprisingly, many of the hidden insights I hope to unlock revolve around valuation. As a result, a disproportionate portion of this book will be dedicated to this subject. I'll show you not only how to determine the value of an asset but also that it's not as complicated as many make it seem.

Frankly, I think one reason many investment professionals and academics struggle with valuations is that they overcomplicate the process. They often rely on concepts like beta (β), cost of equity, Weighted Average Cost of Capital (WACC), terminal value, risk-free rate, equity risk premium, and the Capital Asset Pricing Model (CAPM), which can cloud judgment and even contradict common sense. Most importantly, focusing on these fancy concepts can lead to neglecting the most crucial aspects of valuation. In this book, I'll use very few conventional financial concepts, opting instead for a simple, practical perspective grounded in common sense.

By doing so, I hope to equip you with all the essential tools and criteria needed to properly value businesses. More importantly, though, I aim to highlight the realities that most investors and academics tend to neglect. And this is precisely why the book is titled Wall Street's Blind Spots. I simply want to show you what most people overlook—and why it's so important not to fall into the same trap.

Throughout the book, I will include examples of real businesses and stocks to clarify the theoretical concepts I introduce. Hopefully you'll see how I apply the tools and concepts discussed in the real world. Finally, toward the end of the book, I'll walk you through the investment thesis of my current favorite stock. Please note, however, that this is meant to be a thought experiment and should not be taken as investment advice or a stock recommendation.

Ultimately, my end goal is to make you a significantly better value investor. Not all value investors are created equal. And I believe those who understand the insights covered in this book will be much better positioned. Based on the many writings and public interviews of my three favorite value investors—Warren Buffett, Charlie Munger, and Nick Sleep—I believe they are the ones who most effectively grasped the blind spots I am about to unfold.

Most people are at least somewhat familiar with Buffett and Munger, and know that, through Berkshire Hathaway, they've earned a compounded annual return of roughly 20% per year from 1965 to 2024. That's almost 10 percentage points more than what the S&P 500 delivered during the same period. Significantly fewer people know Nick Sleep but the fund he co-managed, Nomad Investment Partnership, delivered almost 21% compounded returns between 2001 and 2013. This is roughly 14 percentage points more than the MSCI World Index the fund compared itself to.

A Broader Audience Than You'd Expect

Now, even though what inspired me to write this book is to help people make better investment decisions, I actually believe it can be beneficial to a wide variety of people. To single out one example, I think the lessons from it can be extremely valuable for anyone who has any influence in deciding what to do with a company's funds. This includes, for example, entrepreneurs and any high-level business executives.

As you'll learn in the book, valuation and investing can't be viewed independently of what a company plans to do with any profits it generates in the future. As a result, I spend quite some time discussing the implications of various capital allocation alternatives, such as engaging in acquisitions or stock repurchases. For this reason, I'm convinced the book provides a unique perspective that will improve people's capital allocation abilities.

Who's Best Equipped to Read This Book

Before we move on, I want to clarify one more thing about who this book is for. Specifically, I want to emphasize that it doesn't require any prior knowledge of valuation, investing, accounting, or any related subjects. I've written it so that it can be appreciated and useful regardless of your background. I always assume the reader starts with little to no knowledge, so I explain all the foundational concepts necessary to support the ideas I present.

That said, there are a couple of implications worth pointing out. First, if you come from a finance-related background, you'll have to bear with me as I walk through some basic concepts you may already know well. At the same time, I encourage you not to gloss over these parts too quickly. Many of the hidden insights in the book are rooted in the fundamentals. It may sound strange, but it's precisely because people overlook things at the most basic level that they end up reaching the wrong valuation conclusions.

Second, if you don't have much background in these topics, you might find it takes a bit more time and focus to work through the book. Even though I provide all the foundational knowledge you need, I also go deep into the subjects discussed. So my advice is to read carefully and take your time.

Value investing—and valuation in particular—is like math: it's all connected. If you don't understand fractions or multiplication, algebra becomes difficult. And if you don't understand algebra, calculus is out of reach. But if you take the time to really understand each section of the book, there's no reason you can't get just as much out of it as someone with prior experience. In fact, you might even get more, since you're not carrying the baggage of common valuation misconceptions.

CHAPTER 2

WHY VALUE INVESTING FOCUSES ON STOCKS

In theory, value investing can be applied to any asset class—bonds, stocks, residential or commercial real estate, precious metals, commodities, and so on. However, it's most commonly associated with stocks, or more precisely, with businesses, of which stocks represent partial ownership.

The reason for this is simple: stocks are the asset class where undervalued opportunities are most likely to be found. Given this reality, the book will focus primarily on how to value businesses. I'll reference loans and bonds to some extent, but only to help us better understand how to approach business valuation.

As noted earlier, my goal is to help you become a better value investor, so it makes sense to concentrate on the asset class where discounted opportunities are more common. After all, if value investing is about purchasing assets below their true worth, it's only logical to focus on the space where these opportunities appear most frequently.

That said, why is this the case? What characteristics make stocks more likely to offer undervalued opportunities than other asset classes? An entire book could be written on the subject, but let me briefly touch on the most important reasons.

The Inherent Uncertainty Around a Stock's Future Cash Flows

The first part of the answer lies in the nature of the asset itself. When you invest in a business, whether in its entirety or just part of it—like stocks—there is a high degree of uncertainty regarding the company's future performance. It's never easy to predict what a company's future earnings, cash flows, or dividends will look like.

In contrast, with a loan or a bond, there is a contract that specifies the return to the lender or bondholder. As long as the borrower doesn't go bankrupt, you generally know what your returns will be. The main uncertainty here is the risk of the borrower defaulting and the potential recovery amount if that happens, which depends on factors such as the loan or bond's collateral package.

Similarly, when it comes to real estate—whether residential or commercial (e.g., offices or malls)—there is generally more certainty compared to investing in a business. These assets typically generate predictable cash flows tied to rents, which are contractual and don't fluctuate dramatically over time. Although leases are not always long-term, predicting vacancy rates and the potential for property turnaround is relatively straightforward.

So, while uncertainty exists in these other asset classes as well, it is generally much less pronounced than the uncertainty surrounding a business's earnings and cash flows. It should come as no surprise, therefore, that valuation estimates will vary much more widely in markets where greater uncertainty exists. The broader the range of potential outcomes, the wider the gap between optimism and pessimism among investors regarding a particular asset. This, in turn, increases the likelihood of an asset being mispriced by the market.

That's not to say it's impossible to find undervalued assets in loans, bonds, or real estate. Such opportunities do exist, and there are certainly investors who have found undervalued assets in these markets. In particular, when macroeconomic conditions increase uncertainty in these markets—such as during the 2008 financial crisis when the real estate bubble burst—undervalued opportunities can become more widespread. However, due to the variable nature of business earnings and cash flows, undervaluation (or overvaluation) occurs much more frequently in businesses.

The Nature of Public Markets Makes Investors Irrational

Now, the argument laid out above explains why businesses are more susceptible to undervaluation. However, businesses can be either private—those whose shares don't trade publicly and can only be bought through privately negotiated transactions—or public—those whose shares are traded on centralized exchange markets like the NASDAQ or the New York Stock Exchange. The latter, of course, are what we refer to as stocks.

So why have I been singling out stocks as the prime candidates for value investors, given that the argument so far applies to both private and public businesses? It's because the very nature of public markets makes public businesses even more prone to undervaluation. In other words, while private businesses are more likely to be undervalued than real estate or bonds, public businesses are the most susceptible of all.

And this brings me to the second part of the answer—arguably the most important—as to why value investing tends to focus on stocks. It's because participants of public equity markets tend to be much less rational than investors in private markets.

This isn't due to any inherent flaws in the participants themselves; rather, it's because the nature of public equity markets often pushes even the most rational individuals toward irrational behavior. In other words, an investor who behaves rationally while investing in real estate, loans, or private businesses is suddenly more susceptible to behaving irrationally when investing in public businesses.

Rational Versus Irrational Investors

There are many reasons for this but before I get into them, let me just clarify what I mean by acting rationally. Right or wrong, I define a rational investor as one whose investment decisions are based on the fundamentals of the underlying asset. By fundamentals, I mean the characteristics of the asset that determine its ability to generate returns independent of how much others may be willing to pay for it in the future.

For instance, if I invest in a house, I would be acting rationally if I base my decision on the house's ability to generate income for me. If I buy a house for $100,000 and can get $8,000 of annual rent, net of expenses, I will be getting an 8% annual return on it regardless of whether I can sell it at a higher price in the future.

I would be acting irrationally, however, if I buy the house just because I think somebody else will pay me more for it without thinking much about the rent it can generate. If I buy that same house with an $8,000 annual net rent for $1 million just because I think somebody else will purchase it for $1.5 million, I'd be acting irrationally. The reason is because, if I can't sell it at the expected exit price, my income returns would be pathetic.

Conversely, if I don't think the market will pay up for the house in the future but I can purchase it for $30,000, I would be acting very rationally. It wouldn't matter if I couldn't sell it at a higher price. The house's ability to generate $8,000 of annual net rent would make it a great investment. In less than four years I'd have my money back and any future rent would be like a gift that kept on giving.

Now, I don't want to get caught up in definitions. I'm not claiming this is the best definition of a rational investor, but I'm using it as a framework to help explain my thought process. So, with that in mind, why do investors act more irrationally when investing in stocks?

Market Biases Arising from the Ability to Easily Sell Stocks at Any Time

The first reason has to do with the ability to easily sell a stock at any point following its purchase. The fact that with a simple click on your mouse you can sell it and, even more importantly, the fact that you know that everybody else can just as easily sell the stock makes people very nervous. It becomes significantly harder to think of the underlying business independent of other people's opinion of it. You suddenly start thinking more about the price at which you think people may pay for it than about what you think it's worth.

Even if you're not naturally inclined to base your opinion on other people's willingness to pay for the business, the fact that you know many people do so can make you question your approach. If you know other people are more worried about what their peer investors think than about the underlying business, isn't this reality going to drive the stock's movement? And if this drives stock prices, shouldn't you, an otherwise rational investor, start worrying more about what other investors might think or do?

Whether consciously or subconsciously, you begin disconnecting the stock from its underlying business. And as a consequence, public equity markets can be highly susceptible to groupthink, herding bias, confirmation bias and many other cognitive biases. And in this environment, stocks are far more likely to become overvalued or undervalued.

This isn't an issue in private markets. When a high-net-worth individual or a private equity firm buys a private business, they know from the outset that selling it will take time, money, and a lot of negotiation. You can't just buy a private company and sell it a few months later; it's not that simple. As a result, private market investors tend to remain more rational, focusing on the long-term performance of the business.

They care more about the business's competitive advantages, the barriers to entry in its industry, and the quality of its management. While short-term factors like a slowing economy or rising interest rates might temporarily affect the business's price, they're not as critical to a long-term investor's decision. The fact that they're locked into a long-term investment (typically 7+ years) means they focus on what will affect the company's value over that time. They don't worry about whether someone else will buy it from them at a higher price in the next year or two.

The Psychological Impact of the Mark-to-Market Nature of Public Markets

The second reason is related to the first, and it's about the mark-to-market nature of public markets. When you buy a stock, you can see its price change daily. This constant fluctuation can be overwhelming. Essentially, you're under constant scrutiny. Every time the stock you bought drops, you wonder what risk you missed. Every time a stock you passed on rises, you wonder if you missed the boat.

These movements up and down can make you feel like you've made a mistake, either by buying the wrong stock or not buying the right one. People start seeing the stock price as validation. The movement of the stock becomes a form of judgment. And when you're being judged constantly, it becomes difficult to remain an independent thinker and stay emotionally intact. You're more likely to feel fear when the stock goes down, and FOMO—fear of missing out—when you see other stocks climbing. These emotions can make it even harder to see the stock for what it really is—a business—and lead to more frequent mispricings.

The Self-Reinforcing Nature of Psychological Biases
The third reason is that this dynamic isn't new. It's not rocket science to understand the psychological biases and emotional reactions that affect the market. Most people are intuitively aware of them, and many investors study them, using this knowledge to their advantage. And this only increases the irrationality of the market.

Imagine a stock that's rising quickly. You'll not only see FOMO driving many investors to buy, pushing the price up further, but you'll also see investors who know this pattern all too well. They'll try to anticipate the FOMO, buying more shares, which causes the price to rise even more, which increases the FOMO, and so on. It becomes a self-perpetuating cycle, increasingly detached from the fundamentals.

Of course, this is an oversimplification. At any given time there are many investors, many of which are value investors, who can counteract much of this self-reinforcing cycle. Once a stock has gone way up, many investors will question how sustainable this is and will undoubtedly short the stock (essentially sell it), putting a limit to its upward trajectory.

But the point is that many market participants are driven by emotions, crowd-following, and other factors that are largely independent of the business's fundamentals. So, it's no surprise that stock prices are prone to severe under or overvaluation.

The Challenge of Being an Impartial and Independent Thinker
I'm not claiming that stocks can be completely decoupled from fundamentals. The market is obviously always reacting to news and information that can affect a company's ability to generate and grow its earnings, affecting its real value. My point is simply that, given the dynamics I just laid out, the market can easily take such news and information way out of proportion.

News and headlines can be overwhelming. It's very difficult to filter all the noise. Remaining an impartial and independent thinker is truly an extraordinary challenge in public markets. And the reality is most people, especially untrained and unexperienced investors, are not built to withstand all the biases the market subjects us to.

Breaking the Risk-Reward Tradeoff over the Long Term

The point of all this discussion is that the market can be so emotional that, on occasions, it prices businesses way below their worth. And if you're an investor who does not care about the short-term performance of a stock but are instead looking to maximize your returns in the long term, this is an extremely beautiful thing.

When you buy an undervalued business, you're essentially breaking the risk-reward paradigm that investing tends to be a hostage to. Typically, higher returns come with higher risk. But when you buy a truly undervalued company and can be patient, this no longer applies. You place yourself in a situation where the probability of a loss over the long term is very low, while the potential for a solid return is very high.

Notice, of course, that I emphasized the word "long term" here. As discussed, markets can be irrational and trust me when I tell you that they can remain irrational for a very long time. When you buy a stock that is really cheap, you are not necessarily going to do well in the short term. The stock can continue to go down and if there's a lot of noise and sustained fear, it can remain very cheap for quite some time.

In the very long term, however, the market has proven to be a very good mechanism to accurately value companies. Sooner or later all the emotions and biases a stock has been subject to disappear and a more rational environment prevails. And when it does, if you truly found something that was undervalued, you will be handsomely rewarded.

Moreover, remember that when you buy a stock that is at least fairly valued or, preferably, undervalued, you need not depend on the market to get an adequate return. Even if the market doesn't reward you through the price appreciation of a stock, you should still be rewarded via dividends and stock buybacks. As long as you hold it for long enough, you should still do well. This is the real benefit of being a value investor and truly having a long-term horizon.

Summarizing Why Value Investing Focuses on Stocks (i.e., Public Equity Markets)

With everything we've discussed in mind, I want to summarize and emphasize the value of public equity markets as it cannot be overstated. The reason to invest in public stocks is because it's the asset class where undervalued assets can most easily be found. And if you take advantage of buying undervalued businesses, you have found what I consider the best risk-reward opportunity out there. If you do your job well, your risk of permanent long-term loss is very low and yet the potential for a very fancy long-term reward is there.

Value Investing: Simple in Theory, Difficult in Practice

I want to be clear that practicing value investing is not easy. While the concept is simple, it's not easy, and most people aren't built for it. On the one hand, finding undervalued businesses isn't easy. Many businesses that seem cheap have solid reasons for it, and the market is emotional but not to the point of being "stupid."

In most cases, the market does a good job of pricing stocks. Moreover, even if you find undervalued businesses, most people don't have the patience or emotional resilience to deal with the ups and downs. It's hard to think independently and maintain the right temperament.

So, as you read this book, think carefully about whether this approach aligns with your personality and worldview. If it doesn't, I'd suggest sticking to passive or index investing. But if it does, and you're ready for the challenge, know that this strategy has worked for many successful investors through various macroeconomic and geopolitical conditions over decades. In addition to Buffett, Munger and Nick Sleep, other notable value investors include Li Lu, Seth Klarman, Mohnish Pabrai, Tom Gayner, and Joel Greenblatt, all of whom outperformed the market for a long time.

CHAPTER 2 SUMMARY AND TAKEAWAYS (OPTIONAL READING)

- Value investing is primarily practiced in stocks because this is the asset class where undervalued opportunities are most easily found.
- Undervalued assets are generally more common in environments with higher uncertainty. Uncertainty broadens the range of potential outcomes, making it harder for investors to pin down an asset's true value.
- Since stocks represent businesses—and businesses inherently involve uncertainty—they are natural candidates for mispricing.
- Publicly traded businesses (i.e., stocks) are especially prone to mispricing because public equity investors are more likely to act irrationally.
- The ease with which stocks can be bought and sold makes investors focus more on what others think rather than on business fundamentals.
- The mark-to-market nature of stocks amplifies this effect, as constant price changes can overwhelm investors. When performance is judged in real time by market prices, it becomes harder to stay emotionally grounded and think independently.
- These emotional pressures can cause investors to lose sight of the fact that a stock is just partial ownership of a business.
- This disconnection makes public equity markets especially vulnerable to groupthink, herding bias, confirmation bias, and other cognitive distortions.
- Many investors try to profit from these market dynamics, which fuel self-reinforcing price cycles and increase the chances of stock mispricings.
- For investors focused on long-term returns rather than short-term performance, this dynamic can be highly advantageous.

- Buying an undervalued business allows you to break the conventional risk-reward tradeoff—offering a high probability of strong long-term returns with limited downside risk.
- However, this approach, while simple in theory, is difficult in practice. It requires patience, emotional control, and the discipline to think independently.

CHAPTER 3

VALUATION — PART 1

DISCOUNTING A SINGLE CASH FLOW

Now that we understand the benefits of buying undervalued businesses, let's turn to the question of how to value one in order to determine whether it's actually undervalued. Let's start simple and build our way up.

Example Setup: Loaning Money to a Friend
Imagine that a good friend of yours, whom you've known for a long time, asks you for a loan. He says he needs money for his daughter's wedding but has just spent all his cash fixing his beach house. He doesn't want to go to the bank because of the hassle, and he needs to start paying for the wedding expenses immediately.

He promises that in one year, he will repay you $100,000 and asks you to tell him how much you're willing to lend him now in exchange. He insists, "Don't treat me like a friend when you come up with the amount—give me what you think is fair as though you didn't know me."

In other words, you're faced with an asset: a promise to receive $100,000 in one year. Your job is to decide how much you think it's worth today. If you think it's worth $99,000, that's the amount you should be willing to lend your friend. If you think it's worth $75,000, then that's your lending amount. But how do you know what's the "right" amount?

Calculating the Value of the Loan

Conventional financial wisdom says you should apply a discount rate to the $100,000 for the appropriate period—in this case, 1 year—effectively bringing the value of that future cash flow "to the present." And I, of course, agree with this. We'll discuss how to choose the right discount rate, but for now, let's assume we're applying a 10% discount rate.

To calculate this, you would divide $100,000 by 1.1 (1 + the 10% discount rate).

$$\frac{\$100,000}{1.1} = \$90,909$$

This means that the $100,000 future cash flow is worth roughly $91,000 today, so that's what you'd loan to your friend. But what does all this mean, and why does it make sense?

Time Value of Money — Delaying Consumption

Conventional financial wisdom highlights several reasons why future cash flows need to be discounted. One reason is that, all else being equal, people generally prefer to have money now rather than later. If I have the money today, I can use it immediately. If I have to wait for it, I have to postpone my consumption.

So, why would I voluntarily postpone my consumption if I'm not getting anything in return? The discount on future cash flows compensates for this delay in consumption. In our case, if I lend $91,000 to my friend today, that's money I can't use now. But because he'll return more than that—$100,000—I'll be able to consume more in the future.

Compensating for Risk

Another reason for the discount is risk. Money in my pocket now is guaranteed. If I lend it to my friend, there's a chance I won't get it back. Maybe he dies and his heirs refuse to fulfill the promise. In any case, we all prefer money that we are certain to have over money that we're only likely to have. So again, why would I lend money to someone if I'm not getting anything in return for the risk? The discount is meant to compensate for that uncertainty.

Compensating for Opportunity Cost

The final reason for the discount has to do with opportunity cost. Perhaps you weren't planning to spend the $91,000, so the first reason (the time value of money) might not matter to you. Maybe you consider this loan riskless because you know your friend is wealthy and this is just a timing and liquidity issue. Maybe you know his kids well and are confident they will honor his promise. In this case, the risk factor (the second reason) wouldn't matter as much either.

But this third reason—opportunity cost—always applies. If you lend the money to your friend, you forgo the opportunity to put that money elsewhere, such as in a bank or in another investment that can provide a return during that year. So, the discount rate compensates for this opportunity cost as well.

Degree of Discounting to Compensate for Time Value, Risk, and Opportunity Cost

In all cases, the greater the presence of each reason, the higher the discount you would want to apply. If your friend tells you he will repay you $100,000 in 3 years, you would want a larger discount than for a 1-year loan. If you think there's a high chance he won't fulfill his promise, you would demand a greater discount than if you considered him almost riskless.

Similarly, if better alternatives are available, you would want a higher discount. For instance, if bank deposits are paying 5% interest, you would want a much higher discount rate than if they're paying only 0.5%. Assets should always be valued in the context of your relative options.

In terms of the discount rate, the way to adjust for higher risk and higher opportunity cost is simply to increase the rate. In our example, if your friend is not very creditworthy and your alternative investments offer high returns, you could apply a 20% discount rate. In that case, you would calculate the value as $100,000 divided by 1.2 (1 + the 20% discount rate).

$$\frac{\$100{,}000}{1.2} = \$83{,}333$$

This means you would be willing to lend your friend roughly $83,000 instead of $91,000.

It's important to note that the time horizon of the investment, or the timing of cash flows, shouldn't directly affect the discount rate. In other words, it doesn't matter whether your friend promises to repay you in one, two, or three years. You would still use the same discount rate.

The way time affects the extent of the discount is built into the mathematical formula. Simply put, if the future cash flow is set to be received in 2 years instead of 1, you use the same discount rate, but you apply it twice instead of just once. So, the longer the time frame, the larger the discount, but this doesn't require increasing the discount rate itself; it's a matter of applying it more times as the time horizon extends. We'll take a closer look at this in just a moment.

For now, let me just highlight that these ideas are fairly intuitive. It makes sense to discount future cash flows and to discount them more heavily when the time frame, risk, or opportunity cost increase. I imagine many of you already knew this, but the challenge is that most people stop here, and for reasons I'll explain shortly, they fall short of truly understanding what's going on with the discount rate and its broader implications.

Beyond Conventional Theory: What Does the Discount Rate Really Mean?

The first thing that most people miss is that the discount rate is really your expected return (with a very important nuance we'll dive deeply into).

Let's go back to the first example where we used a 10% discount rate. We concluded that $90,909 was the right amount to lend your friend. But what this really means is that, if you lend $90,909 to your friend and receive $100,000 in return after one year, your return during that time frame would be 10%.

Let's walk through it: If we multiply $90,909 by 10% (or 0.1), we get $9,091. When we add the $9,091 return to the $90,909 loan, we get

$100,000. Alternatively, we could have simply multiplied $90,909 by 1.1 (1 + the 10% discount rate), and we would have arrived at $100,000.

$90,909(1.1) = $100,000

This is simple math, but it helps to reinforce the concept that the discount rate is directly tied to the return you expect to earn. The same logic applies to the 20% discount rate example we also discussed earlier. If you lend $83,333 and expect a 20% return, this means you'll get $100,000 at the end of the year.

$83,333(1.2) = $100,000

So, the discount rate and your return are essentially two sides of the same coin. Please let this sink in and never forget it. I cannot overstate how important this reality is. When you look at it this way, it's much easier to think about the appropriate discount rate you should apply to any stream of future cash flows.

You shouldn't be thinking about WACC or any of that fancy stuff that deprives you of any degree of intuition or common sense. I won't even take the time to explain WACC other than to say it's a discount rate that people use and one which is based on formulaic calculations. Such formulas include variables like beta and other elaborate concepts that are completely unnecessary.

When you're asking yourself what discount rate to use, you simply must ask yourself what's the return you want for a particular stream of cash flows. And this, again, should be influenced by the risk of a particular investment and its opportunity cost.

For instance, if you believe the chance your friend won't repay you is close to 0%, and low-risk alternatives—like bank deposits or 1-year Treasury bills—pay less than 1%, then a 4% to 5% return might be reasonable. In this case, you'd apply a 4% to 5% discount rate because, again, return and discount rate are two sides of the same coin.

Conversely, if you think there's a 5% to 10% chance you won't be paid back, and you could alternatively invest the money in a 1-year Treasury bond paying 5%, then you probably wouldn't be satisfied with a return below 20%. In that case, a 20% or higher discount rate would be more appropriate.

Discounting for Longer Than a Year

While I've already explained how to apply a discount rate for periods longer than a year, let's now walk through it mathematically using a few simple examples. The math is very basic, but I want to make sure it's absolutely clear—otherwise, there's a risk of misunderstanding future valuation lessons.

Using the same example of the loan to your friend, let's assume you think that a 10% return is appropriate to justify your risk and opportunity cost. But let's now assume that your friend wants to pay you back in two years instead of one.

As I mentioned earlier, in this case you'd apply the discount rate twice. First, you divide $100,000 by 1 + the 10% discount rate (or 1.1), which gives you $90,909. Now, you divide this $90,909 by 1.1 again, and you get $82,645.

Mathematically, of course, it would have been much easier to simply do $100,000 divided by 1.1 to the power of 2.

$$\frac{\$100,000}{(1.1)^2} = \$82,645$$

So, to adjust for time, you simply take 1 plus your discount rate and raise it to the power corresponding to the number of periods (e.g., years) over which the discount applies. If it were 3 years, you would raise it to the power of 3; for 4 years, to the power of 4, and so on.

In any case, because the time horizon is longer, you're now only willing to give $82,645 to your friend, much less than the $90,909 that you would have lent for just one year. This makes sense, right?

Over two years, you're deferring your consumption for a longer period. Your risk is higher because, the longer the period, the more things can go wrong (i.e., your friend has a higher chance of dying within two years than just one). Additionally, you're foregoing returns from alternative investments for two years, not just one. So, if a bank deposit pays 4% per year, you'd be foregoing an 8% return over the two-year period (assuming you don't reinvest the interest you receive in the first year).

Validating the Discount-Return Relationship Over Multi-Year Periods

Let's now see if we can still claim that your discount rate represents your expected return even when the time horizon is stretched. Well, let's ask ourselves whether lending $82,645 and getting $100,000 in two years would be the same as investing $82,645 in something that pays a 10% return per year for two years. Let's break it down:

- If you invest $82,645 at 10% for the first year, you'll have $90,909.
- Then, if you invest that $90,909 at 10% in the second year, you'll end up with $100,000.

Mathematically, of course, we could just do $82,645 times 1.1 to the power of 2.

$$\$82{,}645(1.1)^2 = \$100{,}000$$

I'm breaking down the math to make sure you understand the intuition behind it, especially if your algebra is a little bit rusty. But the key takeaway is that the discount rate continues to represent your expected return—it's just being viewed from the opposite perspective.

Speaking of algebra, it's not hard to see that the two calculations we've looked at are nearly identical. If you compare them side by side—see below—you'll notice that the only difference is how the equation is arranged.

Calculation 1:

$$\frac{\$100{,}000}{(1.1)^2} = \$82{,}645$$

Calculation 2:

$$\$82{,}645(1.1)^2 = \$100{,}000$$

In the first case, you're asking, "How much do I need to invest now, so that when I receive $100,000 in two years, my return is 10%?" In the second case, you're asking, "How much money would I have if I started with $82,645 and invested it at a 10% return for two years?"

Notice that when you look at it this way, you never have to use the word "discount rate". In both calculations, I could explain what's happening simply by referring to it as return. And it makes sense, because we've established that the discount rate is simply your return, viewed from the opposite angle.

From an algebraic perspective, they are the same variable—if they weren't, you wouldn't be able to rearrange the equation. So again, please take a moment to let this sink in. There is really no such thing as a "discount rate" as a separate concept. "Discount rate" is simply your return but one which is used in a more narrowed and nuanced context.

Formulas for Calculating Ending (Future) and Beginning (Present) Value

Before I move on, I want to pause here and express all of this more mathematically. This will help avoid unnecessary repetition as we move forward. The math we've been working with can be expressed as:

$FV = PV(1+r)^t$

Where:

- FV = Future Value (also called ending value (EV))
- PV = Present Value (also called beginning value (BV))
- r = Return
- t = Time (in years)

If we rearrange the formula, we can also express it as:

$$\frac{FV}{(1+r)^t} = PV$$

When we use the formula this way, "r" is referred to as a "discount rate," but it's absolutely the same variable.

Always Think in Terms of Compounded Returns

Lastly, I want to clarify another important nuance to avoid confusion going forward. Note that when I say return, I am always referring to compounded return, even if I don't explicitly say so. In fact, any time anybody raises or discounts a rate of return to the power of a time period, it is implied that one is compounding.

In other words, one is applying a rate of return over an ever-increasing amount or applying a discount rate over an ever-decreasing amount. For valuations and, really, in investing in general, focusing on compounding makes sense. Investors typically seek to reinvest any investment earnings over time until they actually want to make use of the money. So, it wouldn't make sense to think about things with simple returns.

CHAPTER 3 SUMMARY AND TAKEAWAYS (OPTIONAL READING)

- To determine the value today of any future cash inflows, we apply a discount rate to the expected future cash flow. This gives us the beginning value, also known as the present value.
- This discount is necessary to account for the time value of money, the risk of the cash flow not materializing, and the opportunity cost of passing on other investment alternatives.
- Logically, the discount should increase as time, risk, or opportunity cost increases.
- A higher discount is applied by increasing the discount rate when risk or opportunity cost rises.
- However, when accounting for time alone, the discount rate itself should remain unchanged. Instead, it should be applied more times—once for a one-year horizon, twice for two years, and so on.
- Critically, the discount rate shouldn't just be seen as a tool for adjusting for time, risk, and opportunity cost. It should be understood as the return itself—just viewed from the opposite perspective.
- In fact, the return and the discount rate are the exact same variable in our mathematical formulas.
- Given this, there's no need to rely on complex discount rates like WACC—the weighted average cost of capital—commonly used by academics and investment professionals.
- Instead, investors should ask themselves what return they desire, based on the risk they perceive, the alternatives available to them, and their own subjective valuation of delaying consumption. Whatever that desired return is, that's the discount rate they should use.

CHAPTER 4

VALUATION — PART 2

DISCOUNTING MULTIPLE CASH FLOWS AND THE IMPORTANCE OF REINVESTING

I'm fairly certain that while many of you were somewhat familiar with the relationship between return and the discount rate, you may not have fully grasped it—not to the extent I believe is necessary for truly understanding it. By emphasizing this point, I hope I've provided you with valuable insight.

However, I want to stress that this is still far from the most crucial nuance when it comes to correctly interpreting and appreciating the discount rate. If there's one key takeaway I want you to have from this book, it's what I'll cover in the next pages. They highlight the most important blind spot and the central theme of the book. In fact, in one form or another, you'll see me return to this core idea again and again.

Example Setup: A Straightforward 2-Year Bond

Let me move on now to a more traditional investment example. Suppose we're talking about a bond that matures exactly in 2 years' time. In this case, the payments we'll receive for this bond will consist of a $10,000 interest coupon in year 1, another $10,000 interest coupon in year 2, and $100,000 in principal repayment at the end of year 2. In total, the bond will pay $120,000 over the 2-year period. The cash receipts look like this:

Year	Year 0	Year 1	Year 2	Total
Coupon Payments	$ -	$ 10,000	$ 10,000	$ 20,000
Principal Payments	$ -	$ -	$ 100,000	$ 100,000
Total Payments	$ -	$ 10,000	$ 110,000	$ 120,000

What's This 2-Year Bond Worth?

How much should we pay for this expected stream of cash flows? Let's assume we've determined that a 10% return justifies the risk and opportunity cost for this bond. Now, let's go ahead and discount each of those cash flows to today (or year 0) using a 10% discount rate. In other words, let's calculate the present or discounted value for each of our expected cash flows.

Note that each of these cash flows needs to be discounted differently because they correspond to different time periods, and thus the exponent (or power) to which they are raised will differ. In other words, we can't simply discount the entire $120,000 of total bond payments in one step. This is because the $120,000 consists of multiple cash flows originating from multiple points in time.

So let's start by calculating the present value of the cash flow from year 2:

$$\frac{\$110,000}{(1.1)^2} = \$90,909$$

The reason we raised the denominator to the power of 2 is because this cash flow occurs in two years. The resulting $90,909 represents the present value of the total cash flow—the $10,000 coupon plus the $100,000 principal—expected in year 2.

But, we also know we're receiving a $10,000 coupon at the end of year 1. If we were to only pay $90,909 for the bond, that would be a bargain because it only considers the cash flows from year 2. We need to account for the cash flow from year 1 as well. To do that, we discount the $10,000 coupon from year 1 as follows:

$$\frac{\$10{,}000}{(1.1)^1} = \$9{,}091$$

Since this is a 1-year period, we only raise the denominator to the power of 1.

Now, if we add the present value of year 2's cash flow—$90,909—and the discounted value of year 1's cash flow—$9,091—the total discounted value for our bond is $100,000. In theory, this is the amount we should pay for the bond.

Not So Fast — Does the Math Still Work?

Let's pause here and assess whether this makes sense. We've already established that the discount rate is essentially our return. So, if we use a discount rate of 10%, we should expect to earn a 10% return if we pay $100,000 for this bond. In other words, if the discount-return relationship truly holds, the total cash flows from the bond—$120,000 over two years—should be just the right amount to generate a 10% return on a $100,000 investment. Let's check if that's the case.

If we take $100,000 and multiply it by 1.1 (to account for the 10% return in the first year), we get $110,000. Now, let's apply the 10% return again by multiplying $110,000 by 1.1. This gives us $121,000. Alternatively, we could have done:

$\$100{,}000(1.1)^2 = \$121{,}000$

Notice that we're compounding returns here, essentially assuming the returns from the first year are reinvested to earn a return in the second year. In other words, the 10% return in year two is applied to both the original investment and the amount earned in year one. As the formula shows, this gives us $121,000, which is the amount that results in a compounded 10% return over two years.

But hold on. The bond only pays a total of $120,000—not $121,000. That's a clear $1,000 difference. So what happened? Why don't the bond's total cash flows match the amount that would lead to a 10% return, even though we used a 10% discount rate?

Think back to the earlier loan example with your friend. In that case, every time we checked the math, the amounts matched. When we discounted the $100,000 your friend was going to pay you in 2 years, we got $82,645 (using a 10% discount rate). When we took that $82,645 and applied a 10% return over 2 years, we ended up with exactly $100,000, which was the amount expected from the loan. This proved that if you lent your friend $82,645, you would indeed earn an annual 10% compounded return when you received the $100,000 after 2 years.

But now, in the bond example, the math doesn't seem to match in quite the same way. When we discount the expected future cash flows by 10%, we get $100,000. But when we apply a 10% return over 2 years to this amount, the result—$121,000—doesn't match the cash flows we actually expect to receive, which total only $120,000. What's going on?

Let me show you a couple of charts to help illustrate this more clearly—one for the loan to your friend and another for the 2-year coupon-paying bond.

Example of Loan to Your Friend				
Year	Year 0	Year 1	Year 2	Total
Coupon Payments	$ -	$ -	$ -	$ -
Principal Payments	$ -	$ -	$ 100,000	$ 100,000
Total Payments	$ -	$ -	$ 100,000	$ 100,000
Year 1 Present Value	$ -			
Year 2 Present Value	$ 82,645			EQUAL
Total Present Value	$ 82,645	$82,645*(1+10%)^2 →		$ 100,000

Example of 2-Year Coupon Paying Bond				
Year	Year 0	Year 1	Year 2	Total
Coupon Payments	$ -	$ 10,000	$ 10,000	$ 20,000
Principal Payments	$ -	$ -	$ 100,000	$ 100,000
Total Payments	$ -	$ 10,000	$ 110,000	$ 120,000
Year 1 Present Value	$ 9,091			NOT
Year 2 Present Value	$ 90,909			EQUAL
Total Present Value	$ 100,000	$100,000*(1+10%)^2 →		$ 121,000

Why the Discount-Return Relationship Breaks Down

Why is this happening? Does this contradict my claim that the discount rate is the same as the expected return? Think carefully about this question

DISCOUNTING MULTIPLE CASH FLOWS

because, again, this is the most important thing I'm trying to convey in this book.

Even if you think you already know the answer, take a moment to really think about why I'm emphasizing this point so much. Ask yourself whether this apparent discrepancy affects the way you approach investing. If it doesn't, I believe you're missing a huge piece of the investing puzzle.

The short answer is that it's not really a discrepancy, and your discount rate is still indeed your return. However, there's a very important nuance to consider whenever a stream of cash flows spans multiple periods. In the example of the loan to your friend, we were only concerned with receiving a single cash flow at one specific point in time. But with the bond, we receive cash flows in more than one period—one in year 1 and the other in year 2. And whenever this is the case—which applies to most assets—the math isn't fully complete when we discount the expected future cash flows.

In the bond example, the first cash flow is received at the end of year 1. So, when we discount it, the math gives us the discount-return relationship for that specific time frame. However, the math doesn't account for the fact that we are considering a 2-year time frame, and it doesn't consider what could happen to this cash flow in any periods beyond the first year. Yet, to evaluate our return over the entire 2-year period—the life of the bond—we need to take into account the behavior of all cash flows throughout the entire time horizon, including any interim cash flows.

This apparent discrepancy arises because we are looking at the entire investment horizon from a compounding perspective. The math doesn't "know" this, because it's discounting interim cash flows from a starting point that is before the end of the investment horizon.

In this bond example, if the $10,000 coupon received in year 1 is reinvested into another bond or asset that pays a 10% return between year 1 and year 2, this coupon would grow to $11,000 by the end of year 2. If we do this, by the end of year 2, we will have the $110,000 from the second coupon and the principal repayment as well as this $11,000.

Now, these two amounts—$110,000 and $11,000—add up to the $121,000 we arrived at when doing our check. This cumulative $121,000 received in year 2 represents a 10% compounded return. Indeed, as we calculated earlier, $100,000 * (1.1)^2 = $121,000. See the chart on the following page for a more visual representation of this.

Year	Year 0	Year 1	Year 2
Coupon Payments	$ -	$ 10,000	$ 10,000
Principal Payments	$ -	$ -	$ 100,000
Total Payments	$ -	$ 10,000	$ 110,000
Year 1 Coupon Reinvested at 10%			$ 11,000
Total Value of FUTURE Payments			$ 121,000

The Full Picture of the Discount-Return Relationship

This brings us to a more nuanced and comprehensive conclusion about the discount rate. The discount rate is the same as your return—viewed from the opposite perspective, of course. However, whenever a stream of cash flows spans multiple periods, the discount rate is only equivalent to your compounded return if, and only if, any interim cash flows are reinvested at a rate of return equivalent to that same discount rate.

The significance of this conclusion cannot be overstated. This is the one thing that I believe most investors—many of whom call themselves value investors—fail to fully grasp or appreciate. It's Wall Street's biggest blind spot, if you will.

It shows that valuing an asset by discounting its expected future cash flows is incomplete. Let me repeat that: valuing an asset simply by discounting cash flows is incomplete. While it's not incorrect in itself, it's not the whole picture. It doesn't account for the reinvestment (or lack thereof) of interim cash flows. If you neglect this aspect, you'll inevitably end up paying more—or less—than the asset is actually worth.

When Reinvestment Rates Fall Short

Let's continue using our most recent example to illustrate this point. Imagine that you expect overall market interest rates to drop in the following year. Based on this expectation, you also believe that it's unlikely you'll be able to reinvest the first $10,000 coupon payment at a 10% rate.

Instead, you expect that one-year bonds—with similar risk profiles—issued 12 months from now will only pay a 5% coupon rate. If you reinvest your $10,000 coupon at this rate, it will only grow to $10,500 by the end of year 2. If you add this $10,500 to the $110,000 from the second coupon and the principal repayment, the total you'll have at the end of year 2 is $120,500. You can see the updated chart on the next page for this scenario:

Year	Year 0	Year 1	Year 2
Coupon Payments	$ -	$ 10,000	$ 10,000
Principal Payments	$ -	$ -	$ 100,000
Total Payments	$ -	$ 10,000	$ 110,000
Year 1 Coupon Reinvested at 5%		⮕	$ 10,500
Total Value of FUTURE Payments			$ 120,500

This scenario wouldn't give you a 10% compounded return if you paid $100,000 for the bond—the value according to our discounting exercise. Remember, a 10% compounded return would result in $121,000. Since $120,500 falls $500 short, it's clear that the 10% return wouldn't have been achieved.

Let's do some easy algebra to see what our exact compounded return would be. As a reminder, our relevant formula is:

$FV = PV(1+r)^t$

Where:

- FV = Future Value (also called ending value (EV))
- PV = Present Value (also called beginning value (BV))
- r = Return
- t = Time (in years)

In this case, we know all the variables except for our return (r). So, we can rearrange the formula to solve for "r":

$$r = \left(\frac{FV}{PV}\right)^{\frac{1}{t}} - 1$$

The future value is $120,500, which represents the total of all cumulative cash payments received at the end of the investment period, including earnings from reinvesting the coupon. The present value is $100,000, the amount our discounting exercise suggests we should be willing to pay. The investment period is 2 years, as this is the bond's maturity.

Using these values, we can solve for the compounded rate of return and determine that the compounded return over the 2-year period is 9.77%.

This implies that you shouldn't be willing to pay $100,000 for that bond. Remember, you selected a 10% discount rate because you believed a 10% compounded return was appropriate for a bond of this risk level, given your alternatives. However, if your expectations for reinvesting the interim coupon suggest that you will not achieve a 10% compounded return, why would you still pay $100,000 for it?

In my view, you shouldn't. The most you should be willing to pay is $99,589. I won't dive into the math here, but if you pay this amount, your compounded return will be an annual 10% over the 2-year period, assuming a 5% return on the reinvested coupon.

For additional context, the chart below shows the actual compounded return based on different assumed reinvestment rates for the first year's coupon.

First Year Coupon Reinvestment Rate	0.0%	2.5%	5.0%	7.5%	10.0%	12.5%	15.0%	17.5%
Compounded Return in 2-Year Period	9.5%	9.7%	9.8%	9.9%	10.0%	10.1%	10.2%	10.3%

The Long-Term Impact of Reinvestment Rates

You might be tempted to think that this range isn't that wide. The difference in compounded returns between 9.5% and 10.3% can appear trivial at first glance. But the reality of compounding is that it's exponential. Over long periods, even a small difference can make a huge impact. In fact, the difference in this case might seem small because we're dealing with a relatively short-term asset.

Let's extend this exercise to a 10-year bond and examine the compounded returns for different reinvestment rates of the coupons over the bond's life. Let's assume a 10-year bond that pays a 10% coupon every year on a $100,000 face value—the principal amount. Again, we'll use a 10% discount rate to see what a discounted cash flow analysis suggests we should pay for it. The exercise would look like this (due to space limitations, I'll use vertical charts now):

DISCOUNTING MULTIPLE CASH FLOWS

Year	Coupon Payments	Principal Payments	**Total Payments**	Present Value Formula	Present Value	**Total Present Value**
Year 0						$100,000
Year 1	$ 10,000		$ 10,000	$10,000 / (1+10%)^1	$ 9,091	
Year 2	$ 10,000		$ 10,000	$10,000 / (1+10%)^2	$ 8,264	
Year 3	$ 10,000		$ 10,000	$10,000 / (1+10%)^3	$ 7,513	
Year 4	$ 10,000		$ 10,000	$10,000 / (1+10%)^4	$ 6,830	
Year 5	$ 10,000		$ 10,000	$10,000 / (1+10%)^5	$ 6,209	
Year 6	$ 10,000		$ 10,000	$10,000 / (1+10%)^6	$ 5,645	
Year 7	$ 10,000		$ 10,000	$10,000 / (1+10%)^7	$ 5,132	
Year 8	$ 10,000		$ 10,000	$10,000 / (1+10%)^8	$ 4,665	
Year 9	$ 10,000		$ 10,000	$10,000 / (1+10%)^9	$ 4,241	
Year 10	$ 10,000	$100,000	$110,000	$110,000 / (1+10%)^10	$42,410	
Total	**$100,000**	**$100,000**	**$200,000**			

The chart above shows that over the 10-year period we'll receive a total of $200,000 in payments from this bond and that our present value is $100,000. However, if we invested $100,000 in an asset that produces a 10% compounded return, we would have a total of $259,374 in cumulative payments, calculated as:

$$100,000(1.1)^{10} = \$259,374$$

This represents a huge difference. My bond gives me $200,000 in cumulative payments, but a 10% compounded return would leave me with roughly $260,000—almost 30% more. This is a significantly greater difference than when we looked at our 2-year bond example, where we were comparing $121,000 against $120,000, a difference of barely 1%.

Just like with the 2-year bond, we need to reinvest each interim coupon at a rate of 10% to achieve the total of roughly $260,000 in cumulative payments. Refer to the chart on the next page:

Year	Coupon Payments	Principal Payments	Total Payments	Reinvesting Coupons	Value in Year 10	Total Value in Year 10
Year 0						
Year 1	$ 10,000		$ 10,000	$10,000 * (1+10%)^9	$ 23,579	
Year 2	$ 10,000		$ 10,000	$10,000 * (1+10%)^8	$ 21,436	
Year 3	$ 10,000		$ 10,000	$10,000 * (1+10%)^7	$ 19,487	
Year 4	$ 10,000		$ 10,000	$10,000 * (1+10%)^6	$ 17,716	
Year 5	$ 10,000		$ 10,000	$10,000 * (1+10%)^5	$ 16,105	
Year 6	$ 10,000		$ 10,000	$10,000 * (1+10%)^4	$ 14,641	
Year 7	$ 10,000		$ 10,000	$10,000 * (1+10%)^3	$ 13,310	
Year 8	$ 10,000		$ 10,000	$10,000 * (1+10%)^2	$ 12,100	
Year 9	$ 10,000		$ 10,000	$10,000 * (1+10%)^1	$ 11,000	
Year 10	$ 10,000	$100,000	$110,000	$110,000 * (1+10%)^0	$ 110,000	
Total	$100,000	$100,000	$200,000			$ 259,374

Note that each coupon is reinvested over a different period. The first coupon is reinvested and compounded for 9 years, as there are 9 years remaining in the 10-year investment horizon. The second coupon is reinvested and compounded for 8 years, the third for 7 years, and so on.

It's important to understand that the impact of not reinvesting the first coupon is far greater than that of the last. This makes sense—by not reinvesting the first coupon, we forgo 9 years of compounding. Since compounding is exponential, the effect of not reinvesting the first coupon is much larger than not reinvesting, say, the 9th coupon.

Anyway, if we don't reinvest the coupons, we're left with only $200,000 in cumulative cash flows. And if we used our rearranged formula to solve for the compounded rate of return, we get 7.2%.

$$7.2\% = \left(\frac{\$200,000}{\$100,000}\right)^{\frac{1}{10}} - 1$$

Once again, I'd ask you to stop for a second and let this sink in. By not reinvesting the interim coupons, a 10-year, 10% coupon paying bond would only give us a 7.2% compounded return. And remember, in theory we chose a 10% discount rate because we thought a 10% return—presumably compounded—would justify the risk and opportunity cost of the bond. But a 7.2% compounded return is not even close to the 10% we'd hope for.

So, I'll reiterate; you should never value an asset without considering whether it allows you to compound any interim cash flows at your desired return. Over long periods of time, this makes a significant difference. Let's now look at the actual compounded returns for this bond based on different assumed reinvestment rates.

Coupons Reinvestment Rate	0.0%	2.5%	5.0%	7.5%	10.0%	12.5%	15.0%	17.5%
Compounded Return in 10-Year Period	7.2%	7.8%	8.5%	9.2%	10.0%	10.8%	11.7%	12.7%

Hopefully you can now see that compounded returns can vary significantly for the same asset depending on the reinvestment rate. Comparing a 0% reinvestment rate with a 17.5% reinvestment rate leads to a range of compounded returns between 7.2% and 12.7%, respectively. Variations in compounded returns weren't as high with the 2-year bond, but it certainly does now. And this variation gets exponentially wider as we expand the investment horizon.

Why Reinvestment Rates Matter Even More for Businesses

The issue of not finding adequate reinvestment opportunities is less relevant for bonds than it is for stocks (i.e., businesses). The rates at which one can reinvest interim cash flows in bonds have a practical limit to how much they can vary. But the situation is entirely different for businesses.

The rate of return that businesses can earn by retaining and reinvesting their annual profits can vary greatly. In fact, it's not uncommon for businesses to earn a negative return on their reinvested profits. On the other hand, some businesses can reinvest their earnings at rates exceeding 50% or even 100% during certain stages of their life.

While such high rates are unsustainable in the long run, many businesses can reinvest profits at returns above 20% for extended periods—20 to 30 years in some cases. In fact, this is essentially how most Fortune 500 companies have achieved their success. They grew their profits exponentially by reinvesting them into endeavors with high rates of return over long periods.

Yet, most investors don't seem to consider this, let alone factor it into their investment decisions. It's astonishing that people often value businesses simply by discounting profits or cash flows. This approach doesn't just give you half the picture; it focuses on the least important half.

The rate at which profits are reinvested is the most critical factor for businesses. I cannot emphasize this enough: your compounded returns over time depend so heavily on the reinvestment rate that you can't accurately determine the fair price of an asset, especially a business, without considering it.

I can't say for certain, but I'm convinced this is why Warren Buffett famously said, "It's far better to buy a wonderful company at a fair price than a fair company at a wonderful price." A great business will compound its profits at such high rates that paying a premium is justified—even if your discounted cash flow analysis suggests you may be overpaying. On the other hand, a fair company may no longer have the ability to reinvest its profits at high rates of return. In this case, even if it appears cheap, it's unlikely to perform well over the long term.

CHAPTER 4 SUMMARY AND TAKEAWAYS (OPTIONAL READING)

- While understanding the discount-return relationship from the previous chapter is crucial, it's not the complete picture.
- In fact, Wall Street's biggest blind spot lies in an important nuance of that relationship—and if there's one thing you should take from this book, it's this nuance.
- Specifically, whenever a stream of cash flows spans multiple periods, the discount rate is only equal to your compounded return if—and only if—any interim cash flows are reinvested at a return equal to that same discount rate.
- This happens because we're viewing the entire investment horizon from a compounding perspective. The math, however, doesn't "know" this—it's simply discounting each cash flow back from its own point in time.
- In other words, the math gives us the discount-return relationship for each specific cash flow's timeframe. It doesn't take into account what happens to a cash flow in any periods beyond when it's received.
- This reality means that valuing an asset by discounting expected future cash flows is incomplete.
- While not incorrect on its own, this method doesn't give the full picture because it fails to account for the reinvestment (or lack thereof) of interim cash flows.
- This is crucial to understand because if interim cash flows are reinvested at a rate lower than the discount rate, your compounded returns will be lower than the discount rate.
- Conversely, if interim cash flows are reinvested at rates higher than your discount rate, your compounded returns will be higher than the discount rate.

- So, you should never value an asset without considering whether it allows you to compound any interim cash flows at your desired return.
- This might seem trivial for short timeframes, but over longer periods, the impact cannot be overstated.
- While always important, it's particularly crucial for businesses because the rate of return they can earn by retaining and reinvesting their annual profits can vary greatly. In fact, reinvestment rates for businesses can range from negative returns to beyond 20% for extended periods of time.

CHAPTER 5

VALUATION — PART 3

ACCOUNTING CONSIDERATIONS IN CASH FLOW EXPECTATIONS

Before diving into other valuation considerations, I want to pause and introduce a few accounting-related concepts. For simplicity, I'll limit the discussion to the concepts necessary to understand upcoming topics. However, I want to emphasize that a strong understanding of accounting is crucial for value investors.

When we looked at bond examples, it was clear what interest and principal payments were—they were simply cash receipts. If you're paid $50,000 in interest, you essentially receive $50,000 in cash. So, when we performed a discounted cash flow calculation, we could easily assume that those interest and principal payments were our cash flows. But it's different with businesses.

A company's accounting profits don't necessarily reflect cash received so you can't always use profits as your cash flow source for a discounted cash flow analysis. As such, without a solid grasp of accounting, even if you master the valuation tools and criteria from this book, you'll struggle to become a great value investor.

I don't expect you to grasp every single point I discuss. As long as you understand the conclusions I reach and recognize their importance, that should be enough. In other words, a basic understanding of the concepts in the following pages will help you absorb future lessons and appreciate the significance of accounting. However, if you're serious about value investing, it's up to you to further develop your accounting skills.

Lastly, if you're already well-versed and knowledgeable in accounting, you could probably skim or even skip the section on accounting accruals. However, I wouldn't advise you to skim through the rest, as I'm convinced you'll find valuable new insights and perspectives. At the very least, read carefully the parts on stock-based compensation and depreciation. Not only do I believe they'll offer you a fresh perspective, but they're also important for understanding later lessons in the book.

Accounting Accruals

As many of you are likely aware, accounting follows the principle of accruals. In simple terms, this means businesses don't record revenue (or expenses) when cash is actually received (or paid). Instead, they record revenue when the product or service has been fully delivered to the customer, and they record expenses when the obligation to pay a supplier or service provider arises. In most cases, cash is not received when the product or service is delivered, and similarly, cash is not paid when the obligation to pay a supplier arises.

Understanding Accrual Accounting Through a Simple Example

For a simple example, consider a law firm working on a legal opinion for a client. When the firm delivers the completed opinion, it has fulfilled its client's request, earning the right to be paid for the service—let's say the agreed price is $5,000. At the same time, the client now has an obligation to pay for the service. However, the client won't likely pay for the service the day they receive the legal opinion, but will instead pay 30-90 days later.

And yet, the legal opinion represents an expense for the client and revenue for the firm at the moment it's delivered. At this time, therefore, the correct accounting practice would be for the client to record a $5,000 expense and for the firm to also record $5,000 in revenue.

While accounting isn't perfect, it aims to provide all materially relevant information to stakeholders, such as owners, investors, bondholders, and regulators. If the client and the firm don't record these transactions when the legal opinion is delivered, this objective won't be achieved.

Think about it: if you were an investor in either the firm or the client, wouldn't you want to know that the firm has the right to receive payment or that the client has the obligation to pay for the service? Recording these transactions, even without an immediate cash exchange, provides this essential information.

So, accruing in general makes a lot of sense. I'm not suggesting it's bad practice. But the reality is, profits and cash flows don't always match. The $5,000 in revenue that the firm records increases profits, but part of those profits may not be converted into cash until next year. This would be true, for example, if the legal opinion is delivered to the client in November or December. Conversely, the $5,000 in expenses the client recognizes reduces its profits, but those reduced profits may not reduce cash flow until next year.

Most Accruals Can Be Ignored — But Not All

In this simple example, the timing difference between profits and cash flows likely isn't significant enough to affect our expectations of future cash flows. After all, we're only dealing with a 30- to 90-day gap. In other words, within 90 days, the firm will collect the cash for the increased profits it had previously recognized, and the client will pay the cash for the reduced profits they had already accounted for. When projecting cash flows over many years, how much of an impact can a short delay like this really have?

In most cases, the timing differences created by accounting accruals won't materially impact results over the long term, and therefore shouldn't prevent us from using accounting profits as a reasonable proxy for cash flow. This is not only because these differences are typically short-lived, but also because many of them offset each other.

If we think about the law firm, while it may not immediately receive cash for services rendered, it also isn't immediately paying cash for expenses it has incurred. Take, for example, employee bonuses that are expensed throughout the year but paid a few weeks or months into the following one.

Besides, like Warren Buffett, I also agree with John Maynard Keynes' view that "It's better to be approximately right than precisely wrong." Trying to adjust for every timing difference caused by accounting accruals in order to estimate future cash flows is misguided. Not only is it nearly impossible to accurately predict future timing differences, but it also diverts attention from more important matters. It's far more valuable to focus on studying the business to assess whether it is likely to reinvest profits at very high rates of return.

That being said, accounting profits are not a perfect proxy for cash flow, and I do believe that making ballpark adjustments to profits is sometimes necessary. Since accounting is not the focus of this book, I won't provide a comprehensive list of scenarios where adjustments are justified or how to make them. Even if I tried, I'd likely overlook many examples given the variety of businesses, industries, and business models. However, to provide you with some perspective, I will cover a few common and highly relevant situations.

Asset Revaluations That Don't Involve Cash When Recognized

Let's begin by examining the impact of asset revaluations. Occasionally, accounting rules require a reduction in the value of an asset. For instance, in 2018, The Kraft Heinz Company (Kraft) disclosed in its Form 10-K filing that it had to declare impairment losses totaling nearly $16 billion. These impairments were related to intangible assets from its U.S. refrigerated and Canadian retail operations, as well as two of its trademarks (Kraft and Mayer).

Following accounting guidelines, Kraft determined that the recorded value of these assets was overstated, meaning management believed the future profits they would generate didn't justify their recorded value. To put this in perspective, at the beginning of 2018, Kraft had total recorded assets of $120 billion, but by the end of the year, that number had dropped to $103.6 billion.

While many factors influenced the change in total assets, the largest impact came from the $16 billion impairment loss. Since this event affects the profit and loss statement, Kraft was unprofitable in 2018, posting a negative profit of roughly $10 billion.

I think we can all agree that, as owners or potential investors, we would all want to know if management believes certain assets are overstated. This is why it's crucial for accounting rules to require such adjustments.

However, this impairment loss did not affect the cash Kraft generated from operations during the period. It was a non-cash expense, merely an accounting adjustment, with no direct impact on cash flow for 2018. In fact, it had a positive effect, as it helped reduce the amount of taxes owed.

Therefore, when assessing a company's future cash-generating ability, non-cash expenses like this should be adjusted because they don't reflect the business's true cash flow potential. In other words, when calculating Kraft's 2018 cash flow, you should add back the $16 billion impairment loss—minus any cash tax benefits it may have generated—to the reported negative $10 billion in accounting profits.

This adjustment gives you a much more realistic view of Kraft's cash flow for that year. And if you believe the company's future will closely resemble its 2018 performance, then this adjusted figure can serve as a reasonable proxy for projecting future cash flows.

Sunk Costs Don't Hurt Today's Value

Now, don't misunderstand me—expenses recorded in accounting should always reflect some kind of cash outlay. The cash impact may not occur at the moment the expense is recognized—as in this example—but it must have occurred either in the past or be expected in the future. Otherwise, why would it make sense to call them expenses in the first place?

So, what's the case here? Well, the $16 billion in impairment losses do represent a cash outlay—but one that was made in prior periods. Specifically, Kraft paid for these assets, and at that time, they were recorded at a value equal to the cash spent. No expense was recorded at the time of purchase because the assets were expected to generate cash flow benefits over an extended period.

However, the impairment loss now recognizes that it was a mistake to pay so much for these assets. And since the company is not receiving the minimum expected value from them, it must adjust their value accordingly. This, of course, is important to understand—but it represents a sunk cost: an expense whose cash impact occurred when the decision to purchase those assets was made. That cash outlay affected the business owners invested at the time—not future owners.

If you believe management will continue to make such mistakes, you clearly can't ignore it in estimating your future cash flow projections. But if you think this was a one-time mistake that won't be repeated—perhaps because management has learned its lesson or because new leadership is in place—then it can likely be disregarded. The value of the business today depends entirely on the future cash flows it will generate. The past, including these impairments, is irrelevant.

Don't Confuse Asset Sales with Real Earnings

Similar to impairment losses, gains from selling assets can show up on a company's profit and loss statement. But unlike regular income from core business operations, these gains aren't reflective of the ongoing cash flow the business will generate in the future.

For example, if a company sells a piece of real estate for more than it paid for it, it might recognize a large gain. This gain will boost the company's reported profits, but it doesn't represent cash that will continue flowing in every year from the business's normal operations.

Consider a company that sells a factory or a piece of land and makes a $10 million gain. This is a non-recurring event—once the asset is sold, it's gone. While the company may show a significant profit on its income statement from this sale, the gain doesn't reflect the cash flow the business will generate moving forward. In fact, this gain might even indirectly suggest that future cash flows could be lower. If the asset sold was contributing positive cash flows, the company will no longer benefit from that recurring cash flow stream.

In any case, just like with impairment losses, if you believe that the sale of assets is a one-off event with little impact on future cash flows, you should disregard the gain. The $10 million gain is not something that will repeat year after year. Therefore, when projecting future cash flows, you should focus on the company's core operations—the revenue it generates from its products or services—because those are the consistent drivers of cash flow, not sporadic asset sales.

That said, if the company is in the process of selling off more assets or has a business model heavily reliant on selling assets for large gains, you may need to take these sales into account. But if the sale of assets is a rare occurrence, such as a one-time sale of an underperforming property or factory, it's reasonable to ignore it in future cash flow projections. After all, the key point is that we're interested in understanding the company's ongoing ability to generate cash, not short-term tailwinds from one-off asset sales.

Stock-Based Compensation

Let's now turn to a more complex example: stock-based compensation. This wasn't always the case, but standard accounting practices now require companies to record an expense for compensation paid to employees through stock-ownership programs. While various stock compensation schemes exist, the most common involves granting employees call options that vest over a period of time (typically 3 to 7 years). A call option is a financial instrument that gives the holder the right to buy stock at a predetermined price in the future.

How Stock Options Work

As an example, let's say you worked at Microsoft in 1995, and the company decided to give you a bonus in the form of 100 call options, which together give you the right to purchase 10,000 shares of Microsoft stock at $4 each, starting in the year 2000. The $4 price in this example is called the strike price.

Fast forward 5 years to 2000, and Microsoft's stock price has risen to around $50 per share. Since $50 is much greater than $4, you'd exercise your option to purchase the stock at the strike price, and then you could sell it for $50. For each share, your gain would be $46, and for 10,000 shares, you would have made $460,000.

You may have noticed that at no point did Microsoft actually pay any cash to the employee for this benefit. This is precisely why, in the past, stock compensation wasn't recorded as an expense. But the reality is, while the business doesn't pay cash out for these options, the owners—shareholders—indirectly do. That's because, when the options are exercised, Microsoft must issue 10,000 new shares, which dilutes the ownership stake of existing shareholders.

Visualizing The Real Cost of Call Options to Shareholders

Imagine that, before issuing these new shares, Microsoft had 100,000 shares outstanding. If an existing shareholder owned 20,000 shares, they would have a 20% stake in the company. However, when Microsoft issues 10,000 new shares, the total number of shares becomes 110,000. So, the original 20% stake is now reduced to roughly 18.2%.

This dilution means the existing shareholder now has less ownership of the company, which directly affects their entitlement to dividends. For example, if a $100,000 dividend were to be paid, the shareholder would receive approximately $18,200 instead of the $20,000 they would have received prior to the dilution.

As I've pointed out before, it wouldn't make sense to expense something that doesn't result in a cash outlay at some point. So how does this apply to stock-option compensation? The key is that there is an outlay—it just occurs in a different form, impacting shareholders rather than the company's cash flow. In our example, the stock-option scheme resulted in a very real $1,800 cash outlay to the owner, stemming from a reduced dividend payout.

In typical cases, an expense reduces cash flow, which in turn reduces the amount available to pay dividends to owners. With stock-option compensation, a company's cash flow remains unaffected, so the ability to pay dividends stays the same. However, the ownership stake of the shareholders is reduced and, as a result, they receive less dividends.

And, as an owner, you're indifferent as to how you receive less cash flow. Whether you receive a smaller share of the same-sized pie, or the same share of a smaller pie, the result is the same. Given this reality, we can confidently conclude that stock-option compensation does, in fact, have a real cash impact.

The Challenge of Accounting for Stock Options

To account for this dilution, modern accounting practices now attempt to recognize the cost to shareholders. The problem is that the actual cost of granting stock options is uncertain when the options are granted.

For example, imagine that Microsoft's stock price hadn't reached $50 but instead stayed below $4. In that case, the employee would not exercise the options because it wouldn't make sense to buy shares at $4 when they could purchase them on the market for a lower price. In such a scenario, no new shares would be issued, and therefore no dilution would occur. The owner's share of future dividends would remain unchanged.

So, there's a dilemma. On one hand, stock-option compensation clearly represents a cost to shareholders, so it makes sense to expense it. Even though it doesn't directly affect the company's cash flow, it does affect the owners' rights to future cash flows. This is material information that any rational investor would want to know.

On the other hand, nobody can accurately quantify this expense because the final outcome won't be known until years down the line. As is often the case with accounting, we must settle for imperfect estimates.

Uncertainty Does Not Justify Exclusion

I won't go into exhaustive detail, but in short, the cost of these stock compensation schemes is recorded by estimating the fair value of the options. But even with the sophisticated methods available to estimate this, it's far from perfect. I can guarantee that the fair value estimate won't match the actual cash cost to owners over time. So, the key question is: should we disregard stock-option compensation and exclude it from our estimates of future cash flows?

You may have guessed that my answer is no. We can't ignore it, and yes, we should take it into account. To me, it's simple. If we consider it an expense and don't disregard other expenses, then there's no reason to ignore this cost. If you're a short-term trader, this might not affect you, and you may choose to disregard it. But if you're a long-term investor who expects returns from a company's future cash flows, ignoring it would be a mistake.

Let's use Uber as an example. According to the company's Form 10-K filings, from February 2020 to February 2024, Uber's share count increased from roughly 1.72 billion shares to approximately 2.08 billion shares—a roughly 21% increase over just 4 years. In practical terms, if you owned 10% of Uber in February 2020, you would only own 8.3% by 2024. It's like selling 17% of your shares without receiving anything in return. If this isn't a cost, I don't know what is.

Is the Standard Accounting Method Good Enough?

With all this in mind, I prefer to account for this expense differently. Specifically, I do ignore the stock-based compensation as recorded by accounting guidelines. Not only is it an imperfect estimate, but it's also hard to grasp intuitively.

My preferred approach is to estimate the dilution of my ownership based on the company's stock-based compensation policies and adjust my future cash flow expectations accordingly. For instance, if I estimate that the share count will increase by around 2% per year, I would reduce my future cash flow expectations by roughly 2% annually, all else equal.

The chart below illustrates this idea more clearly. The number of shares increases from 100,000 to 102,000 between today and the end of year 1—precisely a 2% increase. This means that an investor who buys shares today will hold only 98% of their original ownership stake by the end of year 1. So, if I expect the company's year 1 cash flows to be $25,000, I would adjust that figure to 98% of it, or roughly $24,500. That's because this revised figure represents the portion of cash flows the investor is actually expected to be entitled to in year 1. This approach is more intuitive, and at the same time, it better reflects the reality that the investor won't receive the full $25,000.

If this 2% annual growth in the number of shares continues, the investor's ownership stake would fall to roughly 91% by year 5. As a result, even if the company's cash flows stay at $25,000, the investor's entitlement to those cash flows would drop to roughly $22,600.

Year	Year 0	Year 1	Year 2	Year 3	Year 4	Year 5	Year "x"
Total Share Count (increasing 2% per year)	100,000	102,000	104,040	106,121	108,243	110,408	...
Original Share Count as a % of Current Share Count	100%	98%	96%	94%	92%	91%	...
Expected Company Cash Flow (000s)	$25,000	$25,000	$25,000	$25,000	$25,000	$25,000	...
Investor Cash Flow Expectations (000s)	$25,000	$24,510	$24,029	$23,558	$23,096	$22,643	...

The example and chart above assume that this company's cash flows remain flat over time. However, the concept would still apply in the case of a company with growing cash flows.

Imagine the same company, but with expected cash flow growth of

2% per year. The chart below illustrates this new scenario, showing that, from the investor's perspective, the 2% growth in share count completely neutralizes the company's cash flow growth. In other words, even though the company's cash flows increase from $25,000 to roughly $27,600 over five years, this growth has no positive effect on the investor's cash flows. Due to ownership dilution, the investor would still only be entitled to the same $25,000 from year 0.

Year	Year 0	Year 1	Year 2	Year 3	Year 4	Year 5	Year "x"
Total Share Count (increasing 2% per year)	100,000	102,000	104,040	106,121	108,243	110,408	...
Original Share Count as a % of Current Share Count	100%	98%	96%	94%	92%	91%	...
Company CF (000s, increasing 2% per year)	$25,000	$25,500	$26,010	$26,530	$27,061	$27,602	...
Investor Cash Flow Expectations (000s)	$25,000	$25,000	$25,000	$25,000	$25,000	$25,000	...

This method of adjusting cash flow expectations is more realistic and intuitive than using the stock-based compensation expense recorded by standard accounting practices. Moreover, it also allows for easier estimation. In the footnotes of a company's audited financial statements, you can find a wealth of information about stock-based compensation awards and the expected dilution from them. Additionally, you can look at the company's recent history and management commentary to get a sense of what to expect going forward.

Conclusion: How to Think About Stock-Based Compensation

In summary, stock-based compensation is an expense that reduces accounting profits, but it doesn't have a direct cash impact at the time it's recorded. In fact, the cash impact is never reflected in the company's books because the company doesn't pay cash for this type of expense. Instead, it affects the owners by reducing their ownership stake over time, which in turn reduces their share of future dividends. Because it does affect owners (both current and future), it can't be ignored. However, since the accounting treatment for stock-based compensation is imperfect and not always intuitive, I believe it's better to estimate the expected dilution and adjust future cash flow expectations accordingly.

Depreciation

Let's now move on to the last case I want to discuss: depreciation. This accounting expense reflects the gradual recognition of a purchased tangible asset with a long useful life. Think about factory equipment, computer hardware, furniture, office space, solar panels, water and gas pipelines, and so on. These assets are useful for more than a year, often lasting for several decades. So, when a company purchases these items, it wouldn't make sense to record the full expense all at once.

The Logic Behind Depreciation

Let's use IT equipment in data centers as an example to explain how it works. Suppose you estimate that the useful life of servers, CPUs, GPUs, storage devices, and networking hardware is, on average, 4 years—not necessarily because the equipment stops functioning, but because technological improvements make it obsolete. Let's say you purchase $400,000 worth of equipment.

If you recorded an accounting expense for the entire amount today, your profits for this year would be drastically reduced by that full $400,000. However, the equipment will allow you to provide cloud data services over the next 4 years, creating a mismatch between when the expense is recorded and when it helps generate revenue. This would also cause your accounting profits to be highly volatile—this year's profits could even show a loss, while future years would show comparatively much higher profits.

It's easy to see that, if this were the common practice, assessing a company's cost structure and ongoing profitability would be very difficult. Therefore, accounting accrual practices require you to recognize the expense gradually over the asset's useful life.

Accounting Mechanics: How Depreciation Is Applied

Continuing our example, you first need to recognize at the time of purchase that you have an asset worth $400,000—essentially its cost. Then, each year, you reduce the value of the asset by $100,000, so that by the end of its 4-year useful life, its accounting value is reduced to $0. This $100,000 annual reduction in the asset's value is the depreciation expense recognized each year for 4 years.

However, this expense is almost entirely non-cash at the time of recognition. Specifically, while the full $400,000 is paid upfront, only 25% of that payment is recognized as an expense in the first year. The remaining 75% is recognized gradually over the next 3 years, with no additional cash being spent during that time. See the chart below for a simple illustration.

Year	Year 1	Year 2	Year 3	Year 4	Total
Timing of Cash Payment	$ 400,000	$ -	$ -	$ -	$ 400,000
Timing of Non-Cash Expense Recognition	$(100,000)	$(100,000)	$(100,000)	$(100,000)	$(400,000)
Cash Payment In Excess of (less than) Expense	$ 300,000	$(100,000)	$(100,000)	$(100,000)	$ -

Why Depreciation Still Matters for Cash Flow

The non-cash nature of depreciation has led many to disregard such costs in varying degrees. However, in most cases, this doesn't make sense. Depreciation represents a cash outlay that is necessary to keep the data center running.

In contrast to the non-recurring nature of the asset revaluation example, there is a recurring need to replace the equipment. Cash will continue to be spent over time to replace it, reducing the available cash flow for investors. So, even though there are timing differences between when the expense is recognized and when the cash is spent, depreciation is still a true cost.

In a perfect world, for valuation purposes, you would project cash flows exactly as they are expected to occur. For instance, if you're buying a data center a year after it was set up, you'd ignore depreciation for the remaining useful life of the equipment—3 years—then reduce the cash flow for the cost of replacing it, and repeat the cash flow reduction every 4 years. However, as I've mentioned before, it's better to be approximately right than precisely wrong, and attempting to project these precise replacements is an overkill.

Additionally, no one invests in a company with just a single data center or a single long-life asset. Asset purchases within a business are made gradually over time, so they are also replaced gradually. As a result, on a net basis, the timing differences between expense recognition and cash outlay tend to be relatively small.

In our IT equipment example, at any given time, you're depreciating 1/4th of all the equipment purchased in the past 4 years. But since the equipment is acquired gradually, you likely only need to replace about 1/4th of it at any given time.

The chart below provides a visual representation of this concept using our IT equipment example. While there is a difference between cash outflows and expense recognition in the first 3 years, this difference disappears in year 4.

	Year 1	Year 2	Year 3	Year 4	Year 5	Year 6	Year 7	Year 8
Cash Payments for Equipment ($ in thousands)								
Data Center 1	$ 400				$ 400			
Data Center 2		$ 400				$ 400		
Data Center 3			$ 400				$ 400	
Data Center 4				$ 400				$ 400
Total	$ 400	$ 400	$ 400	$ 400	$ 400	$ 400	$ 400	$ 400
Depreciation Expense Recognition ($ in thousands)								
Data Center 1	$ (100)	$ (100)	$ (100)	$ (100)	$ (100)	$ (100)	$ (100)	$ (100)
Data Center 2		$ (100)	$ (100)	$ (100)	$ (100)	$ (100)	$ (100)	$ (100)
Data Center 3			$ (100)	$ (100)	$ (100)	$ (100)	$ (100)	$ (100)
Data Center 4				$ (100)	$ (100)	$ (100)	$ (100)	$ (100)
Total	$ (100)	$ (200)	$ (300)	$ (400)	$ (400)	$ (400)	$ (400)	$ (400)
Difference	$ 300	$ 200	$ 100	$ -	$ -	$ -	$ -	$ -

In reality, of course, these timing differences are rarely as neat, and cash flow and expense will always vary. However, because these differences are difficult to predict and are likely to be immaterial over time, depreciation expense serves as a reasonable proxy for recurring fixed asset replacement needs.

Since depreciation is a real expense and provides a good estimate of actual cash outlays over time, I believe it is generally unwise to ignore depreciation. In other words, the fact that depreciation is a non-cash expense should not prevent you from using profits as a reliable proxy for cash flow in most cases.

Why Depreciation Sometimes Requires Adjustment

That being said, depreciation recognition is not perfect, and you should evaluate each case individually. If this general thought process doesn't apply, it's wise to adjust for depreciation in some way. Ultimately, what matters when valuing a business is the cash flows available to owners over time. If, for any reason, depreciation is not accurately and materially reflecting cash flows, you should definitely make adjustments.

In my view, the most common case where depreciation may need to be reconsidered is when you have a fixed asset with essentially an indefinite life. Take, for example, a business that relies heavily on real estate. Let's think about a grocery chain that owns—as opposed to leases—the real estate it operates in.

According to accounting rules, this real estate must be depreciated over a period of 30 to 40 years, depending on the situation. If we use 30 years as an example, the annual depreciation expense would amount to roughly 3% of the asset's total cash cost. And I see several reasons why this depreciation may not reflect future cash outlays accurately.

Depreciation Doesn't Always Signal Future Spending

It's unclear whether real estate will actually need to be replaced in 30 to 40 years. If maintained and remodeled properly, real estate can last much longer than that. Therefore, using depreciation as a proxy for replacement costs may not be necessary.

Furthermore, any real estate already in place when you purchase the business is a sunk cost. If there's no foreseeable need to replace it, then the gradual recognition of the original cost through depreciation becomes irrelevant.

With the IT equipment example, it was different. In that case, we knew as a fact that several years down the line it would be necessary to replace it. And the cash spent in the recent past—revealed in depreciation—could be seen as a reasonable estimate of the cash that would be needed for replacement over time.

Far-Off Replacements Don't Affect Today's Value

Even if the real estate does need replacement 30 to 40 years from now, the timing of that potential expenditure is so far into the future that it would barely impact today's valuation. You'll understand this better once we explore the topic further in the next couple of chapters.

For now, let me just emphasize that because the real estate will help generate many cash flows before it ever needs to be replaced, what matters most is how those cash flows are managed. If they're reinvested effectively over time, then the cash spent decades from now for a replacement becomes practically irrelevant.

In other words, an investor's compounded annual return over the next 40 years will be largely unaffected by whether or not the real estate is eventually replaced. So, reducing today's cash flow expectations by the full amount of current depreciation would lead to unnecessarily conservative projections—and, as a result, we risk undervaluing the business.

Don't Confuse Depreciation with Reinvestments

It wouldn't be accurate to argue that depreciation is relevant simply because it reflects the cash outlays required to expand the store count. While it's true that opening new stores requires capital, the cash flows from existing stores should be treated separately from those generated by new locations. The proper approach is to focus on the cash flows produced by the existing business, and then separately evaluate the reinvestment returns from investing and expanding into new stores.

Think back to the 10-year bond example from the previous chapter: nobody would argue that the bond's value should be depreciated just because reinvesting the interest is necessary to grow the bond pool. This is an important point—one we'll explore more thoroughly in later chapters—so don't worry if it doesn't fully click just yet.

How to Adjust for Depreciation in Our Grocery Store Example

For all these reasons, I don't believe depreciation is particularly useful in our grocery store example. Instead, I would disregard depreciation and focus on the actual cash costs of maintaining the business over time. Specifically, when considering future cash flows, I would add back depreciation to my profits and then subtract the actual maintenance costs—commonly referred to as maintenance capital expenditures, or maintenance CapEx.

To be clear, this adjustment to profits applies to the cash flows of the existing business and its current grocery store count. If I believe the company will retain all or part of these cash flows to reinvest in new store development, I wouldn't treat those future investments as a cash cost that reduces my future cash flows.

Instead, I would view those cash outlays as reinvestments, and the correct approach would be to evaluate the rate of return on those investments and how they impact my forward-looking compounded annual growth rate. Think again about the 10-year bond example: when we reinvest any coupons earned over time, we don't consider that reinvestment as a future cash cost. Again, we'll explore this concept in more detail later.

Conclusion: How to Think About Depreciation

In conclusion, depreciation is a nuanced concept that can vary greatly depending on the nature of the asset and the business model in question. While it serves as a useful accounting practice for recognizing the cost of long-term assets over time, it doesn't always reflect the true cash flow dynamics of a business.

For companies with assets that have indefinite lives or those in industries like real estate, depreciation may not be the most accurate proxy for future cash outlays. In such cases, it's more useful to focus on maintenance capital expenditures and adjust cash flow projections accordingly. Ultimately, the key to valuing a business is to understand its true cash flow potential, and by carefully analyzing depreciation alongside other factors, you can more accurately assess the long-term prospects of the business.

The Cash Flow Statement

With the examples in the prior sections, you can see that accounting profits are not perfect, and adjustments may be necessary when translating historical profits into projected cash flows.

At this point, you might be wondering about the best way to determine any potential adjustments and how significant they are. Given the variety of businesses and business models out there, mastering this process requires more than just an accounting course and some experience. This is why I've emphasized that you can't become a great value investor without a solid grounding in accounting knowledge.

That said, there is one accounting report worth spending time on, not only because it will make future valuation lessons easier to understand but also because understanding its basics can give you a significant head start. And this report is called the cash flow statement or the statement of cash flows.

In short, this statement is an accounting report that links accrual-based accounting practices with actual cash coming in and out. It shows you which parts of your profits are a result of accounting practices versus transactions that actually affected cash flow.

The Structure of the Cash Flow Statement

The cash flow statement is broken down into three main parts. The first part deals with cash flow from operations. It starts with accounting profits and then adjusts for revenue and expenses that didn't directly impact cash during the period.

The second part focuses on cash flows from investing activities. This section highlights cash outlays for long-lived asset purchases, like equipment or property, that are not immediately expensed because they provide benefits over multiple years. Because they are not expensed right away, these outlays don't affect profits directly, but this section informs stakeholders that cash left the business for these purchases.

The third and final section covers cash flows from financing activities. It shows the sources or uses of cash from debt or equity holders, including borrowing or repaying debt, paying dividends, repurchasing stock, issuing new equity, and so on.

Costco: A Real-World Cash Flow Statement

Let's look at Costco's cash flow statement below to make this more tangible. For clarity, I've made some minor adjustments to the wording, order, and grouping compared to how the company presents it publicly. These changes, however, don't affect the substance. Also, to avoid any confusion, note that Costco's fiscal year ends on the Sunday closest to the end of August, rather than on December 31 as is typical. For example, fiscal year 2024 refers to the 12-month period ending on September 1, 2024.

Statements Of Cash Flows - USD ($) in Millions	2022	2023	2024
Net Income / Profits	$ 5,915	$ 6,292	$ 7,367
Adjustments to reconcile net income to cash provided by operating activities:			
Depreciation & amortization	1,900	2,077	2,237
Stock-based compensation	724	774	818
Impairment of assets and other non-cash operating activities, net	39	495	(9)
Merchandise inventories	(4,003)	1,228	(2,068)
Accounts payable	1,891	(382)	1,938
Other operating assets and liabilities, net	549	172	741
Other non-cash items	377	412	315
Net cash provided by operating activities	**7,392**	**11,068**	**11,339**
CASH FLOWS FROM INVESTING ACTIVITIES			
Additions to property & equipment (or CapEx)	(3,891)	(4,323)	(4,710)
Sales and purchases of short-term investments, net	24	(685)	320
Other investing activities, net	(48)	36	(19)
Net cash used in investing activities	**(3,915)**	**(4,972)**	**(4,409)**
CASH FLOWS FROM FINANCING ACTIVITIES			
Short and long-term debt issuances and repayments	(753)	(93)	(571)
Repurchases of common stock	(439)	(676)	(700)
Cash dividend payments	(1,498)	(1,251)	(9,041)
Other Financing Activities	(1,593)	(594)	(452)
Net cash used in financing activities	**(4,283)**	**(2,614)**	**(10,764)**
Effect of exchange rate changes	(249)	15	40
Net change in cash & cash equivalents	**(1,055)**	**3,497**	**(3,794)**

Source: Costco Wholesale Corporation, fiscal year 2024 10-K.

Breaking Down Costco's Cash Flow from Operations

Let's examine Costco's 2024 fiscal year to see how we can interpret the accounting statement. While we start with roughly $7.4 billion in profits, it's clear that this does not represent the actual cash the company generated from its operations. In reality, Costco received approximately $11.3 billion in cash during the period.

The gap between cash from operations and profits can be explained by breaking it down into two separate buckets. The first bucket relates to expenses that reduced profits but had no cash impact during 2024. These include depreciation, stock-based compensation, impairments, and other non-cash items. You should already be familiar with this bucket, as we've discussed these concepts in depth.

The second bucket relates to short timing differences between when cash is spent or received and when the related expense or revenue, respectively, is recognized. For example, the roughly $2 billion in merchandise inventory shows that the company has spent this amount purchasing inventory. However, because the inventory hasn't been sold yet and remains on the shelves, it hasn't been expensed.

This reflects the accounting principle of matching revenues with expenses, which ensures that profits are recognized consistently and in alignment with when they are earned. If the inventory hasn't been sold, no revenue has been recognized for it yet, so expensing it immediately upon purchase would violate the matching principle.

Similarly, the roughly $1.9 billion in accounts payable reflects the opposite scenario when compared to merchandise inventory. In this case, the company has already recognized an expense for the goods and services purchased from vendors but hasn't yet paid those vendors. In other words, profits were reduced by $1.9 billion, but the cash hasn't been spent yet.

Finally, the roughly $740 million in other operating assets and liabilities would also fall into this second bucket. This line item represents timing differences, typically short-term in nature—less than a year, often between 30 to 120 days. These short-term timing differences are often grouped under the term "working capital." Examples of working capital include insurance paid upfront but not yet utilized, employee benefits earned but not yet paid, or sales that have been earned but the payment hasn't been made by the customer yet.

Why Cash Flow from Operations Isn't Investor Cash Flow

As a side note, please don't be tempted to use cash flows from operations as your primary basis for valuing a business. As I've emphasized before, accounting accruals are generally valid because they represent real cash outflows and inflows, even if there are timing differences. Cash flow from operations, however, removes these accruals, which distorts the true picture.

Moreover, cash flow from operations can be very difficult to interpret and work with. Not only are working capital movements very volatile and unpredictable, but for many types of businesses, cash flow from operations can be quite misleading.

Consider the case of insurance companies as an example. Insurers receive large cash inflows upfront in the form of premium payments from policyholders. However, these cash inflows do not reflect immediate revenue for the insurer. Instead, revenue is recognized gradually over time as the insurer earns it by providing ongoing coverage. Simultaneously, insurers must also recognize estimated loss expenses as soon as they expect claims to be made, even though these losses may not be paid until much later.

So, when you look at an insurer's accounting profits, you're looking at an estimate of how much money will ultimately be available to shareholders. In contrast, cash flow from operations simply reflects premiums coming in and claims going out, which will likely overstate the cash truly available to shareholders—especially for insurers that haven't yet reached a mature stage.

Think about it, for a fast-growing insurer, you're quickly growing your inflows from premiums paid upfront but there's a substantial lag with respect to claims that are going to be paid. And because your inflows are not timely paired with your outflows, cash flow from operations will poorly represent what's available to investors.

Breaking Down Costco's Cash Flows from Investing Activities

Let's now return to Costco's cash flow statement and examine the second section: cash flows from investing activities. Additions to property and equipment are commonly categorized as capital expenditures, or CapEx. For Costco, most of these outflows represent cash spent on developing new stores (growth CapEx) or maintaining existing ones (maintenance CapEx).

As we've discussed, it's crucial to closely examine this line item to determine whether depreciation accurately reflects the ongoing maintenance CapEx needs. If it's not, accounting profits might not be the most reliable proxy for the cash flows available to investors.

In essence, you need to determine what portion of Costco's $4.7 billion in CapEx is allocated to new store development versus maintaining existing stores. You can do this by reviewing Costco's regulatory filings, earnings call transcripts, and other publicly available information.

If you find that most of the CapEx was spent on growth initiatives and that recurring maintenance CapEx needs are low, it's likely that depreciation is overstating the future cash outlays for the existing business. On the other hand, if the majority of the spending went toward remodeling existing stores—and you expect this to be a recurring need—then depreciation may be understating the actual cash required to maintain the current store infrastructure. In either case, adjustments to accounting profits may be necessary, as discussed in depth earlier.

A Brief Note on Financing Activities

Lastly, we move to the section on financing activities, but I won't go into too much detail here since it's relatively self-explanatory. What I do want to emphasize is that, along with investing activities, this section provides insight into what management is doing with the company's profits. This is vitally important because, remember, our investment returns are always tied to how effectively an asset's interim cash flows are being reinvested.

As an investor, you want management to retain and reinvest profits only if they can achieve a high reinvestment rate of return. If that's not the case, you'd prefer management to return profits to shareholders via dividends or stock buybacks. In other words, you want management to be mindful of the damage done to investors when profits are poorly utilized. And, as we'll see in later chapters, this section is crucial for helping us assess whether management has that mindset.

Conclusion: Why the Cash Flow Statement Matters

In conclusion, analyzing the cash flow statement is essential for understanding a company's finances—especially when trying to translate accounting profits into realistic cash flow expectations. By carefully examining the operating activities section and assessing any necessary adjustments to depreciation or other non-cash items, you can form a more accurate view of the potential cash flows available to shareholders. Additionally, reviewing the investing and financing activities reveals important insights into how a company manages its profits and reinvests them. This, in turn, helps you develop a clearer picture of the company's ability to allocate cash efficiently—an essential component of any accurate valuation.

Chapter Conclusion: Bridging Profit and Cash Flow

In this chapter, we explored the critical role of accounting in valuing a business, with a particular focus on how to interpret and adjust accounting profits to more accurately reflect cash flows. We began by examining the importance of understanding accounting accruals and how they impact the translation of profits into cash. While accounting practices make sense in most cases, I emphasized that exceptions exist and may require thoughtful adjustments.

I highlighted the need to adjust for impairments and asset sales, as these can significantly influence cash flow expectations. We also discussed how stock-based compensation, though non-cash, dilutes shareholder value and must be factored into cash flow projections. However, because current accounting practices don't offer an intuitive or accurate way to measure this expense, I suggested a different approach: rather than accounting for this expense at the company level, I suggested evaluating the impact of shareholder dilution at the owners' level.

Additionally, I pointed out the challenges of working with depreciation for businesses that own assets with very long useful lives, such as real estate. In these cases, I recommended focusing on maintenance capital expenditures and ignoring depreciation when projecting cash flows.

Through these examples, we saw how accounting accruals can obscure or distort a company's true cash flow-generating ability. And to better assess that potential, I emphasized the importance of examining the cash flow statement—the financial report that bridges the gap between accounting profits and actual cash flows.

With all this in mind, I hope it's clear that valuing a business goes far beyond a superficial glance at financial statements. It requires a careful analysis of the cash flow statement, a strong understanding of accounting accruals, and the ability to make nuanced adjustments to form meaningful projections. While this section may have felt dense and theoretical, having covered these accounting considerations, we're now well-prepared to return to more valuation-focused topics. With this base, I'm confident you'll better grasp what's ahead and appreciate it on a deeper level.

CHAPTER 5 SUMMARY AND TAKEAWAYS (OPTIONAL READING)

- With bonds, any interest essentially represents cash received by investors. With businesses, however, accounting profits are not a perfect proxy for cash.
- Accounting profits are subject to accrual practices that may hide or distort a company's cash flow-generating ability.
- This doesn't mean accounting conventions are flawed—they provide necessary and material information to shareholders.
- But because what matters for valuation purposes is the expectation of future cash flows, accounting profits may need to be adjusted to reveal a company's real cash flow picture.
- In other words, when accounting profits serve as a proxy for cash flows—which is true in most cases—they can be used as the basis from which investors form their cash flow expectations. However, when they obscure the true picture, adjustments should be made.
- Asset impairments, for example, are a non-cash expense when recognized and, moreover, represent a sunk cost.
- Asset impairments basically imply that a poor investment decision was made in the past and, if such mistakes are no longer expected, they can be ignored and adjusted for.
- Gains from asset sales should also be viewed with caution, particularly for one-off sales with little impact on future cash flows. If they don't represent a recurring activity, they should be excluded from cash flow expectations.
- Stock-based compensation is another very important case. It's not a typical expense since it doesn't reduce a company's ability to generate cash flow.
- However, stock-based compensation results in shareholder dilution, which in turn reduces an investor's share of future dividends.

- Because dilution impacts an investor's future cash flows, stock-based compensation shouldn't be ignored.
- However, accounting practices don't offer the best solution for how to account for stock-based compensation. The expense recognized is nothing more than an imperfect estimate and, more importantly, it's not intuitive.
- Rather than reducing cash flows by relying on the stock-based compensation expense recorded by standard accounting practices, it's better to estimate the expected dilution and adjust future cash flow expectations accordingly.
- Depreciation is the last example discussed and, while it's a non-cash expense at the time of recognition, it does represent a true cash cost.
- In most cases, depreciation does a materially good job at measuring the cash flow impact associated with long-lived asset costs and, as a result, shouldn't be ignored.
- However, in some cases, depreciation may overstate a company's cash outlays. This can happen in businesses with assets that essentially have indefinite lives, such as real estate.
- Because real estate may never actually be replaced and represents a sunk cost, depreciation may unnecessarily reduce cash flow expectations.
- Furthermore, even if the real estate is replaced, if it's set to happen far into the future, it's practically irrelevant for valuation purposes.
- As a result, for these types of long-lived assets, it's better to ignore depreciation and focus instead on the cash cost of maintaining the asset—also known as maintenance CapEx.
- As this adjustment is considered, be careful not to confuse depreciation with a proxy for growth CapEx needed for reinvestments. You should always focus on the cash flows produced by the existing business, and then separately evaluate the reinvestment returns from any expansions.

- Given that accounting profits are not a perfect proxy for cash flows, and that adjustments may be needed as a result, it's advisable to review a company's cash flow statement.
- Because this statement links accrual-based accounting practices with actual cash inflows and outflows, it can help bridge the gap between profits and real cash flow.
- The section on cash flow from operating activities can help assess whether any adjustments to depreciation or other non-cash items are needed.
- Be careful, however, not to think of cash flow from operations as equivalent to investor cash flow. Not only is it difficult to work with the volatile impact of working capital movements, but cash flow from operations can also be misleading.
- The remaining two sections of the statement—investing and financing activities—reveal important insights into how a company manages its profits and reinvests them. Given the importance of reinvesting properly, these sections cannot be overlooked.

CHAPTER 6

VALUATION — PART 4

LOOKING BEYOND 10 YEARS

Before we took a detour into accounting considerations, we were laying the groundwork for how to value an asset, and I highlighted a couple of important concepts that are often overlooked in conventional financial analysis.

First, I emphasized that the discount rate is not some abstract variable; it's simply our expected compounded return viewed from the opposite perspective. Because of this, when we are determining the appropriate discount rate for a stream of future cash flows, the question we should be asking is: "What return do we want?" And the answer should be based on what we think justifies the risk, the opportunity cost, and the fact that we are deferring consumption. Understanding this improves our judgment while allowing us to base decisions on common sense.

The second key point we covered was the limitation of applying a discount rate to future cash flows. When we deal with multiple cash flows over time, the discount rate only accurately represents our compounded return if one condition is met: any interim cash flows must be reinvested at the same rate as the discount rate.

If the reinvestment rate is lower than the discount rate, our actual compounded return will fall short, and conversely, if the reinvestment rate is higher, our compounded return will exceed the discount rate. The longer the life of the asset, the more significant the impact of the reinvestment rate on our compounded returns becomes. We saw this difference in the context of a 2-year bond versus a 10-year bond.

While this comparison was helpful, it's still incomplete when we think about valuing stocks or businesses. The key difference lies in the nature of bonds versus businesses: bonds have a defined maturity date and a contractual obligation to repay the principal, while businesses do not.

In layman's terms, this means that, in addition to interest coupons, investors will receive the initial invested amount when the bond matures. When you purchase a stock, however, there's no fixed time horizon, and there's no expectation that your initial investment will ever be returned.

This means that the value of a business depends exclusively on the ongoing cash flows it generates for investors until it ceases to exist. Because of this, it's important to now explore how the valuation framework we've discussed applies to assets with an indefinite useful life and no contractual obligation to return the original invested amount.

Terminal Value and Perpetual Discounting

Not surprisingly, conventional financial wisdom suggests that we should project all future cash flows, applying a discount rate to each one, and then sum up their present values. However, projecting 30, 50, or even 70 years into the future is rarely practical.

Thankfully, even those who tend to predict down to the finest detail don't typically extend projections that far. Instead, in practice, people often project cash flows for 5 to 10 years and then calculate what's known as a terminal value. This terminal value assumes that, beyond those initial years, cash flows will either remain steady or grow at a consistent rate, which simplifies the math and avoids the need for long-term projections. In essence, the terminal value reflects the present value of an ongoing stream of cash flows that extends indefinitely.

As an example, the chart on the following page illustrates this idea for a hypothetical company that is expected to generate a growing set of cash flows until the 10th year and then return $10,000 per year in perpetuity. For simplicity, it assumes a 10% discount rate:

Year	Total Cash Flows	Terminal Value	Present Value Formula	Present Value	Total Present Value
Year 0					$ 91,898
Year 1	$ 7,750		$7,750 / (1+10%)^1	$ 7,045	
Year 2	$ 8,000		$8,000 / (1+10%)^2	$ 6,612	
Year 3	$ 8,250		$8,250 / (1+10%)^3	$ 6,198	
Year 4	$ 8,500		$8.500 / (1+10%)^4	$ 5,806	
Year 5	$ 8,750		$8,750 / (1+10%)^5	$ 5,433	
Year 6	$ 9,000		$9,000 / (1+10%)^6	$ 5,080	
Year 7	$ 9,250		$9,250 / (1+10%)^7	$ 4,747	
Year 8	$ 9,500		$9,500 / (1+10%)^8	$ 4,432	
Year 9	$ 9,750		$9,750 / (1+10%)^9	$ 4,135	
Year 10	$ 10,000	$10,000 / 10% = $100,000	$110,000 / (1+10%)^10	$42,410	
Year 11					
Year 12					
Year …					
Year …					
Year …					

Perpetuity

To clarify, this chart shows the expected cash flows for the first 10 years plus the value of all cash flows from year 11 onward (i.e., the terminal value). This terminal value tells us what a $10,000 cash flow stream in perpetuity would be worth in year 10. But because we want to know what that terminal value is worth today, we have to further discount it to the present, or year 0.

I'm not particularly fond of relying on this approach, so I won't go into the details of how terminal values are typically calculated or the reasoning behind it. For our purposes, just understand that terminal values are straightforward to calculate and don't require you to assume cash flows remain constant, as we did in the example above. You can instead assume that the last projected cash flow will grow at a consistent rate. For example, rather than assuming a flat $10,000 in year 11 and beyond, you could project that those cash flows will grow at a steady 2%, 3%, or 4% annually.

The Terminal Value Is Abstract and Yet Overly Influential

Conceptually, this approach is not wrong, but it presents several significant challenges. First, it once again fails to address the reinvestment returns of interim cash flows, a critical component that we've already established as essential to accurately understand returns. But the issues don't end there.

The terminal value itself is an abstract concept, preventing us from relying on common sense in our valuation process, particularly because it accounts for a disproportionate share of the valuation. In the case above, the terminal value accounts for over 40% of the total valuation. And if we had calculated it 5 years into the future instead of 10, it would have accounted for almost 70% of the valuation.

The terminal value can represent an even larger portion of the total valuation when we assume that the final projected cash flow will grow over time. This becomes especially concerning for high-growth companies, where the cash flow expected in the later years of the projection period—5 or 10 years out—is significantly larger than that in the first couple of years.

In these cases, the early years of cash flows have much less influence on the final valuation, making the outcome even more dependent on the terminal value. And when such a large portion of your valuation hinges on this one abstract figure, it's hard to make a sound investment decision with this approach.

Terminal Value's Sensitivity to the Discount Rate

The terminal value is also highly sensitive to the discount rate chosen, which further complicates this approach and makes it even more abstract. To put this into perspective, consider the impact of different discount rate scenarios on the terminal value from our example above.

As shown in the table below, reducing the discount rate from 10% to 7% increases the terminal value by over 40%. On the other hand, increasing the discount rate from 10% to 14% reduces the terminal value by nearly 30%. Since the final valuation depends heavily on the terminal value, it's not surprising that variations in the discount rate also significantly affect the overall valuation (see the chart on the next page).

Discount Rate	7.0%	8.0%	9.0%	10.0%	11.0%	12.0%	13.0%	14.0%
Terminal Value	$142,857	$125,000	$111,111	$100,000	$90,909	$83,333	$76,923	$71,429
Final Valuation	$133,983	$116,397	$102,765	$91,898	$83,039	$75,684	$69,484	$64,190

Since we know that the discount rate is essentially our expected return, we can understand this concept better than most people. We know that, for example, if we pay $91,898 for the business—the valuation using a 10% discount rate—we can expect a 10% compounded return, provided that all interim cash flows are reinvested at 10%. Similarly, if we pay $64,190—the valuation using a 14% discount rate—we can expect a 14% compounded return, as long as interim cash flows are reinvested at 14%. Of course, these expected returns will only materialize if our projections hold true.

Reframing Valuation Through Inverse Analysis

In any case, while having a solid understanding of the discount rate helps us better conceptualize the conventional valuation framework, it's not particularly practical. Instead, I prefer an inverse analysis that is more intuitive and places a stronger emphasis on our often overlooked factor: the return on reinvested interim cash flows.

With an inverse analysis, we essentially reverse the process of a discounted cash flow analysis. Instead of projecting future cash flows and discounting them back to the present, we start with an assumed valuation and ask: what needs to happen in the future for me to achieve my desired compounded return?

Since stocks are publicly traded, we can easily see the market's valuation of a company at any time. We can use this market price as our starting point and work backward to determine the conditions required for achieving our target return. This approach is extremely helpful because, rather than dealing with abstract assumptions that lead to overly theoretical valuations, you're left with tangible, practical hurdles that must be met in order to meet your return objective. Ultimately, all you need to do is assess whether the stock can meet these hurdles.

Tailoring Analysis to Mature and Growth Companies

To perform this inverse analysis, it's helpful to categorize companies into two buckets: mature companies and high-growth companies. Mature companies are those you expect to have relatively stable cash flows over time. These companies usually operate in well-established industries, and due to their size and market share, it's difficult for them to experience significant growth.

High-growth companies, on the other hand, are those with substantial potential for cash flow growth in the near future. These businesses often operate in emerging industries or are still small enough to capture market share.

It's important to note, however, that you don't need to define these buckets with precision. Ultimately, the inverse analysis you perform will depend on whether you're dealing with a growth company or a mature company. It's up to you to assess which bucket a particular company belongs to and apply the corresponding inverse analysis based on your expectations for that business.

You Don't Need to Project Forever

That said, we'll detail the process for mature versus growth companies in later chapters. First, it's important to highlight that there's no real need to project cash flows to infinity. While this holds true regardless of the valuation method used, it's especially important to understand in the context of the inverse analysis.

While it's great to believe a business will last for the next 100 years, when valuing it, it's completely unnecessary to project that far ahead. Thinking about a time horizon of 25 to 35 years should be sufficient for mature businesses and 40 to 45 for high growth businesses.

To illustrate this, let's use a simple example: assume the current market value of a mature business is $100,000, and we expect it to generate $10,000 in annual cash flows to shareholders over the next 30 years. Notice that this setup is very similar to the 10-year bond example from Chapter 4. The key differences are that we're now looking at a 30-year horizon instead of 10, and—most importantly—there is no principal repayment at the end of the investment period.

Cash Flow Yield: A Helpful Framing Tool

To make this practical, let's consider our example from the perspective of cash flow yield. This metric is essentially a way to interpret a company's valuation regardless of its size. It tells us what portion of the business's valuation is represented by its expected annual cash flow. It's calculated by dividing the annual cash flow—in this case, $10,000—by the market value of the business—$100,000—resulting in a cash flow yield of 10%.

You can think of this as similar to the coupon rate—or interest rate—in our bond examples, as it highlights the relationship between a company's valuation and its cash flow, much like how the coupon rate reflects the relationship between the bond's interest payments and its principal value. Using the cash flow yield is helpful because, since it's manifesting essentially the same thing, we can interpret and discuss business valuations in much the same way we did with bond valuations.

Calculating Returns from a Stable Cash Flow Yield

Let's move on and ask: what would our compounded annual return be for a company with a stable 10% cash flow yield? To calculate this—just as we did in Chapter 4 with bonds—we need to determine the future value of each interim cash flow after it's been reinvested at a specific rate. For simplicity, let's assume the business reinvests at a 10% rate, matching the cash flow yield. Now, let's look at the chart on the next page to visualize what this looks like:

Year	Total Cash Flows	Reinvesting Cash Flows	Value in Year 30	Total Value in Year 30
Year 0				
Year 1	$ 10,000	$10,000 * (1+10%)^29	$ 158,631	
Year 2	$ 10,000	$10,000 * (1+10%)^28	$ 144,210	
Year 3	$ 10,000	$10,000 * (1+10%)^27	$ 131,100	
Year 4	$ 10,000	$10,000 * (1+10%)^26	$ 119,182	
Year 5	$ 10,000	$10,000 * (1+10%)^25	$ 108,347	
Year 6	$ 10,000	$10,000 * (1+10%)^24	$ 98,497	
Year 7	$ 10,000	$10,000 * (1+10%)^23	$ 89,543	
Year 8	$ 10,000	$10,000 * (1+10%)^22	$ 81,403	
Year 9	$ 10,000	$10,000 * (1+10%)^21	$ 74,002	
Year 10	$ 10,000	$10,000 * (1+10%)^20	$ 67,275	
Year ...				
Year ...				
Year ...				
Year ...				
Year 29	$ 10,000	$10,000 * (1+10%)^1	$ 11,000	
Year 30	$ 10,000	$10,000 * (1+10%)^0	$ 10,000	
				$1,644,940

As you can see in the chart, the cash flow from year 1 is reinvested for the remaining 29 years, the cash flow from year 2 for the remaining 28 years, and so on. When we add up the future value of all these reinvested cash flows at year 30, we get a total of $1,644,940. In other words, if these projections and reinvestment assumptions hold true, our $100,000 investment would grow to roughly $1,645,000 in year 30.

Using the formula from Chapter 4, this represents a 9.8% compounded annual return. See the calculation below for more clarity.

$$r = \left(\frac{\$1,644,940}{\$100,000}\right)^{\frac{1}{30}} - 1$$

What If the Business Lasts More Than 30 Years?

Now, try to think about what would happen if we assumed a 100-year life for the business instead of just 30 years. While it might seem that extending the business's life would lead to significantly higher returns, the compounded annual return would barely increase to 10%.

We'll explain why this is the case in a second but first let me clarify one thing to avoid confusion. In both cases, I'm referring to the returns on an annual basis over the respective periods. In our 30-year example, we would expect a 9.8% compounded annual return over 30 years; in the 100-year scenario, it would be 10% compounded annually over 100 years.

It may seem odd at first to compare returns for periods of different lengths, but that's the advantage of thinking in terms of annual returns rather than absolute figures. This approach lets us directly compare different scenarios, even with varying time frames. Put differently, while the 100-year period would undoubtedly lead to higher absolute returns, you can still compare both scenarios as we're expressing both in annual terms.

That said, to provide further perspective, the chart below illustrates how different time horizons impact our annual compounded returns for this hypothetical business, while keeping all other assumptions constant.

Assumed Life of Business / Time Horizon	Year 15	Year 20	Year 25	Year 30	Year 35	Year 40	Year 45
Forward-Looking Compounded Returns	8.0%	9.1%	9.6%	9.8%	9.9%	9.9%	10.0%

As you can see, the variations in compounded returns become progressively smaller as we extend the time horizon. Extending the life expectancy of the business from 15 to 25 years increases annual returns by 1.6%. However, when we extend the time horizon by another 10 years—from 25 to 35 years—the increase in annual returns is only 0.3%. Extending yet again by another 10 years—from 35 to 45 years—results in an even smaller impact, with annual returns increasing by just 0.1%.

Hopefully, this proves that thinking beyond 25 to 35 years is unnecessary for mature businesses. Now, let's hone in on some key insights and dive deeper into the conclusions we can draw from the results above and the reasoning behind them.

The Diminishing Value of Long-Term Cash Flows

Cash flows far in the future have minimal impact on forward-looking returns. The reason is simple: we can't reinvest them for long periods, so they don't undergo significant compounding. Compounding is exponential, meaning that even small delays can drastically reduce its effect.

For example, if we look at our cash flow chart, we can compare the future values of year 1's cash flow ($158,631) to year 5's ($108,347). The former benefits from 29 years of compounding, while the latter only compounds for 25 years and, as a result, year 1's future value is almost 50% higher than year 5's, demonstrating how much of an impact the extra years of compounding have.

The most striking difference, of course, is between the first and last cash flows in the 30-year period. The future value of year 1 ($158,631) is almost sixteen times that of year 30 ($10,000), and this is essentially the most compelling evidence of why extending the expected life of the business doesn't significantly increase our expected compounded returns.

Beyond the first 25 to 30 years, cash flows generated simply can't match the value of the early ones that have benefited from exponential compounding over that period. In other words, the later cash flows lack the same compounding advantage of the earlier ones, diminishing the impact of extending the business's life.

If you recall our discussion on depreciation from Chapter 5, I had already made reference to this reality. I explained that even if a long-lived asset is eventually replaced, if that replacement is far enough in the future, the cash outlay becomes practically irrelevant for our return expectations. Hopefully, this now makes it much clearer why that's the case: the size of the cash outlay at the time of replacement would simply pale in comparison to the cumulative compounded value of all the cash flows it helped generate over the preceding decades.

Reinvestment Decisions Make or Break Compounding

The successful reinvestment of interim cash flows is the most crucial element in achieving the desired returns. This shouldn't come as a surprise as it's been a key theme throughout the book. However, it's worth emphasizing yet again because, unlike bonds or other assets, we don't control how interim cash flows are reinvested with stocks. Instead, the management team and the company's board decide this.

Whether the company pays dividends, buys back stock, or retains earnings to grow the business, all of these decisions impact how much compounding can actually happen. If management's capital decisions are centered on helping shareholders achieve high reinvestment rates, compounding will likely occur. If not, no matter how accurate our projections of the current business might be, our desired compounded returns simply won't materialize.

Finite-Life Businesses Can Still Create Lasting Returns

It's okay to invest in businesses that may not show much growth or may not be around in 20 to 30 years. For example, a company operating gas pipelines in a basin with finite reserves might only have 25 years of life left. However, if you buy the business at a price that offers a strong cash flow yield, it can still be a solid investment as long as the company reinvests those cash flows wisely.

If the company uses its cash flow to acquire other pipeline businesses in other basins at attractive prices, compounding will work its magic, and you'll likely do well. Even if the company doesn't reinvest the cash flows, significant returns can still be generated if the business returns that money to investors via dividends. In this case, the reinvestment rate would depend on the investor's choice of where to reinvest the funds. Ultimately, the success of the investment depends on how wisely those interim cash flows are reinvested—regardless of who makes the decision.

The Opportunity Cost of Delayed Cash Flows

Be cautious with businesses that have little or no cash flow in the first few years of your investment horizon. The opportunity cost of a lack of early cash flows simply cannot be overstated.

When you invest in a business that produces substantial cash flows relative to the price you pay—like our 10% cash flow yielding example—the compounding effect begins immediately. If, however, you're purchasing a business with little to no cash flows in the early years with expectations that they will materialize later, you're essentially delaying compounding.

This delay can significantly impact your final returns, especially if your growth expectations fall short. If cash flows fail to grow as anticipated, you'll have wasted time and sacrificed valuable compounding with little to show for it.

High-Growth Businesses Need Longer to Compound

This opportunity cost will become even clearer as we explore some examples later. But it's important to note now that high-growth businesses, which often have a low cash flow yield, may require a time horizon of more than 35 years. In other words, extending the time horizon from 30 to 40 years may still have a material impact on expected compounded returns for high-growth businesses—something we saw wasn't the case for mature businesses.

The reason for this is straightforward: a high-growth business with a low cash flow yield won't see as much benefit from the compounding of early cash flows, since those initial cash flows are relatively small. These businesses need more time to allow the early, smaller cash flows to compound and become more significant. Therefore, while a 25- to 35-year time horizon might be sufficient for mature businesses with high cash flow yields, high-growth businesses may need a 40- to 45-year time frame to ensure that you'll achieve your desired compounded returns.

So essentially, when you view the sensitivity chart we last saw, it behaves similarly for high-growth businesses with a low cash flow yield, but the time horizon hurdles shift. In the chart discussed, after the first 25 years, the increments in expected returns become relatively small, and beyond 35 years, they are practically negligible. For high-growth businesses, however, the increments in expected returns become small after 35 years, and negligible after 45 years.

I'm not providing a sensitivity chart for high-growth businesses because the results depend not only on the cash flow yield and reinvestment rate, but also on the business's specific growth rate. Adding this additional variable makes the analysis more difficult to display clearly. That said, the conclusions I just outlined should still hold as a broadly accurate rule of thumb.

CHAPTER 6 SUMMARY AND TAKEAWAYS (OPTIONAL READING)

- Before this chapter, we walked through valuation considerations using various bond examples. However, because businesses don't have a fixed time horizon or an obligation to repay the initial investment like bonds do, it was important to explore a more realistic setup.
- We looked at a business generating a perpetual and consistent stream of cash flows and discussed how it would be valued under the conventional valuation framework.
- In short, people simply project cash flows for 5 to 10 years and then calculate a terminal value for the remaining years.
- The terminal value represents the value of a consistent stream of cash flows extending into perpetuity.
- While there's nothing conceptually wrong with the terminal value, it's too abstract and, because it accounts for a disproportionate share of the valuation, it's not very useful.
- In addition to the difficulty of dealing with terminal values, the conventional valuation framework still fails to address the importance of reinvestment returns.
- Given these challenges, I suggest reframing the valuation process through an inverse analysis, which essentially reverses the steps of the discounted cash flow method.
- Rather than projecting cash flows and discounting them to the present, we can simply take the market valuation already available and ask: what needs to happen in the future to achieve the desired compounded return?
- This method is more effective because, instead of dealing with abstract assumptions and theoretical valuations, investors are given a set of tangible and practical hurdles to achieving their desired returns. Ultimately, all investors need to do is assess whether a given stock can meet those hurdles.

- For the inverse analysis, it's useful to distinguish between mature and growth businesses, but we'll cover exactly how in later chapters.
- For now, it's important to highlight—particularly in the context of inverse analysis—that there's no real need to project cash flows to infinity. A time horizon of 25 to 35 years is typically sufficient for mature businesses, and 40 to 45 years for high-growth businesses.
- To help illustrate this, we began looking at valuations from the perspective of cash flow yield—calculated by dividing the annual cash flow by the market value of the business.
- If we look at a business with a 30-year expected life, a 10% cash flow yield, and an assumed 10% reinvestment rate, the compounded annual return would be 9.8%.
- While this result is materially different from the 8% that would be achieved with a 15-year business—all else equal—it is only slightly lower than the 10% compounded return of a 100-year business.
- The impact of extending a business's life becomes increasingly marginal because of the diminishing value of distant cash flows.
- Early cash flows are significantly more valuable to us because they have more time to compound, disproportionately influencing our forward-looking returns.
- Beyond the first 25 to 30 years, the value of newly generated cash flows simply can't compare to the compounded value of early ones.
- If reinvested adequately, the future value of the first year's cash flow will be magnitudes greater than the value of a cash flow received in year 30.
- This reality underscores the importance of successfully reinvesting interim cash flows—without which investors cannot achieve their desired returns.
- Precisely because successful reinvesting and compounding are so important, investors should be cautious with businesses that have low cash flow yields—typically seen in high-growth companies.

- Businesses with relatively low cash flows today are essentially postponing the exponential benefits of compounding.
- As a result, if the anticipated growth doesn't materialize, valuable compounding time will have been lost with nothing to show for it.
- Additionally, high-growth businesses may need closer to 40 to 45 years—compared to 25 to 35 years for mature businesses—to generate the desired compounded returns.

CHAPTER 7

VALUATION — PART 5

INVERSE ANALYSIS FOR MATURE BUSINESSES

With this background in mind, we can start laying the groundwork for our inverse analysis for mature businesses. As we saw with our stable 10% cash flow yielding company, as long as the company continues to produce that annual yield, and the interim cash flows are reinvested at a 10% rate, you can expect to achieve a compounded return of approximately 10%—9.8% to be exact.

So now we know what conditions need to be present if we're seeking to achieve a 10% compounded return and we encounter a stock yielding 10% at existing market prices. Specifically, the company must maintain that cash flow yield for the next 30 years or so, and the cash flows must be reinvested at the same 10% rate. So, your job now is to determine whether those conditions or hurdles are likely to hold true.

If you believe the company won't last beyond 15 years—or that it will, but with declining levels of cash flow—then you shouldn't purchase it unless you believe the reinvestment rate will be much higher than 10%. Similarly, if you believe the reinvestment rate will be much lower than 10%, you shouldn't purchase it at current prices even if you expect the business to last for 30+ years. Otherwise, you'll have to content yourself with a compounded return below 10% and not achieve your return objective.

Breaking Down Inverse Analysis Across Scenarios

Now, you might be wondering how to apply this approach to businesses with market valuations that result in other cash flow yields. It's clear that the methodology is simple and practical when we have a 10% cash flow yield, but what about the other scenarios? What if we're looking at companies with yields of 5%, 15%, or something else entirely?

Well, rather than bog you down with more math or tables, I've included below a sensitivity analysis across various scenarios. This will make it much easier for you to grasp how different cash flow yields and reinvestment rates affect expected returns. If you're interested in the math, however, note that there's nothing different compared to what we reviewed in our example. The only real difference is the inputs that you apply.

Sensitivity Analysis - Mature Company with Stable Cash Flows and No Growth

		Reinvestment Rate							
		0%	2.5%	5.0%	7.5%	10.0%	12.5%	15.0%	17.5%	20.0%
Cash Flow Yield	2.5%	-1.0%	0.3%	1.7%	3.2%	4.8%	6.5%	8.3%	10.1%	11.9%
	5.0%	1.4%	2.7%	4.1%	5.6%	7.3%	9.0%	10.8%	12.7%	14.6%
	7.5%	2.7%	4.1%	5.5%	7.1%	8.7%	10.5%	12.3%	14.2%	16.1%
	10.0%	3.7%	5.1%	6.5%	8.1%	9.8%	11.6%	13.4%	15.3%	17.2%
	12.5%	4.5%	5.8%	7.3%	8.9%	10.6%	12.4%	14.2%	16.2%	18.1%
	15.0%	5.1%	6.5%	8.0%	9.6%	11.3%	13.1%	14.9%	16.9%	18.8%
	17.5%	5.7%	7.0%	8.5%	10.1%	11.9%	13.7%	15.5%	17.5%	19.5%
	20.0%	6.2%	7.5%	9.0%	10.6%	12.3%	14.2%	16.0%	18.0%	20.0%

Anyway, the table above tells you what your compounded annual return would be under various cash flow yield and reinvestment rate assumptions. In all scenarios, I assumed a 30-year time horizon and that cash flow yields remain constant over that period. The gray-highlighted scenario is the one we just discussed: a company yielding 10% based on its existing valuation and reinvesting at a 10% rate over time. As we know, this leads to an expected compounded annual return of 9.8% over the 30-year period.

To make it even clearer how this chart should be interpreted, let me highlight two more examples. In the upper right corner, we see a company with a 2.5% cash flow yield and a 20% reinvestment rate. In this scenario, you would expect to achieve an 11.9% compounded return over the 30 years. On the other side of the spectrum, the lower left corner shows a company with a 20% cash flow yield, but with a 0% reinvestment rate. In this case, the expected compounded return is only 6.2%.

Knowing how the table works, let me emphasize a couple of important points regarding this sensitivity analysis.

The Most Important Driver: Reinvestment Rate

The reinvestment rate is more important than the cash flow yield—i.e., more important than the valuation. As the key theme of the book, I keep highlighting the importance of the reinvestment rate, but nothing illustrates this point better than this table.

If you look at how expected returns change as we move through the table, it becomes clear that moving from left to right has more impact than moving from top to bottom. Put differently, you achieve a higher expected return by purchasing a company with a low yield and high reinvestment rate than by investing in a high-yielding company with a low reinvestment rate.

So, when we attempt to invest in undervalued companies, we can't ignore this reality. It's not simply about buying cheap companies. It's about finding companies that are highly likely to reinvest cash flows at high rates of return. If such companies are available at cheap prices, that's the ideal investment. But as long as a company is not overly expensive, more importance should be placed on its quality than its price, at least for those of us with long-term horizons. As I mentioned before, I truly believe this is why Warren Buffett and Charlie Munger always emphasize that it's better to buy a wonderful company at a fair price than a fair company at a wonderful price.

Adjusting Cash Flow Yield for Accounting Realities

Don't forget the accounting considerations discussed earlier. When you think about the cash flow yield, it should be based on the cash flow that you expect to be available to owners on a recurring basis. As discussed at length in Chapter 5, accounting profits may often serve as a proxy for cash flows, but they can't be trusted blindly.

You must adjust for those items whose cash impact is not accurately represented by accounting standards. Likewise, be mindful of non-recurring items that won't affect the company's cash flows in the future and don't forget the impact of stock-based compensation schemes. For many mature businesses, shareholder dilution tends to be very low and, as a result, this table would still be materially applicable. If, however, dilution were to be significant, expected compounded returns would be materially lower, requiring higher hurdles for cash flow yields and reinvestment rates.

Don't Confuse Business Growth with Reinvestment Returns

Don't confuse cash flow growth from existing operations with growth driven by reinvested earnings. Many mature businesses do experience at least mild growth in cash flows over time, but this is often due to the company retaining earnings and reinvesting them. While this is great if it's paying off—as we've discussed, that's exactly what we want!—it's important to put it into context.

Cash flow growth resulting from reinvestments reflects the returns on those reinvested funds, not growth from the company's existing operations. Therefore, this type of growth should be considered a result of the reinvestment rate we've been discussing, rather than growth from the current business.

In other words, to assess whether cash flows are stable and consistent, we must imagine what they would look like if management chose to distribute the earnings to shareholders instead of retaining and reinvesting them. This would represent the cash flows from the existing operations. From there, you can evaluate whether reinvesting those cash flows—whether by the company or by you—would generate a satisfactory reinvestment rate.

I can't emphasize enough the importance of making this distinction. Just think about it, no one would claim that a bond has growing cash flows just because reinvested coupons in other bonds result in larger cumulative coupons in the future. This point is so important that we'll explore it in depth in Chapter 11.

For now, let me just highlight that, when you understand this, you realize that many mature companies actually have more stable cash flows than you might think. And as a result, the table above, combined with this mindset, can be extremely helpful in determining whether such companies are worth their market valuation—i.e., cash flow yield.

That being said, it's not uncommon to find businesses that, despite being relatively mature, can still experience moderate growth without needing to retain and reinvest part of their earnings. This could be due to their ability to raise prices or their capability to achieve cost efficiencies gradually over time. Additionally, inflation can certainly contribute to growth in cash flows over time even if it's just in nominal terms. So, to provide you with a bit more perspective for those situations, below is another table that assumes a consistent 3% growth in cash flows over our assumed 30-year period, while keeping all other assumptions the same.

Sensitivity Analysis - Mature Company with 3% Annual Growth									
		\ Reinvestment Rate							
		0%	2.5%	5.0%	7.5%	10.0%	12.5%	15.0%	17.5%	20.0%
Cash Flow Yield	2.5%	0.7%	1.8%	3.0%	4.4%	5.9%	7.4%	9.1%	10.9%	12.6%
	5.0%	3.0%	4.2%	5.4%	6.8%	8.3%	10.0%	11.7%	13.4%	15.3%
	7.5%	4.4%	5.6%	6.9%	8.3%	9.8%	11.5%	13.2%	15.0%	16.8%
	10.0%	5.4%	6.6%	7.9%	9.3%	10.9%	12.5%	14.3%	16.1%	18.0%
	12.5%	6.2%	7.4%	8.7%	10.1%	11.7%	13.4%	15.1%	17.0%	18.9%
	15.0%	6.9%	8.0%	9.4%	10.8%	12.4%	14.1%	15.8%	17.7%	19.6%
	17.5%	7.4%	8.6%	9.9%	11.4%	13.0%	14.6%	16.4%	18.3%	20.2%
	20.0%	7.9%	9.1%	10.4%	11.9%	13.5%	15.2%	16.9%	18.8%	20.7%

Be Approximately Right, Not Precisely Wrong

When using this sensitivity analysis to make decisions, remember that it's better to be approximately right than precisely wrong. In the real world, no company has cash flows as consistent and predictable as bonds. Even a stable business like Coca-Cola will see fluctuations in its cash flows over time.

The key is not to try and predict exact future cash flows, but rather to gauge whether the cash flow yield from current operations will remain fairly consistent. Some years may have slightly higher or lower yields, but these minor variations won't drastically affect your long-term returns. What's important is that you get the general direction of cash flows right, not necessarily the precise numbers.

Likewise, predicting the reinvestment rate is nearly impossible to do with complete accuracy. While we'll discuss at length the reinvestment rate in Chapters 10 - 12, I can tell you now that it's even harder to forecast than the direction of cash flow itself. The reinvestment rate depends largely on management's future decisions, such as whether they retain profits and, if so, what those profits will be reinvested in. Even if you have some insight into those decisions, predicting the returns on those reinvestments is even trickier, given the inherent uncertainty of any company's future endeavors.

Given these considerations, when using the table above in real-world decision-making, focus on being approximately right rather than obsessing over precise predictions. Concentrate on the key factors that drive outcomes, rather than getting bogged down by minor details that are hard to predict. Keep the bigger picture in mind: consider the company's competitive strength, its likelihood of long-term survival, and the quality of management's judgment and capital allocation abilities.

A Margin of Safety Still Matters

When I emphasize the impossibility of being precisely right, I'm not suggesting that being approximately correct is easy. Predicting the future is still challenging, even when you're only trying to gauge the general direction of things. This is why value investors always stress the importance of a margin of safety. The application of the inverse analysis—and especially the use of the sensitivity table—should never imply that a margin of safety can be ignored.

Always buy at a valuation with a cash flow yield higher than what you believe is sufficient to meet your desired return based on your expectations of the future. If you follow this principle, even if cash flows turn out to be directionally less than anticipated or the reinvestment rate comes in lower than expected, you will still have a cushion to protect your investment and a higher chance of achieving the returns you aim for.

Be Wary of Cyclical Businesses

The example we used for our analysis assumes a consistent stream of cash flows, which reflects the approximate reality of many mature businesses. However, this is not always the case. Many companies experience cyclical cash flows, either because they operate in inherently cyclical industries or because they are highly sensitive to economic cycles. Examples include commodity businesses like oil and gas producers, or companies that sell discretionary products that consumers may hesitate to purchase when the economy enters a recession.

Regardless of the cause, it's important not to extrapolate recent cash flow yields into the future for these companies. In fact, you should always be cautious about projecting the recent past forward, but this is especially true when dealing with cyclical companies. When considering the cash flow yield for a cyclical business, it's wise to look at the yield based on the average cash flow of the past 5 to 10 years or a period that includes a down cycle. Additionally, the need for a margin of safety becomes even more crucial in this context.

CHAPTER 7 SUMMARY AND TAKEAWAYS (OPTIONAL READING)

- Based on the learnings from the prior chapter, we now understand what hurdles must be overcome for an investor to achieve a roughly 10% return in the case of a mature company with a market valuation that yields 10%.
- Specifically, the existing cash flows must be maintained for the next 30 years, and each cash flow along the way must be reinvested at a 10% rate.
- With declining or short-lived cash flows, as well as a lower reinvestment rate, the desired return would fall short.
- Even though this is just one example, we can use a sensitivity table to explore any number of scenarios while applying the same thought process.
- The table essentially shows what an investor's compounded annual return would be under various cash flow yield and reinvestment rate assumptions.
- While we didn't go through the math in each case, the calculations are no different from what we did in Chapter 6—the only difference is the set of inputs used.
- In other words, the returns shown continue to assume a business with a 30-year life and a consistent stream of cash flows—with a second version incorporating a 3% cash flow growth rate shown later.
- Importantly, the tables reveal that the reinvestment rate is more important than the valuation—i.e., the cash flow yield.
- This shows that investing in undervalued companies isn't simply about buying them cheap. Doing so is a good start, but greater importance should be placed on the company's ability to reinvest cash flows at high rates of return.
- As these tables are put to use, don't forget how to think about the cash flow yield correctly. It should be based on the cash flow expected to be available to owners on a recurring basis, and the

accounting considerations from Chapter 5 should be taken into account.

- Additionally, be careful not to confuse business growth with reinvestment returns. This distinction helps clarify that the sensitivity tables are applicable to more companies than you might initially assume.

- It's also critical to use the table with a mindset of being approximately right, rather than obsessing over precision. Predicting exact cash flows and reinvestment rates is practically impossible, and trying to do so diverts attention from more important considerations.

- However, even when working with broader estimates, the future is inherently uncertain. As a result, a margin of safety is always advisable. Always aim to purchase at valuations with a higher cash flow yield than you think is sufficient based on your expectations.

- Finally, don't extrapolate recent cash flow yields into the future—especially for cyclical companies. For this type of business, it's always better to use a 5–10 year average and build an even greater margin of safety than usual.

CHAPTER 8

VALUATION — PART 6

INVERSE ANALYSIS FIRST APPROACH FOR HIGH-GROWTH BUSINESSES

The inverse approach for high-growth businesses is not conceptually different from that of mature businesses. The key idea remains to start with a given valuation and work backwards to determine the necessary conditions to achieve our desired returns.

With mature companies, the primary focus was on determining the reinvestment rate required to meet our return expectations. While we also needed to assess the company's ability to last at least 25 to 30 years and the stability of cash flows—at least approximately—these were more binary in nature. Since we can reasonably assume that these two factors are met for many mature companies, we can focus on the reinvestment rate as the key determinant for achieving our objectives under various valuation scenarios.

The Four Variables Behind High-Growth Valuation

For high-growth companies, however, there's an additional factor we need to account for: the growth rate of cash flows. In other words, we need to assess not just how well cash flows will be reinvested, but also how much cash flows will grow over time. Furthermore, we must consider how long the business will remain in a high-growth phase. Eventually, all businesses reach maturity, so assuming perpetual high growth isn't realistic. If we did, we'd essentially be suggesting that the company will eventually dominate the entire economy, which of course, wouldn't make sense.

As a result, we end up with four key variables instead of just two. In addition to the valuation—i.e., cash flow yield—and the reinvestment rate, for high-growth companies we also need to account for the duration of the high-growth phase and the growth rate of cash flows during that phase.

Two Ways to Analyze High-Growth Businesses

Given this added complexity, there are two approaches we can take. One option is to analyze how different reinvestment rates impact the expected return, while keeping the length of the growth phase and its growth rate fixed. This approach keeps the focus on how well the business reinvests its cash flows and is, therefore, more like what we did with mature businesses. Let's call this the first approach.

The other option is to fix a desired return and reinvestment rate—i.e., keep them constant—and determine what growth is needed to meet that target return. This approach places more focus on the growth rate and the duration of the high-growth phase. Let's call this the second approach.

Both approaches have their disadvantages given we must hold some of our four key variables constant while testing the effects of changes in the others. The first approach is more comprehensive and precise. It's also more consistent with how we have analyzed mature businesses, making it easier to compare the merits of a mature company relative to a high growth one.

However, the first approach doesn't allow you to easily sensitize growth rates and the duration of a company's growth phase. And, while not as important as the reinvestment rate, growth assumptions have a significant impact on returns. So, it's harder to get the full picture exclusively from the first approach. Ultimately, which one is more valuable depends on the context of the company being analyzed but, in most cases, my suggestion is to consider both. As I'll cover shortly, the best way to proceed will almost always be to apply the second approach first and then complement it with the first one.

A Brief Detour: Price-to-Cash Flow vs. Yield

Before we dive into each approach, let's first introduce a concept that will be incredibly useful as we go deeper: the price-to-cash flow (P/CF) ratio. Thus far, we've been using cash flow yield as our primary valuation metric. As you now know, cash flow yield is calculated by dividing a company's cash flow by its market value (price). Essentially, it tells us how much return a business is providing in relation to its price. By now, I'm sure you'll agree that the cash flow yield is a very practical metric for determining the price we should be willing to pay for a business.

However, there is a drawback to using cash flow yield, especially when assessing high-growth companies. These companies tend to trade at lower cash flow yields, often below 5%, and sometimes much lower than that. This is understandable, as it makes sense to pay a premium for a business that's growing rapidly. But because high-growth companies often have low cash flow yields, differences in those yields can appear trivial, when in reality, they can represent a significant difference in valuation.

For instance, consider two companies: one with a 1% cash flow yield and the other with a 1.5% yield. A difference of just 0.5% might seem negligible, but in fact, the second company would be valued at a 33% discount, compared to the first.

This is why, in many cases, it's more useful to look at the price-to-cash flow ratio. It's simply the inverse of the cash flow yield formula. Instead of dividing cash flow by the price, we divide the price by the cash flow.

This may sound complicated, but it's actually the same concept, just expressed in a different way. To illustrate this, I've provided a chart below, which compares a set of cash flow yields to their corresponding P/CF ratios.

Cash Flow / Price	1.0%	1.5%	2.0%	3.0%	4.0%	5.0%	6.0%	7.0%	8.0%	9.0%
Price / Cash Flow	100x	67x	50x	33x	25x	20x	17x	14x	13x	11x

The first two columns refer to the examples I just mentioned. A 1% cash flow yield translates to a 100x price-to-cash flow ratio, and a 1.5% cash flow yield corresponds to a 67x ratio. This method makes it much easier to understand that a 67x ratio indicates a significantly lower valuation than a 100x ratio. Looking at it this way helps clarify that one company is being valued at a 33% discount relative to the other.

Moving forward, I'll be using both the P/CF ratio and cash flow yield when evaluating high-growth businesses. But before we continue, it's worth noting that the price-to-cash flow ratio is very similar to the price-to-earnings (P/E) ratio, a metric you've likely heard of. The key difference is that the price-to-cash flow ratio uses cash flows, whereas the P/E ratio uses accounting profits (or earnings).

As you'll recall from Chapter 5, accounting earnings aren't always a perfect reflection of cash flows, and when calculating returns, what truly matters is the cash flow. That's why I prefer to rely on the price-to-cash flow ratio. However, note that in cases where earnings are a reasonable proxy for cash flows, the two ratios—price-to-cash flow and price-to-earnings—would be interchangeable.

Applying the First Approach: Amazon as a Case Study

Let's now move on to the inverse analysis for high-growth companies, starting with the first approach. For this, we'll use Amazon as a real-life example, since it's a company most people are familiar with. For practical purposes, I won't get into a deep dive of its entire financial statements to assess whether accounting profits are an accurate reflection of the company's ongoing cash flow-generating capacity. Instead, we'll assume that Amazon's accounting profits are a reasonable proxy, with the only adjustment being for stock-based compensation expense.

Based on Amazon's 10-K, the company's 2024 accounting profits totaled about $59 billion, which includes the impact of a $22 billion stock-based compensation expense. As we discussed in Chapter 5, stock-based compensation is imperfectly measured, so I'll add it back to calculate cash flow and address it differently in just a moment.

Adding $22 billion to $59 billion gives us a total cash flow of $81 billion, which we'll round to $80 billion for simplicity. With Amazon's market value at the time of this writing at around $2.4 trillion, the existing cash flow yield comes out to roughly 3.3%, or a price-to-cash-flow ratio of 30x.

Assumptions for Amazon's High-Growth Phase

With this context in mind, let's now put our inverse analysis to work. As a brief reminder, this first approach consists of assuming a specific length of time for the high-growth phase as well as a consistent growth rate during that phase. So, let's think about the rate at which Amazon can continue to grow and for how long it can grow at a rapid pace.

I haven't done a detailed analysis of Amazon's business, but I suspect it still has around 10 more years of high growth before it transitions into a more mature business. I also suspect it wouldn't be unreasonable for Amazon's existing cash flows to grow at an annual rate of 7.5% on average during those 10 years.

I know that to many of you, this may seem like an extremely conservative scenario. You may argue that Amazon's historical growth rates, which are closer to 20% and 25% over the past decade, imply that the company can keep growing much faster. You might also point to the new opportunities in artificial intelligence (AI) and Amazon's unique position to capitalize on that. And yes, you could be right, 7.5% may be too conservative. However, before jumping to that conclusion, I'd like you to carefully think about the following considerations.

Refining Our Growth Assumption to Account for Dilution

You have to take into account any expected dilution that may occur as a result of stock-based compensation schemes. Remember, when we calculated the cash flow yield and price-to-cash flow ratio, we added back stock-based compensation expense, essentially assuming it has no impact. But based on Amazon's current stock-based compensation schemes and its history of dilution, shareholders are likely to experience dilution of at least 1.5% to 2% per year.

As discussed in Chapter 5, dilution reduces the benefit of growth to shareholders. When I assume a 7.5% growth, I'm talking about the cash flow growth to me as a shareholder, after accounting for the 1.5% to 2.0% annual dilution I expect. In other words, by assuming 7.5% cash flow growth for existing shareholders, I'm effectively assuming a 9.0% to 9.5% growth from the company's perspective.

Avoid Double-Counting Reinvestment-Driven Growth

As we've discussed before, it's important to distinguish between growth from existing operations and growth driven by reinvested earnings. Otherwise, we risk double-counting growth—particularly the portion that comes from reinvestments, which is already captured in the reinvestment rate.

I do think Amazon is going to grow more than 9.0% - 9.5% annually over the next 10 years just like it has done in the past. However, much of that growth will come from reinvesting the company's earnings, not from the existing data centers, warehouses, and logistics infrastructure.

This was also the case with growth in the past. It's true Amazon's cash flows have grown at an average rate above 20% in the past decade. But what would've been the company's growth if it hadn't retained and reinvested earnings over time? I guarantee you it would have been significantly lower.

Amazon recently reported earnings for the full year of 2024 and they stated they expect capital expenditures to be roughly $100 billion in 2025. Some of that will likely replace existing infrastructure and is thus already accounted for via depreciation expense—again, as discussed in Chapter 5. But a significant portion of it—probably $40 - $70 billion—will go into expanding its infrastructure. And as I've been emphasizing all along, this is great if those investments generate high returns—as I expect will be the case for Amazon. But growth from reinvestment returns is not growth from existing operations or the existing asset base.

As I've said before, no one would claim that a bond has growing cash flows simply because reinvesting coupons in other bonds leads to larger cumulative returns. The same logic applies here. That's why, when thinking through our growth assumptions, we need to base them exclusively on the growth we believe will occur independent of any reinvestments. As I've noted before, we'll explore this in more depth in Chapter 11. But this high-level overview should be enough to clarify why a 7.5% growth rate for shareholders—net of dilution—is a reasonable estimate. In fact, I think it may even be too aggressive.

Focus on the Logic, Not the Assumptions
That said, I'm not an expert on Amazon's business, and I could definitely be wrong about this growth estimate. My goal here isn't to convince you of my perspective on Amazon's growth potential; rather, it's to walk you through the thought process so you can understand how to apply the inverse method effectively. If you disagree with my assumptions, feel free to substitute your own and apply them to the method. Just be sure to take into account these two considerations.

Final Assumptions for the First Approach (Amazon)
One last thing before we can lay out the sensitivity analysis of our inverse analysis with our first approach. For reasons we discussed before, I have assumed a 40-year life for this business as opposed to the 30-years we used for mature businesses. Additionally, after the high-growth period, I've assumed the company's cash flows will grow at a consistent 3% growth rate. While I prefer to be conservative and assume no growth, I do want to account for future inflation, and this terminal growth rate will help address that.

Reading the Sensitivity Results for Amazon
All that being said, what would be our expected returns for Amazon, or any company, which is expected to grow its existing business by 9% - 9.5% annually—equivalent to 7.5% after dilution—for the next 10 years and then grow 3% for 30 years after that. Well, the chart on the next page gives us our expected return based on various valuation and reinvestment rate scenarios.

It's to be interpreted in practically the same way as the sensitivity tables we discussed with mature businesses. In the case of Amazon, the most relevant row is the third one—highlighted in gray—since the company's valuation is very close to the 3% yield—or 33x price-cash-flow ratio—shown in that row.

Now, let's say you've determined that a 10% return is needed to justify the risk and opportunity cost of investing in Amazon. Well, you need to review the third row and find the reinvestment rate column that results in a roughly 10% compounded return. By doing so, you learn that if our growth assumptions hold true, Amazon would need to reinvest earnings at roughly 12.5% for 40 years to achieve your desired return at the current valuation.

Sensitivity Analysis - Investment to Grow 7.5% annually for 10 years and then 3%

P / CF	CF / P	\multicolumn{9}{c}{Reinvestment Rate}
		0%	2.5%	5.0%	7.5%	10.0%	12.5%	15.0%	17.5%	20.0%
100x	1.0%	0.4%	1.4%	2.6%	4.0%	5.5%	7.2%	8.9%	10.7%	12.6%
50x	2.0%	2.1%	3.2%	4.4%	5.8%	7.4%	9.0%	10.8%	12.6%	14.5%
33x	3.0%	3.2%	4.2%	5.5%	6.9%	8.5%	10.1%	11.9%	13.8%	15.7%
25x	4.0%	3.9%	5.0%	6.2%	7.7%	9.2%	10.9%	12.7%	14.6%	16.5%
20x	5.0%	4.5%	5.6%	6.8%	8.3%	9.8%	11.6%	13.4%	15.2%	17.2%
17x	6.0%	5.0%	6.1%	7.3%	8.8%	10.3%	12.1%	13.9%	15.8%	17.7%
14x	7.0%	5.4%	6.5%	7.7%	9.2%	10.8%	12.5%	14.3%	16.2%	18.2%
13x	8.0%	5.7%	6.8%	8.1%	9.5%	11.1%	12.9%	14.7%	16.6%	18.6%
11x	9.0%	6.0%	7.1%	8.4%	9.9%	11.5%	13.2%	15.0%	16.9%	18.9%

A Brief Detour on the Math

On a side note, for those of you curious about the math behind this sensitivity analysis, it's not too different from what we did with mature businesses. The main difference is that instead of assuming cash flows remain constant, we're assuming they grow at our projected rates.

After that, the process is essentially the same: you take each year's projected cash flow, reinvest it at the assumed rate for the remaining time horizon, and calculate its future value. Then, you sum up all those future values and compare the total with your initial investment amount to determine your compounded annual return. Once this is set up, you simply adjust the reinvestment rate and initial investment amount—i.e., your valuation—to explore different scenarios.

Let the Hurdles Guide Your Research

In any case, once again, we have a set of conditions that must be met for an investment in Amazon to generate a 10% compounded return at the current valuation. The inverse analysis, therefore, serves as a compass, offering clear direction. It's intuitive and based on tangible hurdles, acting as a guiding "north star" for our qualitative research. This framework helps us focus on the key questions that need answering. In the case of Amazon, you might want to consider the following:

- Is Amazon competitive enough to sustain a 9% cash flow growth rate for the next 10 years based solely on its existing operations? Given its size and market share in retail and cloud services, can it sustain such growth?
- Are Amazon's profit margins likely to expand and support this cash flow growth, or could they contract due to competitive pressures?
- Can Amazon reinvest its cash flows to achieve the 12.5% reinvestment rate we need, or will the AI frenzy cause irrational spending on data centers that fail to generate the desired returns?
- As the company matures, will management prioritize returning cash to shareholders, or will they invest in questionable ventures in search of more growth at all cost?
- Are Amazon's competitive advantages solid enough to keep it competitive for 30 or more years once it transitions to a mature phase? Or could competitors like Temu or Shein undermine the company's ability to maintain stable cash flows once it matures?

As you can see, all these questions are centered around the hurdles that our inverse analysis produced. And it's the answer to these types of questions that will ultimately determine whether Amazon is a good investment at the current valuation.

Comparing Amazon to a Mature Business: Bank of America

As I mentioned briefly before, one of the benefits of this first approach is that it's consistent with how we analyze mature businesses. As a result, we can more easily compare an investment in Amazon—or any high-growth company—with that of a more mature one. As an example, let's consider Bank of America, a business that most people are also familiar with, and compare it to Amazon.

As of this writing, the bank's market value is roughly $320 billion, and according to its Form 10-K filings, it reported accounting profits of around $27 billion for 2024. Given that banks are cyclical and highly sensitive to interest rate changes, it makes sense to focus on average profits over the past 5 to 10 years—preferably 10. In the case of Bank of America, the 10-year average is roughly $24 billion.

Additionally, we'll assume that accounting profits serve as a reasonable proxy for cash flows, meaning no adjustments are necessary. Based on these assumptions, Bank of America's cash flow yield is roughly around 7.5%—$24 billion divided by $320 billion.

For ease of reference, I've included one of the sensitivity charts we discussed earlier for mature businesses. Specifically, I'm showing the chart that assumes a 3% consistent growth rate in cash flows starting in year 1 to account for inflation. Remember, we assumed this for Amazon in its mature phase as well. And just as a reminder, this sensitivity table assumes only a 30-year time horizon for the underlying business.

Now, let's assume that we're looking to achieve the same 10% return we hoped for with a potential Amazon investment. As always, you need to review the row that matches the existing cash flow yield and find the reinvestment rate column that results in your desired return. In this case, the exercise leads us to the conclusion that a roughly 10% reinvestment rate would be required to achieve our desired returns.

Sensitivity Analysis - Mature Company with 3% Annual Growth

		\multicolumn{9}{c}{Reinvestment Rate}							
		0%	2.5%	5.0%	7.5%	10.0%	12.5%	15.0%	17.5%	20.0%
Cash Flow Yield	2.5%	0.7%	1.8%	3.0%	4.4%	5.9%	7.4%	9.1%	10.9%	12.6%
	5.0%	3.0%	4.2%	5.4%	6.8%	8.3%	10.0%	11.7%	13.4%	15.3%
	7.5%	4.4%	5.6%	6.9%	8.3%	9.8%	11.5%	13.2%	15.0%	16.8%
	10.0%	5.4%	6.6%	7.9%	9.3%	10.9%	12.5%	14.3%	16.1%	18.0%
	12.5%	6.2%	7.4%	8.7%	10.1%	11.7%	13.4%	15.1%	17.0%	18.9%
	15.0%	6.9%	8.0%	9.4%	10.8%	12.4%	14.1%	15.8%	17.7%	19.6%
	17.5%	7.4%	8.6%	9.9%	11.4%	13.0%	14.6%	16.4%	18.3%	20.2%
	20.0%	7.9%	9.1%	10.4%	11.9%	13.5%	15.2%	16.9%	18.8%	20.7%

So, let's now compare the conditions that must be met in each case to achieve a 10% annual compounded return. For Amazon, its cash flows need to grow by 9% - 9.5% for 10 years and then 3% for 30 years after that. In total, Amazon needs to deliver strong, enduring cash flows for at least 40 years. Otherwise, the cash flows for the first 5 to 7 years don't have enough time to compound sufficiently, given they are small relative to the existing valuation. Finally, Amazon's cash flows need to be reinvested at a rate of roughly 12.5%.

In contrast, with Bank of America, its cash flows don't need to grow much to achieve the 10% return. As long as they grow in line with inflation (3%), it should be enough. Furthermore, Bank of America's existing cash flows only need to endure for 30 years. Since the cash flow yield is relatively high, less time is required for the early cash flows to compound meaningfully. Therefore, the time horizon hurdle is lower for Bank of America than for Amazon, which is why the sensitivity table for Amazon assumed a 40-year life, while Bank of America is assumed to have a 30-year life. Finally, Bank of America's cash flows only need to be reinvested at roughly 10%.

With these conditions in mind for each case, let me highlight a couple of key points.

The Best Company Isn't Always the Best Investment

Investing is not just about identifying the best companies. Like most people, I believe Amazon is a far superior company with better prospects than Bank of America. However, this doesn't necessarily mean Amazon is the better investment. Due to their differing cash flow yields—i.e., valuations—the hurdles that need to be overcome to achieve similar returns are very different for each company.

In this case, Bank of America's valuation demands less growth, a lower reinvestment rate, and a shorter time horizon to meet our desired returns. So, the right question isn't which company is better. Instead, we need to ask which company is more likely to meet or exceed the hurdles implied by its valuation.

This dynamic is quite similar to golfing. In any group of friends playing golf, there are likely to be players of varying skill levels. However, because of the handicap system, the best player doesn't always win. A higher handicap reflects a less-skilled player, but it also means this player doesn't need to have the best score to win. In the same way, a lower cash flow yield—i.e., higher valuation—might indicate a better company, but the hurdles to make it a worthwhile investment are more ambitious.

Think about it this way, when it comes to betting on a golf game, you wouldn't necessarily bet on the best player, you'd bet on the player most likely to perform better than his or her handicap. Similarly, when choosing which company to invest in, you don't necessarily have to go with the best company. Instead, you should invest in the one that you believe has the greatest chance of beating the hurdles set by its current valuation.

High-Growth Businesses Usually Come with Unrealistic Hurdles

It tends to be harder to find undervalued opportunities with high-growth businesses than with mature ones. The reason is precisely because the hurdles their valuations command tend to be very demanding.

Due to recency bias, the market is highly susceptible to extrapolating current trends into the future and, as a result, it's very common for the market to become very optimistic about a company's long-term potential when it's growing very quickly. Such optimism can drive valuations very high, making it very difficult to find undervalued high-growth companies, particularly for disciplined investors who require a wide margin of safety. This is why most value investors tend to invest in companies that are more mature and less popular.

Don't get me wrong, however, once in a while high-growth businesses can be very undervalued and those opportunities should be taken advantage of. Just be mindful that high-growth businesses generate significant hype and, as a consequence, their growth potential tends to be more than priced in by market valuations. Only invest in them if you have a clear understanding of why the market may be underestimating the potential of a given company despite the optimism that already surrounds it.

We'll discuss the dangers of investing in high-growth companies later. For now, the most important take away is that high-growth companies tend to be richly valued and because this implies more ambitious hurdles, it's less common for them to be undervalued.

Sustaining High Reinvestment Rates Over Decades Is Challenging

Don't forget that the reinvestment rate hurdles apply to every year within our assumed time horizons. This point is crucial because it helps us understand the real difficulty of achieving these hurdles.

It may seem reasonable to believe that Amazon can achieve a reinvestment rate at or above 12.5% in the next 3 to 7 years, maybe even 10 years. But as the company matures, the number and scope of attractive reinvestment opportunities will diminish. This will not only lead Amazon to achieve lower reinvestment rates over time but eventually the reinvestment results will depend on the investor. As Amazon matures, the company will be increasingly forced to return capital to shareholders, much of which will be through dividends, delegating reinvestment decisions back to investors.

Trust me when I tell you that, while possible, it's difficult to achieve a consistent 12.5% reinvestment rate for us as investors. If you think about the S&P 500's history, for example, it has only achieved a roughly 9% - 10% annual compounded return over the last century and this is including dividends. There are decades where it's higher than this but there are also periods where it's much lower. As a result, over long periods of time it averages out to around 9% - 10%. So, reinvesting any future dividends into the S&P 500 wouldn't be sufficient to meet the 12.5% hurdle required for Amazon.

The only way you can reasonably expect to consistently achieve a higher than 10% reinvestment rate is if you delegate reinvestment decisions to companies that can do this on your behalf. But if you invest in a company whose ability to do so may soon diminish, then it becomes less likely to occur. So, when comparing Amazon's 12.5% reinvestment hurdle over 40 years with Bank of America's 10% hurdle over 30 years, don't forget to take this reality into account.

Furthermore, don't underestimate the magnitude of a 2.5 percentage point difference in reinvestment rate hurdles. Since these rates are expressed annually and apply over long time horizons—30+ years in our case—these seemingly small differences are actually very large due to the exponential nature of compounding.

The Significance of Understanding What's Priced In

I emphasize these key points because if you don't understand the expectations embedded in a company's valuation, it's easy to fall into the trap of thinking that a great company is automatically a great investment.

I can't tell you how often people share their favorite stock picks with me in casual conversations. However, it's almost always clear that the person has no idea what hurdles the current valuation implies. Instead, they focus on the business merits and potential market opportunities, but they never stop to ask themselves whether the market has already priced in their views. So, please be cautious. The investment potential of a business must be evaluated in light of the expectations already factored into its valuation.

This is the real beauty of the inverse analysis approach. It helps us understand what the market is implying about a company's potential.

As investors, our job is to assess whether the market is overestimating or underestimating that potential. If, at any point, you believe the market is clearly and significantly underestimating a company's future prospects, that's when you make your move and buy.

Modeling Different Growth Scenarios Under the First Approach

As is probably obvious, the first approach for high-growth businesses doesn't limit us to just one growth scenario. In fact, you must consider various growth assumptions to gain a clearer understanding of the potential investment's upside and downside risks. To do this, we can simply create a sensitivity table that incorporates different growth assumptions. For example, let's consider a more conservative scenario for Amazon. Imagine a case where the growth phase lasts only 3 years, and cash flows to shareholders grow by just 5%—i.e., at 6.5% - 7.0% before accounting for dilution. With these new assumptions, we can create the table below to illustrate the resulting expected returns.

Sensitivity Analysis - Investment to Grow 5% annually for 3 years and then 3%

P / CF	CF / P	Reinvestment Rate								
		0%	2.5%	5.0%	7.5%	10.0%	12.5%	15.0%	17.5%	20.0%
100x	1.0%	-0.5%	0.6%	1.8%	3.2%	4.8%	6.5%	8.3%	10.1%	12.0%
50x	2.0%	1.3%	2.3%	3.6%	5.0%	6.6%	8.3%	10.2%	12.0%	14.0%
33x	3.0%	2.3%	3.4%	4.7%	6.1%	7.7%	9.4%	11.3%	13.2%	15.1%
25x	4.0%	3.0%	4.1%	5.4%	6.9%	8.5%	10.2%	12.1%	14.0%	16.0%
20x	5.0%	3.6%	4.7%	6.0%	7.5%	9.1%	10.9%	12.7%	14.6%	16.6%
17x	6.0%	4.1%	5.2%	6.5%	8.0%	9.6%	11.4%	13.2%	15.2%	17.1%
14x	7.0%	4.5%	5.6%	6.9%	8.4%	10.0%	11.8%	13.7%	15.6%	17.6%
13x	8.0%	4.8%	5.9%	7.3%	8.7%	10.4%	12.2%	14.0%	16.0%	18.0%
11x	9.0%	5.1%	6.3%	7.6%	9.1%	10.7%	12.5%	14.4%	16.3%	18.3%

By comparing this sensitivity table with the one from the original, more aggressive scenario, we can extract the following conclusions.

Reinvestment Rate and Valuation Still Dominate Return Potential

For each pair of reinvestment rate and cash flow yield scenarios, the conservative scenario naturally results in a lower expected return. More specifically, our annual compounded returns for Amazon would decline between 0.6% and 0.9% as compared to the original growth scenario we contemplated. Due to the exponential nature of compounding, this would have a significant impact on absolute returns over our lengthy time horizons.

That being said, you likely expected the difference in expected returns across each scenario to be much larger. After all, we did meaningfully change our growth assumptions. Most people would intuitively agree that 5% annual growth over 3 years is significantly less than 7.5% annual growth over 10 years. And yet, when we look at the results for each growth scenario, the difference doesn't seem as large as we might have anticipated.

This demonstrates that our most important variable still remains the reinvestment rate and, to a lesser extent, the valuation—i.e., cash flow yield. In other words, even with high-growth companies, the rate at which earnings are reinvested over time will matter more than the inherent growth prospects of a business's existing operations. The expected growth is certainly important, no doubt. But don't let yourself lose sight of the fact that successfully compounding earnings through reinvestments is always a necessary condition to achieve meaningful returns.

When Reinvestment Is Weak, Growth Assumptions Matter More

Precisely because the reinvestment rate is so critical, the difference in expected returns is more pronounced in the lower reinvestment rate columns compared to the higher reinvestment rate columns. In the higher reinvestment rate scenarios, variations in growth assumptions lead to only about a 0.6% difference in annual compounded returns. For example, under the 20% reinvestment rate column for Amazon, the expected return in the original scenario is 15.7%, while the more conservative growth scenario results in 15.1%. The difference isn't as large because, even with slower growth in the conservative scenario, the strong benefits from reinvesting at high rates help offset the impact of lower growth.

However, in the lower reinvestment rate columns, the impact is more significant, with a difference of around 0.9%. For instance, in the 0% reinvestment rate column, Amazon's expected return would be 3.2% in the original scenario, compared to just 2.3% in the conservative scenario. In this case, the lack of reinvestment—0% rate—means that the reduced growth in the conservative scenario cannot be mitigated by the more influential benefits of a good reinvestment rate.

Why the First Approach Isn't Always Enough

With all these considerations in mind, hopefully you now have a clear understanding of how the first approach of our inverse analysis for high-growth companies works. As useful as this approach is, it does have a major drawback. Specifically, we are required to fix both the growth rate and the length of the growth phase for each scenario we analyze.

This can be problematic because it forces us to compare scenarios one by one, which can be time-consuming and distract us from more important considerations. In an ideal world, we would want to explore multiple growth scenarios to fully understand the impact of being wrong about our growth-related assumptions. And this is exactly where the second approach of the inverse analysis for high-growth companies becomes particularly useful.

CHAPTER 8 SUMMARY AND TAKEAWAYS (OPTIONAL READING)

- The inverse approach for high-growth businesses is not conceptually different from that of mature companies.
- However, because two new variables are introduced—the length of the company's growth phase and the respective growth rate—there are two ways to approach it.
- The first approach is to fix these two new variables at specific levels and analyze how returns are affected across valuation and reinvestment rate scenarios.
- It's essentially the same approach as with mature companies, except the underlying cash flows assume elevated growth—as opposed to flat or consistent cash flows.
- The second approach fixes the reinvestment rate while analyzing the growth needed to meet a specific—and fixed—desired return.
- Both approaches have their advantages and disadvantages, and as such, it's often best to use both. This chapter focuses primarily on the first approach.
- To apply these approaches in practice, we introduced the price-to-cash flow ratio (P/CF).
- It's essentially the inverse of the cash flow yield, but it's more practical for low-yielding companies. The cash flow yield can make large valuation differences seem trivial, and this ratio corrects for that.
- As a case study, we used Amazon to apply the first approach. Because this is consistent with how we analyze mature companies, we then compared it to Bank of America.
- For Amazon's growth assumptions, we initially assumed 7.5% cash flow growth—which effectively means 9.5% growth before dilution—for 10 years, followed by consistent 3% growth to account for inflation.

- While these assumptions may seem conservative at first glance, they may in fact be aggressive when properly put into context.
- These growth assumptions must be based on expectations for the company's existing operations—they must be independent of any growth driven by reinvested earnings.
- Otherwise, reinvestment-driven growth would be double-counted, as this type of growth is already captured in the reinvestment rate.
- With these assumptions in mind, we reviewed a sensitivity table showing Amazon's potential returns across various reinvestment rate and valuation scenarios.
- At Amazon's current price-to-cash flow ratio of 33x, we can determine the hurdles required to meet any desired return—we used 10% for this exercise.
- To achieve this return, Amazon must not only deliver the assumed growth, but also reinvest earnings at a 12.5% rate, and—once the growth phase ends—maintain its mature cash flows for another 30 years.
- With these hurdles established, investors gain a compass and a clear direction for what to focus on. Any qualitative research should aim to determine whether these conditions can realistically be met.
- We then compared Amazon's hurdles to those of Bank of America, which currently trades at a roughly 7.5% cash flow yield.
- At this valuation, to achieve the same 10% return we targeted for Amazon, Bank of America doesn't need meaningful growth—just 3% in line with inflation—and its cash flows only need to last for 30 years. The higher cash flow yield allows early cash flows to compound more meaningfully over a shorter time period than Amazon.
- Additionally, Bank of America's cash flows only need to be reinvested at a 10% rate—significantly lower than Amazon's hurdle when considering the exponential impact over the long term.
- In comparing these two cases, we see that the best company isn't always the best investment. Instead, the best investment is the one

- most likely to exceed the hurdles implied by its current valuation.
- Furthermore, investors must be especially cautious when investing in high-growth businesses precisely because the optimism surrounding them tends to create demanding valuation hurdles.
- To conclude, we then looked at Amazon's potential returns under more conservative growth assumptions.
- In doing so, we learned that, as important as growth is, the reinvestment rate—and to a lesser extent, the valuation—remains the most important driver of future returns.
- In fact, it's because of this reality that, when the reinvestment rate is high, growth assumptions have very little impact on the returns achieved.
- It's only when the reinvestment rate is low that growth assumptions matter more, since in those cases the reinvestment rate can't compete with growth.

CHAPTER 9

VALUATION – PART 7

INVERSE ANALYSIS SECOND APPROACH FOR HIGH-GROWTH BUSINESSES

As mentioned earlier, the second approach is not too different from the first in terms of its overall goal. It's still an inverse analysis in that it focuses on working backwards. Instead of calculating a valuation by discounting future cash flows to the present using a discount rate—i.e., our desired return—we are still starting with an assumed valuation and asking what must happen for us to achieve our desired returns. With the second approach, however, the variables we're sensitizing or measuring are not the same.

In this case, rather than trying to determine the required reinvestment rate, the focus shifts to the required length of the growth phase and its required growth rate. More specifically, the question we're now aiming to answer is: for a given valuation, at what rate do cash flows have to grow, and for how long, in order to achieve our desired annual compounded return?

As with the first approach, we have to keep all other variables constant. For reasons discussed before, let's continue assuming a 40-year time horizon and a 3% growth rate for cash flows after the rapid growth phase ends. Regarding the desired return and reinvestment rate, I propose using 10% in both cases for reasons I'll explain shortly.

Unpacking the Growth Hurdles

That said, the table below shows the sensitivity output based on these assumptions. While it follows a similar format to the tables we've discussed earlier, the columns now reflect a different variable, and the output displayed is also different. Instead of showing various reinvestment rate scenarios, the columns here represent different possibilities for the length of the rapid growth phase. Additionally, the output in the middle no longer shows expected returns; instead, it displays the required growth rate during the growth phase.

Growth Required to achieve 10% Return assuming 10% Reinvestment Rate

P / CF	CF / P	Length of Growth Period (Years)							
		5.0	7.5	10.0	12.5	15.0	17.5	20.0	25.0
200x	0.5%	83%	58%	41%	35%	29%	27%	24%	21%
100x	1.0%	59%	42%	31%	27%	23%	21%	19%	17%
67x	1.5%	46%	33%	25%	22%	19%	17%	16%	14%
50x	2.0%	37%	28%	21%	18%	16%	15%	14%	12%
40x	2.5%	31%	23%	18%	16%	14%	13%	12%	11%
33x	3.0%	26%	20%	15%	14%	12%	11%	11%	10%
29x	3.5%	21%	17%	13%	12%	11%	10%	9%	9%
25x	4.0%	18%	14%	11%	10%	9%	9%	8%	8%
22x	4.5%	15%	12%	10%	9%	8%	8%	7%	7%
20x	5.0%	12%	10%	8%	8%	7%	7%	6%	6%

Let's continue using our Amazon example to show how the output table works. For ease of reference, I've highlighted again in gray the row that corresponds to Amazon's current valuation—a 3% cash flow yield or a 33x price-to-cash-flow ratio.

Looking at the leftmost column, the table shows that to achieve a 10% desired return, Amazon would need a 26% annual cash flow growth rate during its rapid growth phase if that phase lasts only 5 years. If, however, you believe its growth phase can extend to 7.5 years, you move one column to the right, and the table indicates that a 20% annual cash flow growth rate is required during this period to meet the desired return. Continuing to move right, you'll see that the required growth rate decreases as the length of the growth phase increases: 15% growth for 10 years, 14% for 12.5 years, and so on.

How Reinvestment Rates Shift the Growth Hurdle

As just noted in the assumptions, all of these scenarios assume that Amazon is reinvesting its cash flows at a 10% rate. If you believe the reinvestment rate can consistently be higher, then the required growth rate would be lower than what the table suggests. Conversely, if the reinvestment rate is lower, the required growth rate would need to be higher to achieve your desired compounded return.

This is why we can't find the exact scenario we discussed for Amazon in the first approach. If you recall, we concluded that a 7.5% growth rate over a 10-year period could potentially yield a 10% compounded return. But this would be true only if the reinvestment rate was 12.5%.

Since the table on the prior page assumes a 10% reinvestment rate, however, we now need a growth rate higher than 7.5%. As the table above indicates in the third column—the one that matches the 10-year growth phase we assumed for the first approach—the growth rate should be 15%.

This comparison is helpful for interpreting the table correctly and, more importantly, it highlights how even a seemingly small difference in reinvestment rates can significantly raise the growth hurdle we need to overcome. The comparison shows that, to remain indifferent, the growth rate needs to increase from 7.5% to 15% if the reinvestment rate drops from 12.5% to 10%. Remember, these growth rates apply annually over a long period—10 years in the scenarios we're comparing. Consequently, the impact on the required absolute growth is not trivial. So, once again, the importance of the reinvestment rate cannot be overstated.

Why Using a 10% Target Return Makes Sense

Technically, we can run multiple scenarios with this sensitivity analysis. For instance, we could fix our desired returns at 15% or 20%. In fact, it wouldn't be wrong to argue that, for riskier investments, it makes sense to sensitize growth based on these higher target returns.

While this is a valid approach, keep in mind that part of the reason

I recommend using the inverse analysis is to keep things practical and straightforward. If we start creating sensitivity tables for multiple scenarios, we risk losing the simplicity of the approach. Instead of becoming unnecessarily inefficient by exploring other possibilities, we can simply maintain this 10% target return and demand a greater margin of safety as perceived risk increases.

Furthermore, I like using a 10% return hurdle because, as I mentioned earlier, this is roughly the average return that the S&P 500 can be expected to generate. Of course, it's not going to be a straight line, but over time, the average will likely end at around 10%. If we're investing in individual stocks, it's presumably because we aim to achieve a return greater than 10% over time. Otherwise, why waste our time?

Now, using 10% as a return hurdle doesn't mean we should simply settle for it. When the analysis reveals the growth conditions necessary to achieve this 10% return, this doesn't mean we should invest if such conditions are roughly in line with our expectations. At the end of the day, these hurdles are just a point of reference, and, as mentioned before, a margin of safety should always be applied.

This means you should invest in a given stock only if your growth expectations for the business are significantly above the growth hurdles implied by this analysis. And, of course, the higher the perceived risk, the greater the margin of safety you should demand. In other words, as risk increases, your growth expectations should be increasingly higher relative to the growth required to achieve a 10% return.

Remember, it's better to be approximately right than precisely wrong. Ultimately, the 10% hurdle is meant to give us a framework that provides a starting point to assess whether a valuation imposes reasonable growth hurdles. Like the first approach, this second method acts as a north star, guiding us in our qualitative research. It should never be used to pinpoint a precise set of growth hurdles based on rigid assumptions.

What About Our Reinvestment Rate Assumption?

Now, what about the reinvestment rate assumption? Is it reasonable to fix it at 10% and not consider other scenarios? Well, as we know, the reinvestment rate is the most important factor of all. And precisely because of its significance, you may consider exploring one or two additional scenarios to gauge its impact on the required growth conditions. My personal preference, however, is to stick just to this single table for the following reasons.

The Idea Is to Focus on Judgment, Not Precision

All the considerations we just discussed regarding the return hurdle also apply to reinvestment rate. Exploring multiple reinvestment rate scenarios complicates things without providing much additional value. If you believe the reinvestment rate will be higher or lower for a given stock, you know that the growth hurdles would be lower and higher, respectively.

Since the goal is to always maintain a significant margin of safety, there's no need to aim for precision. Ultimately, you need to feel confident that your growth expectations are significantly above those implied by the company's valuation. In this context, relatively small differences in growth requirements shouldn't sway you one way or the other. Finally, this exercise is meant to guide our qualitative research, which is far more important than mathematical precision.

10% Is a Conservative Reinvestment Benchmark

A 10% reinvestment rate is conservative, helping us establish a margin of safety from the outset. Don't get me wrong—there are plenty of businesses that aren't capable of reinvesting at 10% or more. In fact, I know many businesses that struggle to reinvest at even 5%.

However, remember that this approach is intended for high-growth businesses. And if a business is growing rapidly, it's presumably because it's a high-quality company with numerous attractive opportunities to reinvest. But even if that's not the case, I hope it's clear by now that we should avoid low-quality businesses with poor reinvestment capabilities.

So, when you're looking at a high-growth business, you're likely evaluating a company that should be able to reinvest at a rate higher than 10%, and hopefully much higher. This is why I consider 10% to be a conservative figure.

The Second Approach Is a Starting Point, Not the Final Word

This method is not meant to be used in isolation. As I mentioned briefly before, my suggestion is to combine both approaches in most cases. This second method should be the starting point because, as we'll see shortly with some examples, it can quickly help us determine whether a stock's value is reasonable, overhyped, or possibly underappreciated. If the stock appears to be underappreciated or, at most, reasonably priced, you can proceed with qualitative research and then use the first approach once you have a clearer picture of the growth conditions.

Remember, the most important factor in long-term investing is the reinvestment rate, and since the first approach focuses on this variable, it should ultimately guide your final decision. The second approach is extremely useful, but once you've determined what growth scenarios seem reasonable for a particular stock, it's better to move to the first approach and, if needed, explore multiple scenarios with it as we did with Amazon.

There are exceptions to this general rule and, ironically, they apply to the case of my current favorite stock—which we'll discuss in the final chapter of the book. In short, when the margin of safety is wide enough, it might be overkill to apply the first approach as well. Similarly, if the 10% reinvestment rate seems reasonable, it may not be necessary to sensitize this variable.

Moving On: How to Account for Dilution with the Second Approach

Now that we understand the rationale behind the suggested rule-of-thumb assumptions for the second approach, let's move on to shareholder dilution. Remember, because we exclude stock-based compensation from our cash flow calculations, the growth requirements shown in this table do not account for dilution. Fortunately, though, it's very easy to capture the potential impact of dilution with just a minor adjustment.

As we discussed in Chapter 5, dilution effectively reduces the benefits of growth. So, to account for dilution, we can simply add the expected share count growth to the growth rate revealed in the table.

For instance, with Amazon, I estimated that the number of shares outstanding will likely grow by 1.5% to 2% annually. If this holds true, the first 1.5% to 2% of annual cash flow growth will be completely offset by dilution. Therefore, we need to adjust the growth rate required by this expectation.

According to the sensitivity table, if we assume a 10-year growth phase, Amazon's cash flows must grow 15% annually over this period.

However, after accounting for dilution, even if the company achieves this growth, the actual cash flow growth for existing shareholders would only be 13% to 13.5%. This wouldn't be enough to achieve the 10% desired return. To meet that goal, Amazon would need to grow at 16.5% to 17% to provide the 15% growth required for shareholders.

In brief, to get the actual growth required from the company, simply add the expected dilution to the growth rate shown in the table. This adjustment ensures that, net of dilution, you'll receive the growth you need to achieve your desired returns. Of course, this approach is not perfect and is also subject to error. But I am convinced it's a more effective alternative than relying on accounting stock-based compensation expense. Moreover, hopefully you can agree it's a much more intuitive and practical approach.

A Quick Note on the Math Behind the Second Approach

One last point before we move on to a few more examples. Regarding the math, as always, I won't go into unnecessary details. But for those who are curious, the math is essentially the same as what I covered in the first approach for high-growth businesses. The only real difference lies in the variables you're adjusting to obtain the output for a given scenario.

In the first approach, you adjust the valuation—i.e., cash flow yield—and the reinvestment rate. In this second approach, however, you're adjusting the length of the growth phase and the growth rate during that period, searching for the combination of these two factors that will give you a 10% compounded return.

In theory, this is a trial-and-error process since multiple combinations of these two variables can yield the same 10% desired return. In other words, there is no formula that we can algebraically rearrange to determine all the right combinations. Fortunately, however, with Excel we can easily perform a what-if analysis that runs the trial-and-error process for you.

The Second Approach: Some Practical Examples

Now that we've covered the theory, let's examine a couple of additional examples from well-known companies to better understand how this approach works and its practical usefulness. Because of their current popularity, let's look at Tesla, Palantir, Apple and Alphabet (Google's parent company).

For simplicity, and because it's likely the case with these companies, let's assume that, aside from stock-based compensation expense, their accounting profits serve as a reasonable proxy for cash flows. The table below provides a summary of the valuation landscape for each of these companies as of this writing.

2024 Cash Flow and Valuation Calculations						
Company	Accounting Profits ($bn)	Add: Stock-Based Comp ($bn)	Proxy Cash Flow ($bn)	Existing Valuation ($bn)	Cash Flow Yield	Price-to-Cash Flow Ratio
Tesla	$7.1	$2.0	$9.1	$850	1.1%	94x
Palantir	$0.5	$0.7	$1.2	$193	0.6%	166x
Apple	$96.2	$12.0	$108.1	$3,450	3.1%	32x
Alphabet	$100.1	$22.8	$122.9	$2,100	5.9%	17x

Source: Author's analysis based on company 10-Ks, annual reports, and quarterly filings.
Note: All data as of calendar year-end December 31, 2024. Apple's figures reflect a trailing twelve months (TTM) calculation to align with this period, as its fiscal year ends September 30.

Based on these valuation metrics, the second table on the next page shows where each of these companies would fall within our sensitivity analysis. Palantir, and to a lesser extent Alphabet and Tesla, don't fit perfectly into any of the valuation rows in the table. Therefore, for these three companies, we know the required growth conditions will fall slightly above or below the values indicated in the table.

For example, although I placed Palantir in the 200x price-to-cash flow ratio row, its actual ratio is 166x. As a result, the required growth indicated by this row won't be a perfect match for Palantir. The true required growth will fall somewhere between this row and the one below it, skewed closer to the 200x row since 166x is nearer to 200x than to 100x.

So, for the 5-year growth phase column, the required growth won't be the 83% shown in the table, but more like 75%. Since these rough adjustments are relatively simple to make and we're only aiming to be approximately right, this set up should still suffice.

Growth Required to achieve 10% Return assuming 10% Reinvestment Rate											
			Length of Growth Period (Years)								
P / CF	CF / P		5.0	7.5	10.0	12.5	15.0	17.5	20.0	25.0
200x	0.5%	Palantir	83%	58%	41%	35%	29%	27%	24%	21%
100x	1.0%	Tesla	59%	42%	31%	27%	23%	21%	19%	17%
67x	1.5%		46%	33%	25%	22%	19%	17%	16%	14%
50x	2.0%		37%	28%	21%	18%	16%	15%	14%	12%
40x	2.5%		31%	23%	18%	16%	14%	13%	12%	11%
33x	3.0%	Apple	26%	20%	15%	14%	12%	11%	11%	10%
29x	3.5%		21%	17%	13%	12%	11%	10%	9%	9%
25x	4.0%		18%	14%	11%	10%	9%	9%	8%	8%
22x	4.5%		15%	12%	10%	9%	8%	8%	7%	7%
20x	5.0%	Alphabet	12%	10%	8%	8%	7%	7%	6%	6%

Palantir

Let's now look at Palantir. First, it's important to note that its stock-based compensation expense of $0.7 billion isn't large for no reason. Since its IPO in the last quarter of 2020, the company's shares outstanding have grown at an annual rate of roughly 6% to 11%, and it's likely to remain high for many years to come. For the sake of this exercise, let's assume this share count growth rate gradually decreases and stabilizes at around 3%.

As we discussed earlier, this means we need to factor in this dilution by adding the 3% rate to our required growth from our table. So, if we need roughly 75% annual growth in the 5-year growth phase scenario, in reality, the required growth would be more like 78%. According to the table, for the 7.5-year growth period scenario, the growth rate would range between 58% and 42%, with a slight tilt toward the 58%. More precisely, the growth rate would be around 52%, but after considering dilution, the more realistic number would be closer to 55%. And if we continue with these ballpark adjustments, a more realistic set of required growth rates for Palantir would be the following:

Palantir Required Growth Rates After Accounting For Dilution								
Length of Growth Period (Years)								
5.0	7.5	10.0	12.5	15.0	17.5	20.0	25.0
78.0%	55.0%	40.0%	35.0%	30.0%	27.5%	25.0%	22.5%

I'm far from an expert on Palantir, and based on what I know, it appears to be a great company with significant potential. However, I have serious reservations about its current valuation. The growth required to justify this valuation is simply enormous. Regardless of how long we think it can stay in its rapid growth phase, the growth hurdle to achieve a 10% return as a buy-and-hold investor is simply daunting.

Even if we give the company the benefit of the doubt and assume it won't mature until 25 years from now, it still needs to grow cash flows at a compounded rate of 22.5%. This is the equivalent of saying the company should double its cash flows every 3.4 years for the next 25 years. By the end, this growth would mean that the annual cash flow in year 25 would be a staggering $185 billion, more than Apple's existing $108 billion. In other words, in 25 years Palantir's cash flows need to be 160 times larger than what they are today.

And keep in mind that this growth rate needs to hold true for investors to achieve a 10% compounded return. As we discussed earlier, while we use this as a reference point, it's not a return we should settle for, at the very least because we need a margin of safety. So, even without knowing much about Palantir, to me, it's clear that it's not worth considering it as a potential investment. The likelihood that qualitative research would lead to a conclusion that these growth rates are achievable is so low that it's simply not worth the time to pursue the research.

Now, it's true that the required growth rates mentioned earlier are based on the assumption that cash flows will be reinvested at only 10%. And, as we discussed, this is likely a conservative scenario, so the actual growth rates required could potentially be lower. However, even if the required growth rates decrease by 5% to 10% percentage points, the growth hurdles remain very demanding. It would still be hard to argue that there's a wide margin of safety with this valuation.

Furthermore, Palantir seems to operate with a capital-light business model, which means it doesn't require much capital to continue growing. This is great because it suggests Palantir can maintain a high reinvestment rate, using little capital to generate significant profits. However, this can be a double-edged sword because it may also mean the company doesn't need to reinvest much of its earnings. As a result, the reinvestment outcomes will likely be passed on to investors.

In other words, Palantir is likely to accumulate excess cash from its earnings, which may lead the company to pay dividends to shareholders rather than reinvesting it. In such a case, the assumed 10% reinvestment rate can only be considered conservative if you're a skilled capital allocator. You would need to invest those dividends in other companies that, unlike Palantir, are reasonably priced and capable of reinvesting earnings into attractive opportunities. If you do this, Palantir's earnings could indirectly compound at a rate higher than 10%. But the point is, when we put this into context, the 10% reinvestment rate may no longer seem as conservative in Palantir's case.

So, while it's great that Palantir's reinvestment rate potential appears high, these reinvestment rates are unlikely to apply to you as an investor. Palantir simply may not reinvest all of its earnings, and therefore, even if the small reinvested portion generates high returns, the overall reinvestment rate won't necessarily be as high.

Additionally, the reinvestment rate could decrease significantly if management opts to use earnings for share repurchases at these elevated valuation levels. We'll explore this idea more thoroughly in Chapter 12, but in short, when a company repurchases its shares, it's essentially choosing to invest in itself.

If it's questionable for an investor to buy Palantir at these valuations, then it's equally questionable for the company to do so. In other words, the same factors that determine whether investing in Palantir is justified should also apply to the company, not just investors. Again, we'll dive deeper into this concept later, but for now, just take my word for it; share repurchases can be very harmful if done so at high valuations.

The Ideal Scenario: Growth Plus Reinvestment

After discussing Amazon and Palantir, we have enough context to highlight another important point that should help avoid any confusion or misunderstandings. Specifically, I want to emphasize that for any given valuation, the optimal scenario is a company with significant reinvestment opportunities, but one that could still grow its cash flows even without reinvesting its earnings. In this case, we can expect cash flows from the company's existing operations to grow, while also expecting the company to reinvest those growing cash flows at attractive rates.

I know that with Amazon I mentioned the importance of not conflating growth stemming from existing operations with growth from reinvesting earnings. And in doing so, I stated that the growth we're trying to measure with our inverse analysis is specifically that which comes exclusively from the company's existing operations. Otherwise, we would be double-counting growth because growth from reinvested earnings is already accounted for through the reinvestment rate.

Now, by emphasizing this distinction, you might have assumed that the only growth we're interested in is the kind that doesn't require reinvesting. And if that happened to be your interpretation, you may now be wondering why I don't seem thrilled with the fact that Palantir appears to be capable of growing without needing to reinvest.

So, let me be as explicit as I can to avoid any potential misinterpretation. There's nothing inherently wrong with the fact that Palantir might grow without having to reinvest. This kind of growth is certainly desirable and, all else being equal, it justifies a higher valuation compared to a company with no growth. However, it's crucial to remember that even with rapidly growing cash flows, the ability to reinvest those cash flows effectively remains incredibly important. Therefore, while growth accompanied by limited reinvestment opportunities is a good scenario, it's not the optimal one.

Likewise, there's nothing wrong if Amazon's growth mostly comes from reinvesting earnings. I don't necessarily expect this for Amazon, but if it were the case, it wouldn't represent the optimal scenario. As mentioned above, the optimal scenario is one where both engines are working at full speed. As investors, we want growth coming from existing operations, along with ample reinvestment opportunities that allow the company to reinvest all or most of its earnings into high-return endeavors.

Resuming Our Look at Tesla, Apple, and Alphabet

With this in mind, let's now turn to our other three examples: Tesla, Apple, and Alphabet. All of these companies are and will likely continue to be subject to ongoing dilution, especially in Tesla's case. However, for the sake of simplicity, let's assume that the required growth rates from our sensitivity table don't need any adjustments. For this high-level discussion, it's certainly not necessary to make every single modification. Besides, walking through the process would be unnecessarily time-consuming.

That being said, if you had to choose which of these three companies to invest in, the decision shouldn't be based on which one you think is the better company. Instead, the focus should be on which company is more likely to overcome the hurdles implied by their respective valuations. And with that in mind, let's highlight some things about these companies and their existing valuations.

Tesla

Tesla might be more of a mature company than the market tends to believe. In other words, there is a risk that Tesla is being mistakenly viewed as a high-growth company, when in fact it might not be, at least not to the extent commonly assumed. This may be a case where the market is conflating growth from existing operations with potential growth driven by reinvestment.

If Tesla didn't reinvest its cash flows into new manufacturing plants, additional supercharging stations, research and development, compute infrastructure for its Full Self-Driving (FSD) systems, and AI infrastructure for training its Optimus robot, its growth prospects could be significantly lower.

At the end of the day, there's a limit to how many cars and large-scale energy storage units Tesla can produce with its existing manufacturing capacity. Similarly, there's a cap on how much electricity it can sell through its current supercharging network. So, unless Tesla can successfully enhance the monetization of services like its in-car entertainment, the company's potential cash flow growth may be entirely reliant on reinvestments.

Now let's consider this as we assess the required growth hurdles from our sensitivity chart. What this suggests is that it may be unlikely for Tesla to sustain growth from its existing business for more than 5 years. Again, I'm not saying Tesla can't grow rapidly for longer, I'm just saying it's questionable it can do so with its existing business and, remember, that's what the table is focused on.

If we assume a 5-year growth period, Tesla would need to grow its cash flows at around 60% annually during that time. In other words, its annual cash flow in 5 years would need to be 10 times what it is today. Just like for Palantir, this represents an extremely demanding growth hurdle.

To be fair, however, Tesla does appear to have multiple reinvestment opportunities, many of which could offer very high rates of return, especially if you're a strong believer in Elon Musk's vision. As such, in contrast to Palantir, our 10% reinvestment rate assumption embedded in this approach may actually be too conservative for Tesla. So, to complement the analysis we've done so far, let's bring in the first approach of our inverse analysis.

Let's give Tesla the benefit of the doubt and assume that, net of any dilution, Tesla's existing operations can grow at a rate of 20% for the next 5 years, at which point it matures and grows at 3% thereafter for the following 35 years. The table below shows the output based on these assumptions, with the row that most closely applies to Tesla highlighted in gray.

Sensitivity Analysis - Investment to Grow 20% annually for 5 years and then 3%

P / CF	CF / P	Reinvestment Rate								
		0%	2.5%	5.0%	7.5%	10.0%	12.5%	15.0%	17.5%	20.0%
100x	1.0%	1.2%	2.3%	3.5%	4.9%	6.5%	8.1%	9.9%	11.7%	13.6%
50x	2.0%	3.0%	4.1%	5.3%	6.8%	8.3%	10.0%	11.8%	13.6%	15.6%
33x	3.0%	4.1%	5.1%	6.4%	7.8%	9.4%	11.1%	12.9%	14.8%	16.7%
25x	4.0%	4.8%	5.9%	7.2%	8.6%	10.2%	11.9%	13.7%	15.6%	17.6%
20x	5.0%	5.4%	6.5%	7.8%	9.2%	10.8%	12.6%	14.4%	16.3%	18.2%
17x	6.0%	5.9%	7.0%	8.3%	9.7%	11.3%	13.1%	14.9%	16.8%	18.8%
14x	7.0%	6.3%	7.4%	8.7%	10.1%	11.8%	13.5%	15.3%	17.3%	19.2%
13x	8.0%	6.6%	7.8%	9.0%	10.5%	12.1%	13.9%	15.7%	17.6%	19.6%
11x	9.0%	7.0%	8.1%	9.4%	10.8%	12.5%	14.2%	16.1%	18.0%	20.0%

As you can see from the table, for Tesla to achieve a 10% compounded return over 40 years, it would need to reinvest its earnings at a rate close to 15% for 40 years. This is a significant hurdle, not just because compounding earnings at this rate would be extraordinary, but because our growth assumptions are not overly conservative. Additionally, keep in mind that these are the hurdles needed to achieve a 10% return, which, as we've discussed, is not particularly exciting.

Consequently, just like Palantir, Tesla has a valuation that is so demanding that it's probably not worth the time to study it in-depth. And I say this even though I'm a big fan of Elon Musk and believe he's one of the most talented entrepreneurs out there. If anyone can achieve these sorts of reinvestment rates while branching into new ventures, it's him. But this valuation doesn't even come close to offering a margin of safety, so the risk likely isn't worth it.

As a final thought on Tesla, I hope this helps you conceptualize more clearly what I mean by conflating growth from existing operations with growth from reinvestment. Understanding this distinction is key because, once you grasp it, you begin to view many companies differently. With Tesla, for example, you realize it might not be a traditional growth investment, but rather an investment in a somewhat mature company with a venture capital fund attached to it.

This venture capital aspect has the advantage of being linked to the Tesla ecosystem, which increases the chances of success compared to a typical venture fund. However, if the returns from the ventures Tesla is pursuing aren't consistently and significantly high, the company's overall cash flow trajectory will likely suffer. By viewing it this way, you can more realistically assess Tesla's risk and avoid making a questionable investment just because it's surrounded by hype.

Apple and Alphabet

Moving on to Apple and Alphabet, I won't go into much detail because my purpose here is not to discuss individual companies. Instead, my objective is to use some examples so that you learn how to properly think about valuating businesses using our inverse analysis. And with the examples discussed so far, I think we've covered most of the critical learning lessons and conclusions. That being said, I only want to point out the following.

Always Consider What Growth Hurdles Imply in Absolute Terms

Don't forget that the required growth revealed by our sensitivity table is expressed in annual terms. As a result, the hurdle is based on a compounding perspective, meaning that over time, the growth in absolute terms tends to exceed what you might intuitively expect. For example, let's give Apple the benefit of the doubt and assume that, despite its massive size and market share, it can continue growing rapidly for another 12.5 years. According to our table, the required growth hurdle would be 14%.

Now, if we grow Apple's existing cash flows of roughly $108 billion by 14% for 12.5 years, those cash flows would need to reach roughly $550 billion by the end of that period. This is about five times its current cash flow and significantly more than Apple's existing $396 billion in revenue.

So, even though Apple's valuation may seem much cheaper compared to companies like Palantir and Tesla, the growth hurdle in absolute terms is still quite daunting. It's always important to consider what the required growth rate implies in absolute terms and assess whether it makes sense. This is especially true for very large companies like Apple, as their existing size and market share impose a practical limit on how much they can realistically grow.

Don't Forget: Cash Flows Must Be Sustained After Maturity

Don't forget that our analysis of high-growth businesses assumes a 40-year period. If the company we're analyzing doesn't last for at least this long, or if its cash flows decline significantly at some point, we wouldn't achieve the 10% return fixed in our analysis. This holds true even if the growth from the initial growth phase matches the required growth.

When we look at Alphabet, the required growth rates seem reasonable. In fact, of all the companies we've discussed, I think Alphabet could be the only one that's potentially undervalued. However, the reason I'm personally not fully convinced of this is because I'm concerned its cash flows may not be as long-lasting as desired.

Don't get me wrong—I'm confident that Alphabet will be around 40 years from now. But what I'm uncertain about is whether, once it matures, Alphabet will be able to maintain consistently strong cash flows. While Alphabet is a leader in AI, I have reservations about how well it will be able to monetize its AI efforts, particularly when compared to its existing search business. I'm no expert, but I see a risk that the way we navigate the internet might change dramatically.

Instead of Googling for everything, we might be using AI agents, chatbots, or something entirely different. Even if Alphabet adapts and offers what replaces Googling, there's no guarantee it will maintain its dominant position. Moreover, even if Alphabet does, there's no certainty it will be able to monetize this new form of navigation as successfully as it has with search.

Because of my doubts regarding Alphabet's ability to maintain stable cash flows in the long term, I don't feel comfortable labeling it as clearly undervalued. That said, I'm sure many of you have a deeper understanding of Alphabet than I do, and can better assess how much of a threat these technological changes actually pose.

If you conclude that these changes won't have a significant impact, then this valuation could indeed be quite interesting. But again, my goal isn't to convince you one way or the other; it's simply to show you how such considerations should factor into our inverse analysis. Ultimately, you need to decide if the hurdles implied by the current valuation are achievable.

Back to Broader Considerations: Inverse Analysis Isn't Enough

As I hope you agree by now, using the inverse analysis for high-growth businesses, both with the first and second approaches, is intuitive, practical, and relatively easy to apply. However, I want to caution you not to become overconfident simply because you now have this powerful tool at your disposal. Applying the inverse method to determine the conditions that must be met for a particular investment is just one part of the process. In fact, it's the easy part, and it's far from sufficient to make a high-conviction decision.

Once you've clearly identified the hurdles implied by a given valuation, the next step is to conduct an in-depth qualitative analysis to assess the likelihood of those hurdles being met. As you dive into your qualitative research, I'd like you to keep in mind the following considerations.

Sustaining Growth Is Extremely Challenging

Don't assume that recent growth trends are poised to continue. This is one of the most common mistakes I see people make. You have to recognize that when a company is growing quickly, it naturally attracts capital, which, in turn, invites competition. Market participants, both companies and investors, are inherently jealous. Nobody wants to miss out on potential opportunities. If one company is doing something new and achieving success, many others are likely to follow suit.

Just look at the current AI landscape. As soon as ChatGPT was released, it sparked a wave of competition, with everyone trying to launch their own large language models or AI chatbots. Google introduced Bard, Baidu launched Ernie Bot, Microsoft rolled out Copilot, Elon Musk's xAI debuted Grok, Meta introduced Llama, Alibaba unveiled Tongyi Qianwen, and the list goes on.

So, when evaluating whether a particular growth hurdle can be met, be cautious. Recent growth rates can only be sustained if there are strong reasons to believe that upcoming competition won't be able to compete successfully. Otherwise, you risk falling into what I call the "Zoom path".

I call it this because it's what happened to Zoom Communications Inc., the company behind the virtual work communication platform we all relied on during the COVID-19 pandemic. Before and during the pandemic, Zoom experienced explosive growth. According to data reported by Seeking Alpha, in fiscal year 2021 alone, its revenues grew by 325%. But even before that, the company was growing at over 100% annually. For example, from fiscal year 2017 to 2019, Zoom's revenues skyrocketed from roughly $60 million to $330 million in just two years.

Many people became so excited by Zoom's success and future potential that its stock price skyrocketed from around $100 per share at the start of the pandemic to approximately $550 per share at its peak in October 2020. At its highest point, the company's market valuation reached about $165 billion.

The problem with Zoom, however, was that there was nothing really preventing competitors from making strides in the space and gaining market share. And sure enough, both Google and Microsoft aggressively worked to capture Zoom's customers, with Google Meet and Microsoft Teams providing serious competition.

As a result, Zoom's revenue growth began to slow, dropping to 55% in fiscal year 2022, just 7% in 2023, and a mere 3% in 2024. The situation was even worse in terms of profitability; as of fiscal year 2024, Zoom's operating income is still lower than what it was in 2022. Not surprisingly, Zoom's stock price has plummeted to roughly $80, with its market valuation now around $25 billion, significantly lower than its peak.

Zoom's recent stock performance is not surprising and is in fact justified. When people were buying shares at its peak in October 2020, Zoom was trading at a price-to-cash flow ratio similar to Palantir's current levels. Since we covered Palantir at length, we know that the required growth conditions for valuations this high are extremely demanding. So, naturally, as the market came to realize those growth rates weren't even close to being achievable long-term, the stock was repriced very rapidly and strongly.

For those who bought at the peak, it's a tough position to be in because there's little reason to expect the stock price to recover to previous levels. And if you choose to hold onto the stock, the long-term returns are also likely to be very low. The initial cash flow yield was so low that it's hard to see how it could end well. The yield was simply too low to allow time and compounding to work their magic even if Zoom does a great job at reinvesting earnings.

This example should serve as a cautionary tale for investors as many growth companies are at risk of following the "Zoom path". Therefore, if you do invest in these companies, make sure your qualitative research provides solid reasons to believe that the company can successfully fend off competition. Otherwise, the recent growth may not be sustainable long enough to meet the required growth hurdles.

It's Hard to Have the Stomach, Even if You're Right

Even if you're right long-term, the stock price can still perform poorly, and most people don't have the stomach to endure it. Imagine it's December 1999, and after conducting an inverse analysis on Amazon, you conclude that, in the very long term, it could meet the growth conditions implied by your analysis.

You make the investment, and fast-forward 25 years, you clearly would have been right. Both its earnings and stock have done incredibly well since then. In fact, your compounded annual return would be an impressive 16.5%, meaning you'd have made about 45 times your initial investment over the 25-year period.

Despite these phenomenal returns, however, two years into your investment the market value of Amazon would have been roughly 90% lower than when you initially invested. And you wouldn't sustainably surpass your break-even point until sometime in late 2009. It would have taken almost 10 years to realize that your decision had actually been the correct one.

And this is the real danger of investing in high-growth companies. Even if you correctly apply the inverse analysis, the results may only materialize in the very long term. Don't forget that we're assuming 40-year periods, and what we're trying to determine are the returns we would obtain by holding the business and relying on its cash flows. The market, however, doesn't think this way and, as a result, any market doubts about the near-term growth thesis can lead to significant repricing.

So, in general, investing in high-growth businesses can be painful and requires much more patience than investing in mature companies. You need to be aware of this, as most people don't have the stomach for the stock swings that growth companies often undergo.

In the case of Amazon, it would have been extremely difficult to maintain your emotional intelligence for such a long period. When the market is constantly questioning a company, it's easy to doubt your investment thesis yourself. The likelihood that anyone would have given up in the first 10 years is very high, resulting in an unnecessary loss.

Another way to look at it is that with high-growth businesses trading at low cash flow yields, you don't get any immediate benefit from the existing cash flows. They're so low that even if you're reinvesting them successfully, it will take time to see the compounded impact. For the first 5 to 10 years, your potential returns are almost entirely at the mercy of the market.

In contrast, if you invest in a mature business with a 7% or higher cash flow yield, even if the valuation falls significantly, you can rely on those relatively high cash flows to continue compounding more immediately. In this case, you're much less dependent on the market's whims in the medium term.

So, be very careful when investing in high-growth companies. Only invest in them when the margin of safety is extremely high, and even then, understand that the risks are substantial, and share price swings are inevitable. If you're not comfortable enduring this kind of volatility, I would even recommend staying away from these companies altogether.

Conclusion of Inverse Analysis for High-Growth Businesses

While the inverse approach for high-growth businesses is relatively straightforward, we've covered a lot of ground—so let me recap everything we've discussed. This final section of the chapter is intended to replace the usual summary and takeaway bullets. It ties everything together and highlights the most critical insights from our discussion. In this case, though, I don't consider it "optional reading," because given the depth of the analysis, it's essential to bring it all together to ensure we're on the same page.

That said, let me start by reminding you that this method is very similar to the one we used with mature companies. The core idea remains the same. Instead of projecting cash flows and discounting them to arrive at a valuation, we flip the process on its head. We start with the market valuation and ask what conditions must be met for us to achieve the desired return. If these conditions seem achievable and offer a margin of safety, the company may be undervalued.

Now, the challenge with high-growth companies is that there are more variables to consider. The reinvestment rate and starting valuation are no longer the only key factors affecting expected returns. We must also consider how long a company can maintain its rapid growth before it matures and at what rate it can continue to grow during that period. Given these additional variables, the inverse approach for high-growth companies can be divided into two approaches.

The first approach involves assuming the length of the high-growth period and the growth rate during that phase are fixed. These variables are kept constant so we can assess the required reinvestment rate across various valuation scenarios. This approach is more comprehensive and aligns closely with how we analyze mature companies. It's useful for comparing high-growth companies to mature ones, but it does have a major drawback. Specifically, it's harder to assess multiple growth scenarios simultaneously.

To address this drawback, we can complement the first approach with a second one that allows us to explore different growth conditions. In this approach, we assume a fixed reinvestment rate and choose a desired return, helping us determine the required growth conditions to meet that return. While it's possible to explore many scenarios, I recommend using a 10% desired return and a 10% reinvestment rate for practical and conservative purposes.

I've argued that considering multiple scenarios would complicate the analysis unnecessarily. These assumptions simply provide a consistent reference point against which we can compare different potential investments. If a higher return is desired, simply increase your margin of safety when comparing your growth expectations to the required growth. Similarly, if the 10% reinvestment rate seems too conservative, you can revisit the first approach, as we did with Tesla, to analyze the impact of a higher reinvestment rate.

Ultimately, my advice for most cases is to use both approaches as needed. Typically, it's better to start with the second approach because it can quickly help you assess whether a valuation is too optimistic, within reason, or potentially undervalued. If the company seems undervalued or at least reasonably priced based on this approach, you can then proceed to the first approach. From there, you can explore multiple scenarios as needed and, combined with qualitative research, decide whether the investment seems worthwhile.

Now, throughout this analysis, I've highlighted several important conclusions and considerations that shouldn't be overlooked. Most importantly, even for growth companies, successfully reinvesting cash flows remains a necessary condition for achieving high returns in the long term.

While considering reinvestment potential, remember not to double-count growth. Growth from a company's existing operations is not the same as growth from reinvesting. Conflating the two could lead to overly optimistic projections of a company's potential to deliver returns.

I also emphasized that, while high growth is desirable, it's not necessarily the optimal scenario. The ideal situation is when, in addition to having a growing set of cash flows, the company has ample opportunities to reinvest those growing cash flows into high return endeavors. Otherwise, the potential for a high reinvestment rate remains challenging. The company simply can't compound cash flows on the investor's behalf. Instead, the company will have to return capital to shareholders, delegating the fate of the reinvestment rate to investors.

Furthermore, I discussed several reasons why investors should exercise caution when considering high-growth companies. For example, we looked at the challenges of maintaining growth for very large companies like Apple. By examining the "Zoom path", I also highlighted the importance of not assuming that recent growth trends can continue into the future. Additionally, remember that our inverse approach assumes a 40-year time horizon. So, even if you're right about a company's growth over the next 5 to 10 years, achieving the expected returns will depend on whether cash flows continue for another 30 to 35 years once the company matures.

Finally, I hope I've also made it clear that, even if you're right in the long term, the market may not validate your investment decision immediately. High-growth stocks can be extremely volatile, so if you're not comfortable with enduring that volatility, it may be wise to avoid investing in these companies altogether. Otherwise, you risk losing money even if your original investment decision proves correct in the end.

CHAPTER 10

IS PROPER REINVESTING TAKING PLACE?

PART 1 – RETURN ON EQUITY

After reviewing how to properly assess a company's valuation, you now understand that the most critical factor for achieving significant returns over time is the ability to continually and successfully reinvest cash flows. This principle applies to both mature and high-growth companies.

Now, until now, we haven't delved into how to determine whether a company has the capacity to reinvest cash flows effectively. I've only mentioned that this is crucial because, ultimately, it's the management team, not the investor, who decides whether the company retains its cash flows and, if so, how and where those funds are reinvested. So, in the following two chapters, I'll explain how you can gain a good sense of the degree to which a company is likely to reinvest its cash flows successfully.

In short, there are two key things we can examine in a company's financial statements to help us determine this. First, we can look at the company's return on equity (ROE), a financial ratio that indicates how much earnings a company generates in a given year relative to the capital previously invested. Second, we can assess the company's historical financial performance and examine how retaining cash flows has impacted its ability to grow its profitability over time.

As we'll see, neither of these methods is perfect. Just like we combined approaches in our inverse valuation method, my recommendation is to always look at both. Even when we combine these analyses, however, we still can't get a perfect picture just by relying on these financial metrics. There's no guarantee that past performance, whether good or bad, will continue into the future. Therefore, while these analyses are invaluable, they should always be complemented by qualitative research. You must thoroughly consider the company's business model and strategy to assess whether its past performance is a reflection of the future.

Decoding the Balance Sheet for ROE

To interpret return on equity correctly, we must first understand how a balance sheet works. However, as we did in Chapter 5 when discussing accounting, I won't go over every aspect of it. Instead, I'll highlight only the relevant aspects necessary to understand and appreciate the metric of return on equity. But as I've stated before, if you're really serious about value investing, I strongly recommend learning more about accounting, in large part because it will help with the many nuances embedded in return on equity.

In simple terms, the balance sheet provides a snapshot of a company's assets at a specific point in time, along with the sources used to finance those assets. Whether the assets were financed through debt, vendor financing, other liabilities, or equity capital, the total value of the assets always equals the combined value of the liabilities and equity. This is why it's called the balance sheet, because the assets always "balance" with the liabilities and equity.

To stay consistent with the cash flow statement example from Chapter 5, let's take a look at Costco's balance sheet as of September 1, 2024—the end of the company's 2024 fiscal year. As before, I've made minor adjustments to the wording, order, and grouping for clarity, but the substance remains unchanged from the Company's published results.

Consolidated Balance Sheet - USD ($) in Millions As of September 1, 2024			
ASSETS		**LIABILITIES**	
Cash and cash equivalents	$ 9,906	Accounts payable	$ 19,421
Short-term investments	1,238	Accrued salaries and benefits	4,794
Accounts Receivables, net	2,721	Accrued member rewards	2,435
Merchandise inventories	18,647	Deferred membership fees	2,501
Other current assets	1,734	Long-term debt	5,794
Property and equipment, net	29,032	Long-term operating leases	2,375
Operating lease right-of-use	2,617	Other liabilities	8,889
Other long-term assets	3,936	**EQUITY CAPITAL**	
		Investor Equity Capital Raised	$ 7,831
		Retained Earnings	15,791
Total Assets	**$ 69,831**	**Total Liabilities & Equity**	**$ 69,831**

Source: Costco Wholesale Corporation, fiscal year 2024 10-K.

As you can see, the left side of the balance sheet lists all of Costco's assets, which together total nearly $70 billion. Most notably, the company has about $10 billion in cash, almost $19 billion in inventory, and around $30 billion in property and equipment, net of depreciation. Together, these three items make up more than 80% of Costco's total assets.

Now, how has Costco financed this inventory, property, and equipment, while still maintaining almost $10 billion in cash? The answer lies on the right side of the balance sheet which, not surprisingly, also totals nearly $70 billion.

We can see, for instance, that nearly $20 billion of assets have been financed through accounts payable. This means the company has purchased goods from vendors but hasn't paid them yet. Essentially, these vendors have provided Costco with short-term financing.

Costco has also raised almost $6 billion in long term debt and obtained some funding from customers and employees. The deferred membership fees, for example, represent receipt of payments from customers for their membership. It's a form of financing because the company receives payments from customers upfront and yet it gives them access to Costco's store for an entire year. Similarly, the accrued salaries and benefits reflect amounts the company owes to employees for work already performed, but for which it hasn't yet paid. Both of these items fall under "working capital," which we briefly covered in Chapter 5.

For our purposes, the most important section to understand is the equity section, which can be divided into two main items, as shown above.

The first one is what I've labeled as "Investor Equity Capital Raised." In reality, this amount is usually broken down into "common stock" and "additional paid-in-capital," but both essentially represent money that was raised at some point and injected into the business in exchange for an ownership stake. In other words, it's the capital provided by equity investors to help fund the business.

The second section is retained earnings, and as the name suggests, it represents the portion of profits that the company has decided to retain over time rather than distributing it to investors through dividends or stock repurchases. This capital belongs to the investors, but it differs from the first item in that it didn't come directly from them. Instead, it represents capital that could have been paid out as dividends or used to buy back shares from investors.

While it's still funding that ultimately comes from investors, it is only indirectly so. It's not new capital that investors have chosen to inject, but rather capital that investors have temporarily forgone to continue funding the business's investments.

Understanding the Function of Retained Earnings in Equity

The explanation just given on the balance sheet would likely be sufficient to understand what return on equity represents and why it's so valuable. However, I want to take a moment and provide a few more details on retained earnings as it may help make things even more clear. Specifically, I'd like to highlight that retained earnings has the unique characteristic of being indirectly linked to many other items on the balance sheet. And this is important because it helps us understand how certain assets are funded, at least indirectly, by retained earnings.

For example, consider the roughly $2.7 billion in accounts receivable listed under Costco's assets. A significant portion of this amount consists of money that banks owe Costco for amounts earned under co-branded credit card agreements. Costco has recognized the revenue from the credit card fees it's entitled to, but it has yet to receive the money from the partner bank. Since the revenue was recognized, however, profits have already increased, contributing in turn to the increase in retained earnings on the balance sheet.

This essentially means that Costco's shareholders indirectly funded this $2.7 billion asset. The asset represents money that some bank out there owes Costco, and once received, shareholders could use it to pay themselves a dividend. In other words, shareholders have earned the right to the cash this asset will eventually be converted into. But because they technically don't have access to this expected cash receipt yet, they're essentially foregoing the use of that money and, therefore, indirectly funding the asset.

Think about it this way. If the company decided to pay a dividend for the entire $15.7 billion in retained earnings to shareholders, the $9.9 billion in existing cash wouldn't be enough to cover it. The owners essentially have earned an amount higher than what's currently available in cash to them. This is due to the assets the company holds, including the claims it has on its bank partners we just discussed. So, while it's difficult to conceptualize and somewhat indirect, shareholders are indeed financing assets through retained earnings.

Sometimes it's difficult to visualize this because money is fungible. No one can truthfully claim that a specific item on the right side of the balance sheet is being used to finance just one or two specific assets. In practice, money comes in from various sources at different times and is used to fund multiple assets simultaneously. However, this example helps demonstrate that retained earnings is contributing to the funding of assets in general, even if it's not always immediately obvious.

Return on Equity Calculation and Interpretation

All these details aside, the key takeaway regarding the balance sheet is that the equity section essentially represents the total capital that equity investors have cumulatively provided to fund the business. Part of that capital comes from actual injections into the business, and part of it comes from retaining profits that belong to investors but are kept in the business. Either way, it represents equity funding.

This is a great piece of information to have because it allows us to compare how much money a company is generating relative to how much has been put into the business by equity investors. This is precisely what return on equity (ROE) measures.

Mathematically, it's a simple calculation consisting of earnings divided by the equity section of the balance sheet. In Costco's case, we saw in

Chapter 5 that in 2024 the company generated roughly $7.4 billion in profits. If we divide this by the $23.6 billion in total equity, we arrive at a return on equity of roughly 31%.

Linking Return on Equity to the Reinvestment Rate

This means that for every dollar of equity put into the business by investors, Costco is generating 31 cents in annual profits. If this output can be maintained going forward, the implication is that for every dollar Costco retains to invest in opening new stores, its annual profits could increase by 31 cents. And by indicating how much profit can be generated from each incremental dollar invested, return on equity can provide insight into what the reinvestment rate might look like.

Now, I don't want to imply that a 31% return on equity means Costco's rate of return from reinvesting is 31%. In other words, the reinvestment rate is not equal to the existing return on equity.

The reinvestment rate can be higher or lower because return on equity is evaluating a single year's performance. In contrast, the reinvestment rate is concerned with the return from reinvesting over an extended period. While it's expressed in annual terms, it represents the compounded rate of return over multiple years.

In Costco's case, if a stream of 31 cents from a reinvested dollar lasts for 30 years, the return for that stream could approach 31%. However, if the stream of 31 cents produced by each reinvested dollar only lasts for 10 years, the 31% return won't be realized. Ultimately, in both cases, the actual reinvestment rate will depend on how the 31 cent streams are reinvested, and what additional cash flows they generate over time as well.

Furthermore, Costco hasn't and likely won't reinvest all of its earnings in the future. Some of its earnings are paid out as dividends or used for share repurchases. Remember, return on equity tells us the performance of the portion of profits that were retained, but it can never tell us about the performance of the portion of earnings that wasn't retained.

As discussed before, that will depend on you as the investor. So, even if the 31% return on equity corresponds to a 31% reinvestment rate for the retained portion, the overall reinvestment rate to investors won't be the same.

Despite these considerations, return on equity is still extremely useful for gauging the potential of the reinvestment rate. In the case of Costco, if you believe they still have ample room to open new stores worldwide, it wouldn't be unreasonable to assume their reinvestment rate could range between 15% and 30% over time. Personally, I think it's more likely to be closer to 15%, given their size. However, if this were 1999, when they had much more room to expand without the risk of saturation or cannibalization, a 20%+ reinvestment rate wouldn't seem unreasonable.

Over time, Costco's extremely high return on equity has translated into a very high reinvestment rate. In 1999, Costco's profits were relatively modest, around half a billion dollars. Fast forward to 2024, those profits have increased to almost $7.4 billion, representing a roughly 11.5% compounded annual growth rate.

This growth is despite the fact that Costco has paid out a significant amount in dividends and repurchased a considerable amount of shares over the 25-year period. Hypothetically, if Costco had been able to reinvest all of its earnings, today's profits would likely be much higher than $7.4 billion. While it's not worth the time to make a precise calculation with assumptions, I'd imagine that profits would be at least double what they are today if all earnings had been reinvested since 1999.

Return on Equity Considerations

Like any financial or accounting metric, return on equity is not perfect. To use it successfully as a tool for decision-making, it's important to keep the following considerations in mind.

Revisit Accounting Profits Before Relying on ROE

Don't forget the lessons from Chapter 5. The return on equity calculation uses accounting earnings or profits in the numerator. As we know, however, accounting profits may not be a perfect proxy for cash flows and, as a result, adjustments may be warranted in the numerator. As always, what we truly care about is cash flows available to owners. If accounting earnings reasonably represent cash flows, then accounting profits can be used. Otherwise, consider making the necessary adjustments as we discussed before.

Don't Take ROE at Face Value

As we saw with growth trends, be cautious not to assume that the existing return on equity will persist into the future. While return on equity tends to be more stable and consistent than growth, there are no guarantees. Through qualitative research, you must carefully evaluate whether the current economics can be sustained. For this, it's essential to understand the characteristics that contribute to a company's current economics. Without this understanding, you won't be equipped to assess whether these conditions are likely to persist or if there are risks that could alter the company's future return on equity.

Evaluate ROE in Context, Not in Isolation

Don't just focus on last year's return on equity; it's important to consider trends as well. For example, a rising return on equity could signal that a company is becoming more efficient. Costco, for instance, has a much higher return on equity today than it had in 1999 when it was roughly 15%.

As it grew, it likely earned more pricing power with suppliers and vendors, generating efficiencies there. Additionally, Costco may share an increasingly larger portion of non-store-specific costs across a larger number of stores. As a result, the unit economics of each store improved, ultimately allowing each store to generate more profits without the need for additional capital. So, there are many ways in which a company can improve its return on equity through economies of scale.

Conversely, if a company's return on equity is declining over time, it may imply that the company is no longer as efficient in generating earnings for each additional dollar invested. This could be the result of no longer having low hanging fruit in which to invest. Alternatively, it might mean the company is increasingly investing outside its core business and those new ventures may not offer the same economics.

Given these possibilities, a high return on equity doesn't necessarily guarantee that a company can continue to reinvest efficiently. In fact, it's possible for a company with a high return on equity to have reinvestments that generate negative returns. For example, imagine a company that had $100 in equity five years ago and was generating $30 in annual profits at the time. That would translate to a 30% return on equity.

Now, let's assume that for the next five years, the company retained all its profits, increasing its cumulative retained earnings to $250. Now imagine that, despite retaining and reinvesting its profits, the company's earnings today are still $30. If I calculate the return on equity today, it would be 12%, resulting from dividing $30 by $250.

While 12% is not nearly as high as 30%, it's not terrible either. As a result, if you only look at today's return on equity, you might conclude that the company is reinvesting at an acceptable rate. But the reality is that the company invested $150 over the past five years with no additional profits to show for it. Essentially, the company's incremental profits were $0 despite the additional capital of $150 being invested. This means that $150 of invested capital were thrown down the toilet, leading to the conclusion that the company's reinvestment rate has recently been negative.

So again, return on equity can't be trusted blindly. Trends must be considered along with a clear understanding of the company's business model and strategic efforts. Without this, you're likely to make a mistake in assessing whether a company can successfully reinvest its earnings going forward.

Idle Cash Can Distort ROE

Be aware that return on equity may be understated when a company holds a significant amount of cash on its balance sheet. Let's take Alphabet as an example to see how this can affect our view of return on equity.

As of December 31, 2024, the company has accounting equity of approximately $325 billion, made up of $85 billion in equity capital raised and $240 billion in retained earnings. And, as we saw in Chapter 9, Alphabet's annual cash flows are around $123 billion.

Doing the math, we get a return on equity of roughly 38%. If we interpret this metric the same way we did with Costco, it suggests that for every dollar of equity invested or retained in the business, Alphabet generates 38 cents in annual cash flows. There's a very important nuance, however, that can lead us to a materially different conclusion.

Specifically, Alphabet currently holds roughly $95 billion in cash and liquid securities, which means it didn't need the full $325 billion of equity to generate its $123 billion in annual cash flows. Those $95 billion are essentially non-working assets. If the company had decided to distribute them as dividends, its ability to generate cash would have remained the same. If we subtract these $95 billion in cash and equivalents from the $325 billion in equity, we see that the amount actually put to work is only $230 billion.

See Alphabet's balance sheet below for more details.

Consolidated Balance Sheet - USD ($) in Millions As of December 31, 2024			
ASSETS		**LIABILITIES**	
Cash & other liquid securities	$ 95,657	Accounts payable	$ 7,987
Accounts receivable, net	52,340	Accrued compensation & benefits	15,069
Other current assets	15,714	Accrued revenue share	9,802
Non-marketable securities	37,982	Other current liabilities	51,228
Deferred income taxes	17,180	Deferred revenue	5,036
Property and equipment, net	171,036	Long-term debt	10,883
Operating lease assets	13,588	Income taxes payable	8,782
Goodwill	31,885	Operating lease liabilities	11,691
Other non-current assets	14,874	Other long-term liabilities	4,694
		EQUITY CAPITAL	
		Investor Equity Capital Raised	$ 84,800
		Retained Earnings	240,284
Total Assets	**$ 450,256**	**Total Liabilities & Equity**	**$ 450,256**

Source: Alphabet Inc., fiscal year 2024 10-K.

So, when evaluating a company's potential reinvestment rate, using $230 billion as our equity may be more meaningful. Remember, the reinvestment rate reflects the returns generated by the portion of profits that has been retained and reinvested. And if only $230 billion has actually been reinvested over time, this would be the more appropriate figure to use.

Now, if we use this figure instead of the $325 billion, the return on equity jumps to approximately 53%. That means Alphabet is generating 53 cents of annual cash flow for every dollar it has effectively put to work and this is significantly higher than the 38 cents implied by our original calculation.

Of course, this can't be looked at in isolation or without considering the other factors we've discussed. And don't forget that even if the 53% figure is more representative of what Alphabet has achieved historically, it would only apply to the portion of earnings that actually gets reinvested. If Alphabet is unable to find sufficient opportunities to deploy all of its earnings over time, the reinvestment rate will fall short of 53%.

Additionally, Alphabet is currently channeling a disproportionately large share of its earnings into its cloud business. It's possible that this segment may not be as efficient at generating returns for every dollar invested as compared to its more mature Google or YouTube segments.

That said, the main takeaway here is that maintaining a large cash balance on the balance sheet can distort return on equity and its usefulness in assessing a company's economics. Too much idle cash can artificially lower ROE, leading us to underestimate how efficiently a business has traditionally redeployed earnings over time. And this is something you should always account for when thinking about a company's reinvestment potential going forward.

Leverage Can Artificially Inflate Return on Equity

Be aware that return on equity can be significantly manipulated with the use of leverage. To illustrate this let's look at a simple example involving a hypothetical company that produces $10 million in annual cash flows before any interest expense. For simplicity's sake, I've laid out several tables on the next page showing the company's hypothetical situation. Notice, however, that I've provided two different scenarios, each depicting a different debt situation. The only meaningful difference between the two scenarios is the amount of debt assumed and any related effects that stem directly or indirectly from it.

More specifically, Scenario 1 shows the company with no debt and, as a result, a higher equity requirement to finance its assets. In total, this scenario shows $60 million in equity, made up of $59 million in retained earnings and $1 million in equity capital raised. Naturally, since there's no debt, the company doesn't incur any interest expense, so the full $10 million in annual cash flows remains.

Scenario 2, however, shows the company financing a large portion of its assets with debt, $35 million, to be exact. As a result, the portion of assets financed through equity drops to $25 million. The debt is assumed to carry an effective interest rate—net of tax benefits—of 7.5%, leading to an annual interest expense of $2.6 million. This interest cost reduces the company's annual cash flows from $10 million to $7.4 million.

Assets ($ in millions)		Liabilities ($ in millions)	Scenario 1	Scenario 2
ASSETS		**LIABILITIES**		
Cash	$ 5.0	Accounts payable	$ 2.0	$ 2.0
Other current assets	5.0	Accrued salaries	1.0	1.0
Property & equipment	40.0	Other current liabilities	1.0	1.0
Other long-term assets	15.0	Total Debt	-	35.0
		Other Long-term liabilities	1.0	1.0
		EQUITY CAPITAL		
		Equity Capital Raised	1.0	1.0
		Retained Earnings	59.0	24.0
Total Assets	**$ 65.0**	**Total Liabilities & Equity**	**$ 65.0**	**$ 65.0**

Cash Flow Calculations ($ in millions)	Scenario 1	Scenario 2
Annual Cash Flow Before Interest	$ 10	$ 10
Less: Interest Expense, net of tax benefits	-	(2.6)
Annual Cash Flow	**10.0**	**7.4**

Return on Equity Calculations	Scenario 1	Scenario 2
Annual Cash Flow (A)	$ 10.0	$ 7.4
Total Equity (B)	60.0	25.0
Return on Equity (A / B)	**16.7%**	**29.5%**

Now, if you look at the last of the three tables, you'll see that despite being the same company, the return on equity varies significantly across the two scenarios. In the version with no debt, the return on equity is 16.7%, while in the version with debt, it nearly doubles to 29.5%.

This happens because, even though cash flow dropped by about 26% between the two scenarios, the amount of equity dropped by roughly 58%, a significantly larger decline. As a result, in relative terms, more cash flow is being generated per dollar of equity in Scenario 2.

Now imagine you come across a company with characteristics similar to the one in the second scenario. A return on equity of nearly 30% could easily lead you to believe it's an extremely efficient business, one capable of generating significant cash flows relative to the equity capital invested. But I urge you to be cautious. It's not that this conclusion is technically wrong; it's just that it's true only because of financial engineering rather than the strength of the business itself.

So take note that return on equity will always increase with the use of leverage whenever the cost of debt—7.5% in our case—is lower than the return the business could achieve without using debt—16.7% in our example.

What's happening is that, for the portion of assets financed with debt, you're essentially capturing a spread that's almost like a free lunch. Think about it; on the $35 million of debt, you're only paying 7.5%, but the assets financed with that debt are generating a 16.7% return. So the return on your assets can fully pay for the cost of debt and still leave you with an excess return on top.

Given this dynamic, the reality is that many mediocre companies can achieve very high return on equity simply by using debt. My recommendation, however, is to look for companies, like Alphabet and Costco, that can achieve high returns on equity without relying heavily on leverage. Otherwise, you might be taking on too much risk, one that can lead to permanent losses even though the starting ROE implied there was potential for a high reinvestment rate.

Be Wary of How Historical Acquisitions Can Distort ROE

For the purposes of helping us assess a potential reinvestment rate, distortions to return on equity can also happen when a company has made material acquisitions in the past. To better understand why, let's imagine a world where current accounting practices don't apply and two companies are merging. Now, because this ROE consideration is somewhat lengthy, I've bolded the first sentence of some initial paragraphs to signal changes in subject and highlight key points.

Suppose Company A decides to join forces with Company B and, once they merge into becoming Company C, they simply plan to combine their financial statements by adding them up. In this hypothetical case, the balance sheet for Company C would show all of the assets that Companies A and B had acquired over time, along with the liabilities and equity that financed those assets. More importantly for our purposes, the equity of Company C would exclusively reflect the capital injections and retained earnings that both Company A and Company B made or built up over time.

In this scenario, if we were to calculate Company C's return on equity, there wouldn't be any distortion affecting what this metric typically conveys. In other words, we could still claim that its return on equity tells us how much cash flow is being generated annually for every dollar put to work in the combined businesses over time.

The issue is that when acquisitions take place, accounting rules don't

allow companies to simply combine balance sheets. Instead, they require the acquirer to adjust the value of the acquiree's assets and liabilities to reflect their estimated fair value. These revaluations are especially common with assets because the acquiree may have assets that were never recorded on the balance sheet or were recorded at historical cost, often much lower than what a third party would be willing to pay. As we'll discuss shortly, this is particularly true for intangible assets such as brands, customer relationships, patents, copyrights, internally developed software, trade secrets, and know-how derived from research and development.

In addition to revaluing the assets of the acquiree, accounting practices also require the acquiring company to create an intangible asset called goodwill. Without going into unnecessary details, goodwill essentially captures the premium paid for over and above the estimated fair value of the acquired assets minus the acquired liabilities.

As a result, the acquirer's balance sheet is now showing the acquiree's assets at a value much higher than what was actually required to develop and operate that business. There are valid reasons why accounting works this way, and I don't dispute the general rationale. But for our purposes, the issue is that instead of reflecting the amount put to work in the business, equity is essentially reflecting the value paid to the former owners of the acquiree.

As an example of how all this works, imagine Alphabet is acquiring Company X and, before any revaluations, this company's balance sheet looks as follows:

Company X Consolidated Balance Sheet - USD ($) in Millions			
ASSETS		**LIABILITIES**	
Current assets	$ 5,000	Current liabilities	$ 8,000
Non-current assets	15,000	Non-current liabilities	2,000
		EQUITY CAPITAL	
		Investor Equity Capital Raised	$ 2,000
		Retained Earnings	8,000
Total Assets	**$ 20,000**	**Total Liabilities & Equity**	**$ 20,000**

Now imagine we could simply merge this accounting history into Alphabet's balance sheet with no adjustments. We've already seen Alphabet's balance sheet, so we know its equity would rise from the existing $325 billion to about $335 billion, reflecting the additional $10 billion in equity from Company X.

But remember, this equity still includes Alphabet's $95 billion in idle cash, which hasn't been put to work. So, to isolate the equity that has actually been deployed, we need to subtract that amount. Doing so, we arrive at roughly $240 billion in equity that the combined businesses have truly invested to generate their cash flows. For clarity, see the breakdown of the calculation below.

Alphabet's Equity + X's Equity − Idle Cash = Combined Equity Put to Work

$325 + $10 − $95 = $240

Now suppose Company X generates $5 billion in annual cash flow, implying a return on equity of roughly 50% for the standalone business—very similar to the 53% we previously calculated for Alphabet.

To determine the return on equity for the combined company, we simply add Company X's $5 billion to Alphabet's $123 billion in annual cash flow, and divide that total by the combined $240 billion in equity actually put to work. By doing so, we effectively preserve Alphabet's 53% return on equity, even after the hypothetical merger. For clarity, see the breakdown of these new calculations below.

$$\frac{(X's\ Cash\ Flow + Alphabet's\ Cash\ Flow)}{Combined\ Equity\ Put\ to\ Work} = Return\ on\ Equity$$

$$\frac{(\$5 + \$123)}{\$240} = 53\%$$

In a perfect world, this is the kind of information we'd want when trying to assess the reinvestment rate. It precisely shows how much equity capital was actually required to fund the combined businesses and produce the cash flows they generate together. As I referenced before, however, the exercise we just went through is not what actually happens.

To explore a simplified version of what actually takes place, let's assume Alphabet purchases this company for $90 billion and uses the cash on its balance sheet to fund the acquisition. For a business generating $5 billion in annual cash flows, this would imply a price-to-cash flow ratio of 18x, a very realistic scenario.

In terms of possible revaluations, current assets and current liabilities are rarely adjusted because they reflect expected cash inflows or outflows within the next 12 months. Accounting practices simply wouldn't permit their recorded values to differ materially from their estimated fair values.

Similarly, non-current liabilities are also unlikely to be revalued. These typically represent contractual obligations to third parties, such as debt, long-term lease commitments, or deferred taxes, and it would make little sense for accounting rules to allow their amounts not to be aligned with their fair value.

So, when an acquisition happens, it's unlikely that any material revaluations may be required for current assets, current liabilities and non-current liabilities. In all cases, of course, there are exceptions to these generalizations, but for the most part, these soft conclusions tend to be materially accurate. So in our example, let's assume these three line items remain unchanged when Alphabet acquires Company X.

With respect to non-current assets, however, it really depends on what the assets are. If they consist mostly of depreciable items—such as property and equipment, data centers or other technological infrastructure, vehicles, or furniture—there's typically no reason to revalue them. It's rare for these types of assets to have a fair value higher than their historical cost, which is essentially what's reflected on the balance sheet.

There are, of course, some exceptions, the most notable being real estate, such as a company's office building. While technically depreciable, commercial real estate often appreciates in value over time, and yet accounting rules don't require its recorded value to be increased unless an acquisition takes place. So, given these exceptions exist, let's go ahead and assume that Company X's non-current assets are revalued by $5 billion, increasing them from $15 billion to $20 billion.

Let's now move on to intangible assets, the item most relevant for our purposes since it's the balance sheet element that typically undergoes the most significant revaluation. This is primarily because, unless a company is acquired, internally generated intangibles are often not allowed to be recorded on the balance sheet for multiple reasons. To start with, it can be difficult to assign a cost to them, and since accounting values are typically based on cost, this creates limitations. Think about a company's brand: could Coca-Cola have realistically identified every cost associated with creating the Coca-Cola brand?

Faced with this challenge, one might argue that intangibles should be recorded at their fair value, adjusting their value as estimates of it change over time. But the problem is this would be a very difficult endeavor. Intangibles tend to be very unique and so it's hard to estimate what they're worth. And because of this, there would be a risk of earnings manipulation.

To look good, management could increase the value of intangibles under some subjective pretext. Or to reduce a company's tax basis, management could find a reason to reduce their value by recognizing a loss. Anyway, I don't want to get into unnecessary detail. The point here is that, because there are many challenges with intangibles, accounting opts for the conservative view of generally not allowing them to be recorded when they're internally generated.

That being said, when one company acquires another, accounting practices take a different approach. In these cases, they allow, and even require, revaluations based on estimates, despite knowing that such estimates can still be subjective and prone to error. The reason is that an acquisition provides external validation that the intangibles have real value. Their worth becomes less subjective because someone is clearly willing to pay a premium for them.

It may still be difficult to value each intangible asset individually, but at least you know that, collectively, they're worth significantly more than nothing. And because of this outside validation, accounting aims for greater accuracy and requires you to revalue them as best as possible. For our example, let's assume that Company X had a significant amount of intangible assets and their estimated worth is $25 billion, adding this amount to its balance sheet.

As the final part of this thought exercise, let's now take a look at goodwill. As a reminder, goodwill essentially represents the premium paid over and above the estimated value of the acquiree's net assets. In our example, the revalued assets of Company X now total $50 billion, comprised of $5 billion in current assets, $20 billion in non-current assets, and $25 billion in intangible assets that were not previously recorded on the balance sheet. We didn't revalue any of the liabilities, so Company X still has a total of $10 billion in liabilities which consist of $8 billion in current liabilities and $2 billion in non-current liabilities. To get the net assets, we simply subtract the $10 billion in liabilities from the $50 billion in assets to arrive at $40 billion.

Based on these figures, we now know that, following the acquisition, Alphabet should record goodwill of $50 billion on its balance sheet. This simply reflects the $90 billion paid for Company X minus the $40 billion in net assets being brought into Alphabet's balance sheet.

I'll show all of this in a revised balance sheet shortly, but first let me break it down to make it easier to follow.

- No revaluations are made to current assets, which remain at $5 billion.
- Company X's non-current assets are revalued upward by $5 billion, increasing them from $15 billion to $20 billion.
- Company X has a significant amount of intangible assets that were not previously recorded. Their estimated worth is $25 billion, and the full amount is added to the balance sheet.
- With these revaluations, total revalued assets now amount to $50 billion.
- No revaluations are made to current liabilities ($8 billion) or non-current liabilities ($2 billion), so total liabilities remain at $10 billion.
- Alphabet is acquiring Company X for $90 billion.
- Given these assumptions, the calculations are as follows:

Purchase Price – Revalued Net Assets = Goodwill

Purchase Price – (Revalued Assets – Revalued Liabilities) = Goodwill

$90 – ($50 – $10) = $50

The recording of this goodwill serves several purposes. To start with, if we don't include it, the balance sheet wouldn't balance after the acquisition. That's because we're only adding $40 billion in net assets from

Company X, yet we're reducing Alphabet's cash by $90 billion to reflect the acquisition. So, without goodwill, total assets would fall short by $50 billion, creating an imbalance.

Secondly, even though the nature of goodwill can be abstract and sometimes confusing, Alphabet still had to finance it. We need a way to reflect the fact that part of the right side of the balance sheet—whether retained earnings, capital raised, or both—was used to pay a premium above what Company X's assets are worth on a standalone basis. Goodwill makes that premium visible.

Finally, goodwill is not without meaning. It essentially captures the idea that the acquirer believes the value of the acquiree's assets is greater when viewed as a whole than when valued individually. Each intangible asset is revalued on its own merits during the acquisition process, but it's entirely possible that the combination of those assets has greater value than the sum of their parts. In addition, goodwill may also reflect the expectation that the acquired assets will be more valuable when integrated with the assets of Alphabet. In this sense, goodwill reflects the anticipated synergies that justify paying a premium over their estimated fair value.

In any case, to help put our example and its details into perspective, see Alphabet's balance sheet after adjusting for this hypothetical acquisition on the next page. For ease of understanding, I've separated and highlighted the assets that were hypothetically acquired. I've also highlighted the $90 billion decrease in cash that result from the acquisition.

Consolidated Balance Sheet - USD ($) in Millions As of December 31, 2024				
ASSETS		**LIABILITIES**		
Cash & other liquid securities	$ 95,657	Accounts payable		$ 7,987
Amount used for acquisition	$ (90,000)	Accrued compensation & benefits		15,069
Pro forma Cash & other liquid securities	$ 5,657	Accrued revenue share		9,802
Accounts receivable, net	52,340	Other current liabilities		51,228
Other current assets	15,714	Deferred revenue		5,036
Non-marketable securities	37,982	Long-term debt		10,883
Deferred income taxes	17,180	Income taxes payable		8,782
Property and equipment, net	171,036	Operating lease liabilities		11,691
Operating lease assets	13,588	Other long-term liabilities		4,694
Goodwill	31,885	**Acquired liabilities**		
Other non-current assets	14,874	Current liabilities (no revaluation)		8,000
Acquired assets		Non-current liabilities (no revaluation)		2,000
Current Assets (no revaluation)	5,000	**EQUITY CAPITAL**		
Non-current asset (revalued by $5 billion)	20,000	Investor Equity Capital Raised		$ 84,800
Intangible assets not previously on balance sheet	25,000	Retained Earnings		240,284
Goodwill	50,000			
Total Assets	**$ 460,256**	**Total Liabilities & Equity**		**$ 460,256**

Source: Alphabet Inc., fiscal year 2024 10-K; illustrative adjustments by the author for educational purposes.

With all this information in mind, now imagine we're analyzing Alphabet's return on equity after the acquisition takes place. Combining investor equity with retained earnings, we can see above that Alphabet's total equity remains roughly $325 billion. However, due to the $90 billion reduction in cash, Alphabet is now left with only about $5 billion in idle cash.

Before the acquisition, we could adjust equity downward by the full $95 billion in idle cash, since that capital hadn't been put to work. But now that the bulk of that cash has been invested in the acquisition, we can no longer make that same adjustment. In this new case, the $325 billion in equity largely reflects capital that has been deployed. You could still argue that the $5 billion in idle cash should be deducted, but that would only reduce the equity base to $320 billion, a relatively small adjustment.

Now, if we take the $128 billion in combined annual cash flows of the combined business and divide it by the $320 billion in equity, we get a return on equity of 40%. This result is significantly lower than the 53% we obtained when we simply combined Alphabet's balance sheet with that of Company X.

And remember, that 53% figure was actually based on the capital that had been deployed into the combined businesses, which is exactly what we want when assessing how successfully reinvestments can be made within the business. The 40% figure, by contrast, reflects the returns generated when some of the capital is invested at a premium, rather than at the actual cost it would take to build those assets internally.

So, if we suspect that Alphabet will continue to reinvest its earnings into material acquisitions, the 40% figure may be more useful, as it more accurately reflects the results of how capital would be deployed in the future. In fact, if that's our expectation, the 40% might actually be too high, since it represents a blended rate that is still more heavily influenced by Alphabet's internally generated activities than by acquisitions. Put differently, if we believe acquisitions will be the primary driver of reinvestments going forward, then the rate should be more influenced by acquisition economics. And because this 40% figure doesn't fully capture that shift, it's likely overstating the company's true reinvestment rate potential.

That said, if we believe Alphabet will mostly limit acquisitions and continue reinvesting in internally generated projects, then the 53% return on equity is likely a more reliable indicator. This is assuming, of course, that past performance can reasonably be expected to continue.

Either way, the challenge is that in the real world, we rarely get to see the acquiree's balance sheet before asset revaluations are made. And because of that, we can't run through the same kind of exercise we just did with our hypothetical Company X where we just combined the balance sheets.

However, knowing everything we just discussed about how revaluations typically work, we can still make some useful adjustments based on the information available in Alphabet's balance sheet. To keep things simple, let's focus only on the adjustments related to the hypothetical acquisition we walked through. Expanding beyond that would make the exercise unnecessarily long. And by setting aside Alphabet's prior acquisition history, we'll also ensure a cleaner, apples-to-apples comparison.

Now, because we know that the assets most commonly affected by acquisitions are intangibles and goodwill, we can simply remove these amounts from equity. By doing so, we're essentially stripping out any revaluations and premiums paid in connection with acquisitions, at least to a material extent.

In the case of our example, we can reduce the $325 billion in equity by the $25 billion in intangible assets and the $50 billion in goodwill.

And to stay consistent with our earlier adjustments, we'll also reduce the roughly $5 billion in idle cash, even though this amount is no longer particularly material. See calculations below for more clarity.

Equity – Intangible Assets – Goodwill – Idle Cash = Adj.Equity

$325 – $25 – $50 – $5 = $245

As you can see, by making these subtractions, our adjusted equity figure drops to $245 billion. If we now divide the $128 billion in combined cash flows by this $245 billion, we arrive at a return on equity of roughly 52%.

This figure is much closer to the 53% we had obtained by simply combining the balance sheets. As a result, we can conclude that these adjustments provide a materially accurate representation of what return on equity would have looked like had the acquisitions never taken place.

So, to conclude this somewhat lengthy consideration around return on equity, the first takeaway is that past acquisitions can heavily distort the metric. As a result, when assessing a company's future reinvestment potential, return on equity may no longer be a reliable indicator. In particular, it may no longer reflect the company's ability to generate cash flow through reinvestments in internally generated initiatives. Therefore, if you believe the company won't materially reinvest in acquisitions going forward, it would be wise to adjust the equity value before calculating return on equity.

By contrast, if you expect a company's reinvestment opportunities to be limited and believe it will rely on acquisitions to grow, the unadjusted return on equity figure becomes more relevant. However, even in this case, be cautious. Depending on how much acquisition activity you expect, the reported return on equity may still be too optimistic. Companies often pay steep premiums when acquiring businesses that others have built internally, which means that returns on these acquisition-driven investments tend to be much lower. And by extension, this would be true for the reinvestment rate as well. So, once again, be very careful not to take return on equity at face value—especially when acquisitions have played, or are expected to play, a meaningful role.

Conclusion: Interpreting ROE with Context and Judgment

As a broader conclusion to our discussion on return on equity, this metric can be very helpful in assessing a company's potential reinvestment rate going forward. Because it gives us insights into how well capital has been invested in the past, we can gain a better understanding of the degree to which a company might reinvest earnings in the future.

However, return on equity should never be taken as the equivalent of the reinvestment rate and must always be analyzed in context. You should aim to understand the business itself to determine whether its historical performance is likely to persist, and you should focus on the trends in return on equity, not just the most recent figure.

In addition, you must be aware of its limitations, as its usefulness depends on how well you interpret and work with it. There are many reasons why return on equity may not give you a clear picture, and I've walked through some of the more common issues. Things like excessive leverage, significant idle cash, or a history of material acquisitions can meaningfully distort this metric. As a result, it's sometimes appropriate to make adjustments to arrive at a more useful figure.

Naturally, the considerations outlined above are not exhaustive. Given the wide variety of businesses out there, it would be impossible to list every potential nuance. The important thing is to study each case carefully and assess whether other adjustments may be needed. And even if you make all the justifiable adjustments for a given company, you still can't take return on equity at face value. In the end, return on equity is only as good as the story you can justify behind it, and the clarity with which you interpret that story.

CHAPTER 10 SUMMARY AND TAKEAWAYS (OPTIONAL READING)

- While we've reviewed the importance of the reinvestment rate, it isn't until this chapter that we begin to examine how to gauge it.
- There are two ways to get a sense of it: analyzing return on equity (ROE), which this chapter focuses on, and examining the impact of retaining cash flows on a company's profitability over time.
- To understand what ROE is and how to interpret it, we must first understand how a balance sheet works.
- The balance sheet is an accounting statement that provides a snapshot of a company's assets, liabilities, and equity at a specific point in time.
- It's called this because it "balances" assets on one side with liabilities and equity on the other.
- It's structured this way to show that assets are financed either through liabilities—debt, deferred membership fees, accrued salaries, etc.—or through equity—in other words, owners' capital.
- For ROE purposes, the most important item to understand is the equity section, which is essentially a combination of capital injected into the business through capital raises plus retained earnings.
- Retained earnings are essentially the portion of profits that the company has kept rather than distributing through dividends or stock repurchases. It's capital that investors have temporarily forgone to continue funding the business's activities.
- The key point here is that the equity section of the balance sheet represents the total capital that equity investors have cumulatively provided to fund the business. Part of it comes from injections, and part from profits that belong to investors but are kept in the business. Either way, it's equity funding.
- Knowing how much equity has been put into the business is useful because it allows us to compare that invested amount with how much money the company is generating.

- This is precisely what ROE measures. Mathematically, it's a simple calculation: earnings divided by the equity section of the balance sheet.
- And it's precisely because ROE indicates how much profits can be generated from each dollar invested that it can provide insight into what the reinvestment rate might look like.
- However, the existing ROE is not equal to the reinvestment rate because 1) the former only measures a single year's performance, while the latter represents a rate of return over multiple years, and 2) ROE reflects the performance of the portion of profits that were retained, excluding the reinvestment performance of the earnings paid out through dividends and buybacks.
- Despite this, ROE remains a very useful tool for gauging the potential reinvestment rate.
- However, to use ROE effectively, it's important to understand its limitations so you can interpret it correctly.
- Investors must not forget the lessons from Chapter 5. Earnings—the numerator in the ROE formula—may not be a perfect proxy for cash flows, and adjustments may be warranted.
- Always be cautious about extrapolating existing ROE into the future without context. Through qualitative research, investors must assess whether the current economics are sustainable.
- Looking at ROE trends is extremely important. A company with a seemingly high ROE but a declining trend may indicate that recent reinvestments are not bearing fruit. In fact, a company with high ROE can still make reinvestments that generate negative returns.
- Conversely, a rising ROE implies that the company is becoming more efficient at generating earnings from each additional dollar invested.
- ROE can also be distorted when a company holds too much idle cash. Cash is a non-working asset and doesn't represent money being put to work.

- Including idle cash in retained earnings can lead to an artificially low ROE and, by extension, understate the company's actual reinvestment rate potential.
- ROE can also be manipulated through leverage. Whenever the cost of debt is lower than the return the business can achieve without using debt, ROE can increase significantly.
- In these cases, the debt-financed assets generate enough profits to cover interest payments and still leave an excess return. The company essentially captures a spread—almost like a free lunch.
- The use of leverage doesn't make the calculated ROE false. However, caution is warranted because, even though mediocre companies can produce high ROEs with leverage, it's likely at the cost of taking on too much risk.
- ROE can also be distorted when a company has made material acquisitions in the past.
- When acquisitions occur, accounting rules require the acquirer to revalue the acquiree's assets and liabilities at fair value. In addition, goodwill must be recognized to account for any premium paid above the estimated fair value of net assets.
- As a result of these revaluations, the equity figure on the pro forma balance sheet no longer reflects the actual capital invested in the combined business. Instead, it shows the value paid to the acquiree's former owners—an amount almost always higher than what it would cost to build the underlying business organically.
- Therefore, if an investor believes acquisitions won't be a significant reinvestment channel, ROE will appear artificially low and no longer serve as a reliable indicator of the company's reinvestment rate potential.
- In such cases, equity should be adjusted by subtracting goodwill and intangible assets. This adjustment essentially removes the most significant revaluations and premiums typically associated with acquisitions.

- Note, however, that if significant acquisitions are expected going forward, equity should not be adjusted, as it would more accurately reflect the reality that future reinvestments will be made at premium prices—thereby lowering the reinvestment rate's potential.
- Even without adjusting equity, reported ROE might still be artificially high if future reinvestments are expected to come mainly from acquisitions.
- That's because ROE is a blended rate still influenced by the results of internally generated activities. And if acquisitions will be the primary reinvestment channel going forward, then ideally, ROE should exclusively reflect acquisition economics.

CHAPTER 11

IS PROPER REINVESTING TAKING PLACE?

PART 2 — EXAMINING HISTORICAL FINANCIAL PERFORMANCE

P recisely because return on equity is not perfect, it's important to analyze whether proper reinvesting has been taking place from another perspective. As I mentioned earlier, there's a second approach that involves analyzing a company's historical financial performance to study the impact of retaining profits over time.

Understanding Reinvestment Through a Simple Bond Example

Before we dive into real examples to explore this method, however, it's helpful to first take a look at how reinvesting actually works from a theoretical standpoint. And to keep things simple yet practical, let's use bonds as a starting point for the explanation.

More specifically, let's imagine a situation where we invest $100,000 in a bond with a 10% coupon rate, meaning it pays a $10,000 coupon every year. Let's not worry about when the bond is supposed to pay back the $100,000 principal, as that detail isn't necessary for this hypothetical exercise. What we want to focus on instead is what we do each time we receive that

$10,000 coupon, and for simplicity, let's look at a five-year period.

Let's assume that every time we receive a coupon, we reinvest it in another bond that also pays a 10% coupon rate. And every time this second bond pays us a coupon, we also reinvest it in yet another bond with the same 10% rate. In fact, let's just assume that any time we get paid a coupon—whether it's from the first bond, the second, or any thereafter—we reinvest it in successive bonds that continue to pay a 10% coupon rate. For more clarity, the table below shows what would happen in this hypothetical example.

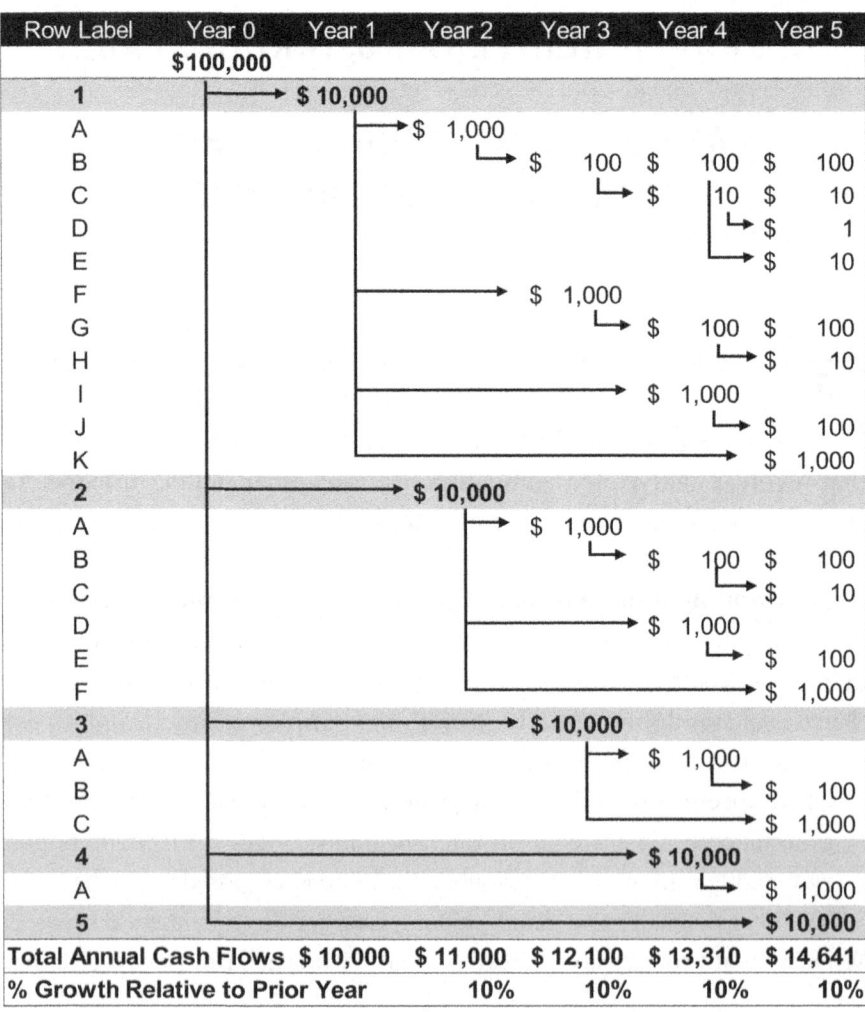

Breaking Down the Reinvestment Chain

As you can see, in year 0 we have the investment in the bond, representing a $100,000 cash investment. The lines I've highlighted in gray show the $10,000 coupons received over the next five years as a direct result of this first bond investment. Below each gray line, you can see the additional coupons that are generated—directly or indirectly—from reinvesting these payments.

For instance, in row 1A, we see the first $1,000 coupon received in year 2 as a result of reinvesting the initial $10,000 coupon from the first bond into a second bond. Rows 1F, 1I, and 1K show the remaining $1,000 coupons from this second bond.

Then, in row 1B, we see the $100 coupons received in years 3 through 5 that come from reinvesting the first $1,000 coupon of the second bond into a third bond. In row 1C, you'll find the $10 coupons generated by reinvesting the first coupon from the third bond into a fourth bond. And if you continue on with this thought process, you'll be able to account for every coupon laid out on the table.

Now, in addition to breaking down the reinvesting process, I've also included the total cash flows we would receive each year under this hypothetical setup. As you can see at the bottom of the table, in year 1 we only receive the initial $10,000 coupon from the first bond. In year 2, however, we receive the second $10,000 coupon from the first bond plus the first $1,000 coupon from the second bond. Then in year 3, we receive the third coupon from the first bond along with the proceeds from all the other bonds we had reinvested in up until year 2. Again, this process and structure continues all the way through year 5.

With these explanations, I trust you now see the structure and logic of the table clearly. If not, I strongly encourage you to take a moment to walk through it slowly until you do, because the importance of this table cannot be understated. The conclusions we can draw from it are simply too valuable, and you may not fully appreciate them unless you truly understand how the reinvestment chain works. That said, let's go ahead and discuss the insights or lessons we can extract from our hypothetical bond example.

Reinvestment Should Eventually Lead to Growth

The first major insight is that if cash flows from an asset are being reinvested successfully, future cash flows should grow over time. Of course, with companies, we can't expect growth in cash flows to unfold as neatly as it does in this bond example. Returns from new projects, geographic expansion, or even acquisitions often take longer to materialize than simply reinvesting in a bond. And even when results do show up, the cash flows these initiatives generate aren't going to rise at a constant rate. However, sooner or later, annual cash flows should begin to rise following a period of retaining and reinvesting them. If this isn't happening, even over long stretches of time, it's likely a sign that something is off.

The Implications of Flat Cash Flows

If cash flows are not growing, the most likely explanation is that the assets into which cash flows are being reinvested are not delivering any meaningful return. It would be the equivalent of taking each of the coupons in our bond example and reinvesting them into bonds that pay no coupons. In that scenario, it's easy to see that annual coupons would remain stuck at $10,000 each year, all of it coming from the original $100,000 bond investment.

That said, with bonds, you still expect to get your principal back. So even if the reinvested bonds paid 0%, you wouldn't be throwing money down the drain. But with companies, it's different. If a company reinvests $10,000 of earnings into a new project, that project doesn't come with a promise to return the capital. So, if the company is continually reinvesting cash flows and yet cash flows aren't rising, it may very well mean that money is being thrown down the toilet, representing negative returns.

There is a second possible explanation for a lack of growing cash flows despite reinvesting earnings. It may be that the initiatives into which cash flows are being reinvested are generating returns, but those results are being overshadowed or hidden by a decline in cash flows from the business that existed prior to the reinvestments. In other words, it could be that, had the reinvestments not been made, cash flows would have declined, but the decline is being offset or masked by the returns from the new investments. To make all of this a little less theoretical, let's examine a couple of hypothetical but realistic examples that reflect what I mean.

Example 1 – A Beer Company's Hidden Decline

Imagine a beer company that, at one point in time, only sells one beer. Now imagine this company decides to retain all its earnings to create a second beer with a completely different brand and a manufacturing process that is significantly different. As a result, in addition to the marketing investments and regulatory costs required for launch, this new beer also requires a brand-new manufacturing plant.

Now imagine that, five years into the investments in the new beer, the company's earnings are roughly the same as they were before it reinvested in this initiative. This scenario would suggest that either the new beer isn't generating any profits, or it is generating profits but the profits from the original beer have declined. In other words, the company is either reinvesting unsuccessfully, or it's a business with declining cash flows that needs to reinvest just to maintain its level of profitability.

Either way, if this pattern is expected to continue, this wouldn't be a company that is achieving a high reinvestment rate. Its reinvestments either don't deliver results, or the cash flows they produce do not last long enough to deliver the desired rate of return over a 30- to 40-year time horizon.

Example 2 – A Car Company's Masked Stagnation

As another example, imagine a car company that is only capable of producing gas-powered cars. Suppose further that the company believes that within the next 10 years, the market for this type of vehicle will disappear because people will be exclusively demanding electric vehicles.

In an attempt to survive this shift in demand, the company expects to retain most of its earnings to invest in R&D, new supply chains, different manufacturing processes, and several acquisitions that will be necessary for it to be able to produce competitive electric vehicles. Now imagine the management team tells investors that, thanks to this strategic shift, they expect to maintain their current profitability levels 10 years from now. In this scenario, many investors would likely find it reasonable and may even be relieved that the company is expected to survive and maintain profitability.

However, for those of us who are thinking about successfully reinvesting and compounding earnings, this is not a great scenario. As our table from the bond example implies, we would need a profitability level significantly higher than what it is today in order to claim, 10 years from now, that successful reinvesting has taken place.

A Common Pattern, Not an Exception

With these examples, you might think I've come up with far-fetched scenarios, but believe me when I say that these types of outcomes are extremely common. I'll go over two real examples shortly, but for now just know that they weren't hard to find. In fact, I would even say that more than half of companies out there are subject to this dynamic.

In other words, most companies are not reinvesting successfully because, for one reason or another, they're forced to retain a significant part of their earnings just to maintain their profitability or barely grow it. In all these cases, if they were to decide to pay all earnings out as dividends instead of reinvesting, they would lose the ability to compete and, sooner rather than later, their cash flows would begin to wither away.

Growing Cash Flows Don't Always Mean a Growth Business

Another very important lesson from our bond example is that a set of growing cash flows doesn't necessarily imply a company is a growth company. I've emphasized this point several times throughout the book, but it becomes especially clear when we look at this table. We can all see that the table shows a set of growing cash flows over time, with the first year yielding a $10,000 coupon and year 5 generating a total of $14,641 in cumulative coupons.

This growth, however, doesn't come directly from the original bond or any of the successive bond investments. The cash flows of each bond remain flat. The reason we see growth is because we're continually reinvesting the coupons. If, at any point, we decided to use the coupons for consumption instead of reinvesting them, the growth in our cash flow stream would stop immediately. Put differently, if our original bond were truly a "growth bond", we could spend the coupons however we liked, and the future coupons would still grow over time.

So, once again, you have to be careful when you're analyzing a company's cash flows. At least at a conceptual level, you have to try to separate cash flow growth that comes from reinvesting from cash flow growth that comes from the existing business. The value of a business will be significantly different if one requires reinvesting to grow versus another that doesn't.

Just think about it: it would be a mistake to base the value of our $100,000 bond on the total cash flows shown at the bottom of the table. You simply can't value a business based on expected cash flows that include the results of reinvesting. If you do, you'll be double-counting and risk wrongly concluding that the implied growth rate from a particular inverse analysis is achievable while also expecting a high reinvestment rate. As explained before, you have to base the valuation on the expected cash flows from the business as it stands, and then think about the results of any reinvesting separately.

The Math Link Between Reinvesting and Cash Flow Expansion

The last critical lesson from our bond example is a bit more technical. Put simply, if all cash flows are retained and reinvested, the rate at which total annual cash flows grow is equivalent to the annual returns the reinvestments are generating.

If you look at our table above, each year the total annual cash flows grow by 10%. Year 1 generated $10,000, year 2 increased by 10% to $11,000, and year 3 grew another 10% to $12,100, and so on.

In fact, instead of breaking down the reinvestment chain one by one, we could have just as easily compounded $10,000 for 4 years at 10% and arrived at the same result we see in year 5 on the table. The math here is fairly straightforward:

$10,000(1+10\%)^4 =$
$14,641 (year 5's total annual cash flows on our table)

To avoid confusion, the reason we're compounding for only 4 years—not 5—is because there are only 4 years between the end of year 1, when we receive the coupon and reinvest it, and year 5, the year we're evaluating.

With that clarified, this result shouldn't come as a surprise—after all, we assumed each reinvestment was made in bonds paying a 10% coupon. But even though it's a result we should mathematically expect, it's not intuitive for most investors. At the very least, it's something they don't pay attention to given how differently they've been taught to value businesses.

Now, as I said before, with companies we can't expect this compounding process to play out as neatly as it does with bonds. But understanding this mathematical reality can help us determine whether reinvestments are bearing fruit and give us some sense as to the extent of their results. Even if cash flow growth doesn't happen in a straight line, we can still examine multiple years at a time to see if, overall, the trajectory is upward, and at what rate.

For instance, if a company retains all its earnings and its cash flows are growing at roughly 10% on average, it's likely that reinvestments are resulting in a roughly 10% increase in annual earnings. Similarly, if cash flows are growing at 15%, 20%, or 25% on average, this might suggest that the annual returns from reinvestments are in that same ballpark; 15%, 20%, or 25%, respectively.

Be Cautious When Equating Growth Rate with Reinvestment Rate

As with return on equity, we can't automatically equate this rate of cash flow growth from reinvesting with the reinvestment rate used in our inverse valuation analysis. It's important to remember that the reinvestment rate in that context represents a return measured over the entire forward-looking investment period. While it's expressed in annual terms, it reflects the return on reinvested earnings over a 30- to 40-year time horizon.

Whether the cash flow growth from reinvesting really represents the reinvestment rate will depend on how long the increased profits last. If the increased cash flows from reinvestments are sustained for 30-plus years, then the growth rate we're seeing now will likely be close to the reinvestment rate. But if those increased cash flows only last for 10 to 20 years, the reinvestment rate won't get anywhere near that growth rate. So it's critical to always think about the sustainability of any positive reinvestment results.

Another important consideration is that, with companies, it's almost impossible to perfectly pinpoint the cause of cash flow growth. It's hard to separate growth that stems from reinvesting from growth that would have occurred regardless. Cash flows can increase due to sustained cost efficiencies, new customers gained through simple business momentum, or many other factors.

On top of that, most companies distribute at least part of their earnings, so they don't retain absolutely everything, and that naturally makes this hypothetical exercise less practical and harder to apply.

But despite all these considerations, examining the link between growth and reinvested results remains both extremely useful and necessary. It may not tell us exactly what the reinvestment rate has been, nor what it will be, but it will always show us whether reinvestments are bearing fruit. It's very simple: if earnings are being retained to at least some extent and cash flow growth isn't materially present over lengthy periods of time, then proper reinvesting isn't happening.

That said, I'd like to remind you that arriving at the most appropriate conclusion requires knowing the business well. Only by understanding the business model—along with its strategy, opportunities, and threats—can we put this analysis into proper context. And, as always, don't forget that past performance shouldn't be extrapolated into the future. A business that hasn't compounded effectively over the past 10 years might still have a chance of doing so going forward. Conversely, a company that has compounded well historically may not continue to do so in the future.

Disney Through the Lens of Reinvestment and Compounding

Now that we've gone through the theory behind reinvesting and compounding, let's turn to a few real-life companies to see how these concepts play out in practice. To start with, let's look at Disney, a company I'm sure all of you are familiar with. For reference, the table on the next page highlights the financial figures most relevant for this analysis over the past nine years. Note that Disney's fiscal year ends around September 30.

Relevant Financial Data for Walt Disney Co

USD ($) in Billions	2016	2017	2018	2019	2020	2021	2022	2023	2024	
Relevant Profitability Figures										
Net Income / Profits	10	9	13	11	(2)	3	4	3	6	
Adjustments										
Asset Impairments	-	-	-	-	5	-	0.2	3	4	
Stock-based comp	0.4	0.4	0.4	1	1	1	1	1	1	2016-24 Total
Non-operating, non-cash (gains)/losses on investments	-	(0.3)	(1)	(5)	(1)	(0.3)	1	(0.2)	-	
Adjusted Net Income	10	9	13	7	2	3	5	7	11	68
Relevant Cash Flow Figures										
Acquisitions	(1)	(0.4)	(2)	(10)	-	-	-	-	-	2016-24 Total
Dividends	(2)	(2)	(3)	(3)	(2)	-	-	-	(1)	
Stock Repurchases	(7)	(9)	(4)	-	-	-	-	-	(3)	
Total Shareholder Return	(10)	(12)	(6)	(3)	(2)	-	-	-	(4)	(37)
Relevant Balances										2016-24 Change
Cash Balance	5	4	4	5	18	16	12	14	6	
Total Debt Balance	20	25	21	47	59	54	48	46	46	
Net Debt (Debt - Cash)	15	21	17	42	41	38	37	32	40	25

Source: Author's analysis based on The Walt Disney Company 10-K and annual report. Totals may not match due to rounding.

As you can see, the table is divided into three sections. The first section shows the company's profitability over time, including a breakdown of the adjustments I considered necessary to more closely reflect the company's actual cash flows available for reinvesting. I'll explain the reasoning behind these adjustments in just a moment, but for now, just note that the "adjusted net income" line is conceptually analogous to the coupon payments from our bond discussion. Since this is the metric we're actually interested in, I've also included the total adjusted net income generated over the entire 9-year period.

The second section primarily shows how much money the company has returned to shareholders, breaking it down between dividends and share repurchases. I've also included the amounts paid for acquisitions to give us a sense of whether part of the reinvested cash flows were directed toward external investments rather than internal initiatives. But the most important metric here is the total shareholder return and so I've also included the total amount used for this purpose in the 9-year period.

Finally, the third section shows the company's cash and debt balances at the end of each financial period. Unlike the first two sections, these values come from the balance sheet rather than the cash flow statement.

That means they don't represent cash inflows or outflows generated or spent during a particular period; they're simply point-in-time balances. As I hope will soon become clear, what matters to us is how these balances change over time. So, the figure you see on the far right isn't the sum of the balances, but rather the difference between the ending balance of our examined period (2024) and the starting balance (2016).

In terms of the adjustments made in the first section, I've basically added or subtracted any material non-cash expenses or gains that didn't affect how much money was actually available for reinvesting during the 9-year period. To avoid any confusion, however, let me clarify a couple of points around some of these adjustments.

Avoiding Double Penalties for Failed Investments

As discussed in Chapter 5, asset impairments do represent a cash outflow, but one that occurred before the year in which the impairment is recognized. It essentially means that cash was used for an acquisition in the past, but because that investment didn't bear fruit, the cash spent should now be considered lost.

So, while the impairment is non-cash in the year it's recognized, it does reflect a real cash outflow in its nature. Given this reality, it could be argued that these impairments shouldn't be added back since they simply reflect a timing difference and, in the end, do reduce how much cash was available.

This interpretation, however, wouldn't be appropriate for the purpose of our analysis. Remember, we're trying to assess whether reinvestments have led to cash flow growth over time. If past investments weren't successful, that failure will already show up in the form of stagnant or declining cash flows. So, if we also keep the impairment expense, we'd be effectively penalizing the poor investment decision twice. Adding the impairment back essentially allows us to look at the real cash flow growth—or lack thereof—of any reinvestment decisions.

While a True Cost, Dilution Doesn't Affect Reinvestment Capacity

With respect to stock-based compensation, we also discussed in Chapter 5 that this is a real expense with a real cash impact to owners. However, the nature of this cost is different as it manifests itself through dilution and the reduced rights to future dividends that this dilution represents.

It doesn't reduce the cash available for reinvestment at any point, nor does it affect how much total cash is available for shareholder return. In other words, it may reduce the portion of dividends a shareholder receives, but it does not affect the size of the dividend pool itself. So, for the purposes of assessing successful compounding, it should be ignored.

Stagnant Profits Despite Years of Reinvestment

All this being said, let's go ahead and break down whether Disney has actually been reinvesting successfully or not. The first thing to note is that the company's cash profits—as measured by adjusted net income—haven't really grown over time. Given the impact of the COVID pandemic, we could reasonably ignore the company's performance from 2020 to 2021, or perhaps even extend that to 2022. But even setting those years aside, the profitability levels in 2023 and 2024 still remain similar to those seen from 2016 to 2019.

Now, if the company had distributed most or all of those earnings to shareholders, maintaining a similar profitability profile would be reasonable. In fact, for a mature company like Disney, it would even be expected. Just think back to our bond case study —if the coupons had been spent rather than reinvested, the coupon payments would have remained flat.

However, the issue here is that Disney retained a significant portion of its profits, and yet, profitability didn't increase. More specifically, over the 9-year period, the company generated almost $68 billion in adjusted profits while only returning about half of that—$37 billion to be exact—to investors. And it's not as if they're sitting on the undistributed portion of profits; the cash balance in 2024 is basically unchanged from 2016. This makes it clear that the company did, in fact, reinvest those earnings into the business.

Disney's Reinvestment Shortfall, Further Masked by Debt

To make matters worse, if you look at Disney's debt balances, they increased from $20 billion to $46 billion. In other words, the company raised $26 billion in debt over the analyzed period—and, once again, it's not as if that debt simply sat in cash. Cash only rose from $5 billion to $6 billion—a mere $1 billion increase. So it's clear that of the $26 billion in new debt, $25 billion was put to use in one way or another.

Now, because money is fungible, we can't precisely pinpoint what Disney's incremental debt directly funded. However, we do know that, had the company not issued this debt, it wouldn't have been able to make the shareholder distributions it did while still funding the investments it made. Without that incremental debt, Disney would have had to cut back on some of its cash uses along the way.

Think about it this way: the company had only $6 billion in cash at the end of 2024. So, if it hadn't issued the additional $26 billion in debt, it would hypothetically be sitting on a negative $20 billion cash balance—which, of course, isn't possible. Not only is a negative cash balance impossible, but in practice, a company always needs to maintain a minimum cash buffer for working capital. In Disney's case, that minimum is likely around $4–5 billion, given that its cash balance hasn't dropped below that range at any point in the past decade.

So, whether directly or indirectly, the issuance of the additional $25 billion in net debt enabled Disney to fund a significant portion of its shareholder distributions. In other words, had the company not issued this debt, its ability to return capital to shareholders would have been reduced by $25 billion. That means it would have only been able to return $12 billion—$37 billion minus the $25 billion funded through debt. This clearly shows that internally generated funds covered only a relatively small portion of Disney's shareholder returns.

Reinvesting Without Compounding: Disney's 9-Year Outcome

The reality, then, is that out of the roughly $68 billion in adjusted net income generated between 2016 and 2024, the company only used about $12 billion for shareholder returns. The remaining $56 billion—or roughly 80% of the total—was clearly retained and reinvested into the business. And the key point here is that, despite this massive level of reinvestment, the company's cash flows haven't grown over time. And remember, cash flow growth is exactly what we would have expected if those reinvestments had had any meaningful impact.

So, with Disney, successful reinvesting and compounding hasn't been happening over the past 9 years. The company is clearly in the position we discussed earlier with our hypothetical beer and car company examples.

Over this period, Disney's investments have either failed to bear fruit, or they have—but the version of Disney without them would have experienced declining cash flows. Either way, compounding is not taking place, which means Disney's reinvestment rate has clearly been low or possibly even negative.

A Useful Lens, But Not the Final Word

All this being said, because I don't know Disney's business well, I can't conclude that its reinvestment rate won't be high going forward. This analysis only tells us that, in the recent past, it has been very poor. But as I've emphasized many times before, we should never extrapolate the past into the future.

The value of this analysis is that it gives us perspective. It tells us that, if nothing changes relative to the recent past, Disney's reinvesting prospects are very low. And because of this, it's likely a good idea to avoid the stock, almost regardless of the price you pay. But if an investor has reasons to believe that the recent past is not representative of what's ahead, then Disney may still be worth considering as a potential investment.

Reinvestment Analysis vs. ROE: A Clearer Lens

Finally, I want to highlight one last key point. There's a major advantage to doing this type of analysis as opposed to relying solely on return on equity. Specifically, this approach is based exclusively on the company's most recent performance, whereas return on equity isn't.

It's true that we can look at return on equity for the most recent year or even examine the trend over the last 5 to 10 years. However, the equity balance used in the return on equity calculation captures the entire history of a company. It reflects the cumulative capital from inception.

Because of this, return on equity ends up being a blend of how efficiently a company deployed capital in its early years and how efficiently it's doing so today. This is why, as we discussed before, looking at ROE trends is so important. But even when looking at trends, return on equity can still hide a company's more recent compounding performance.

That's not the case with the analysis we just did. If a company hasn't been reinvesting successfully over the past 7 to 10 years, this approach will make it very clear. To put it in perspective, while Disney's return on equity has declined since 2016, it's still not a terrible number. I won't bore you with the exact calculations and my opinion of what adjustments are justified, but based on my analysis, Disney's current adjusted return on equity is around 10%.

That's certainly not at the level of Costco or Alphabet, but it doesn't seem terrible either. An investor looking only at that figure might reasonably conclude that Disney is still reinvesting capital adequately. But based on the deeper analysis we just walked through, we know that isn't the case. In fact, we can see that Disney's reinvestment rate in the most recent past is possibly even negative.

A Second Look: Verizon's Reinvestment Story in Brief

With Disney's example, I went into a lot of detail to make sure you got the full picture. But the downside to that is there's a risk you may have missed the big picture. So to provide a more summarized scenario, let's look at one more example by analyzing Verizon, another company I'm sure most of you are familiar with. The table below shows the relevant financial data we'll use to conduct our analysis. Since it follows the same structure and is subject to the same considerations as the Disney table, I won't explain much about it.

Relevant Financial Data for Verizon Communications Inc

USD ($) in Billions	2016	2017	2018	2019	2020	2021	2022	2023	2024	
Relevant Profitability Figures										
Net Income / Profits	14	31	16	20	18	23	22	12	18	
Adjustments										2016-
Asset Impairments	-	-	5	0.2	-	-	-	6	-	24
One-off non-cash tax gain	-	(14)	-	-	-	-	-	-	-	Total
Adjusted Net Income	14	16	21	20	18	23	22	18	18	169
Relevant Cash Flow Figures										
Acquisitions	(4)	(6)	(0.2)	-	(1)	(4)	-	-	-	2016-
Dividends	(9)	(9)	(10)	(10)	(10)	(10)	(11)	(11)	(11)	24
Stock Repurchases	-	-	-	-	-	-	-	-	-	Total
Total Shareholder Return	**(9)**	**(9)**	**(10)**	**(10)**	**(10)**	**(10)**	**(11)**	**(11)**	**(11)**	**(92)**
Relevant Balances										2016-
Cash Balance	3	2	3	3	22	3	3	2	4	24
Total Debt Balance	108	117	113	111	129	151	151	151	144	Change
Net Debt (Debt - Cash)	**105**	**115**	**110**	**109**	**107**	**148**	**148**	**149**	**140**	**35**

Source: Author's analysis based on Verizon Communications Inc. 10-K and annual report. Totals may not match due to rounding.

Verizon's History of Profit Retention

Breaking down the most important pieces, Verizon has generated around $169 billion in total adjusted net income over the past 9 years and has returned to shareholders an amount equal to roughly half of that—about $92 billion.

But, similar to Disney, Verizon clearly couldn't have made all those dividend distributions without increasing its debt balance by roughly $35 billion over the same period. So in reality, its internally generated profits funded only part of the $92 billion in shareholder returns.

More specifically, Verizon's earnings really only funded about $57 billion of shareholder returns—the result of subtracting the $35 billion in debt raised from the $92 billion in total shareholder distributions.

Viewed from another angle, this means that, out of the $169 billion in internally generated profits, only $57 billion were returned to shareholders, implying that around $112 billion was retained and reinvested. In other words, Verizon retained and reinvested about 65% of all its profits—or, more precisely, of all the cash available for reinvestment.

Verizon's Flat Cash Flows Reveal a Lack of Compounding

Now let's think about the results of this history of retention and reinvesting. As you can see on the table, while there are some fluctuations along the way, adjusted net income has largely remained flat over time. It may not look that way if we compare today's profits with those of 2016, but that's only because 2016 was an especially weak year. I couldn't show it due to space limitations, but the company's adjusted net income in 2013, 2014, and 2015 was around or above $20 billion, so still roughly in line with today's $18 billion.

So, despite a significant amount of reinvesting taking place, the company's cash flows are not growing. And yet, as we've stated multiple times already, cash flow growth is exactly what we would have expected if compounding and successful reinvesting were actually taking place.

It would have been a different story if cash flows had remained flat but the company had been able to pay all of them out to shareholders. In that case, it would simply mean that the company didn't have opportunities to reinvest but the generated cash flows would be available to shareholders for reinvesting on their end. But in this case, successful reinvesting is simply not happening, and there's nothing shareholders can do about it.

At the time of this writing, Verizon's cash flow yield is practically 10%. Some investors may consider that cheap, particularly given that the cash flow yield for the S&P 500 is closer to 3.5%. But when you factor in the poor reinvesting results of the past decade, this valuation doesn't seem cheap to me at all.

I'd much rather invest in a 6% coupon bond—where I know I can reinvest the coupons and have the expectation of receiving the principal back—than in Verizon, where the cash flow yield may be 10% but the reinvestment rate is likely very low or, like in Disney's case, maybe even negative.

Another Case Where ROE Tells the Wrong Story

Finally, once again I want to highlight the stark contrast between the conclusion from this analysis and the picture painted by return on equity. As before, I won't bore you with the detailed math, but by my estimates, Verizon's adjusted return on equity is around 15% to 18%.

At face value, this might suggest that Verizon has a strong ability to reinvest at high rates. But as we just discussed, based solely on the company's most recent past, this clearly isn't the case. And so, unless an investor has a reason to believe that the company's capital deployment efficiency is meaningfully changing, I would personally stay away from Verizon despite its relatively high return on equity.

A Third and Final Look: Alphabet's Successful Compounding

Moving on, let's compare these two examples of poor reinvesting results with one where compounding has taken place very effectively. And to keep things consistent with prior examples from the book, let's use Alphabet once more. The table on the next page shows Alphabet's relevant financial data. It follows the same structure, format, and considerations we used in earlier examples, so I won't go into detail explaining all of it again.

Relevant Financial Data for Alphabet Inc

USD ($) in Billions	2016	2017	2018	2019	2020	2021	2022	2023	2024	
Relevant Profitability Figures										
Net Income / Profits	19	13	31	34	40	76	60	74	100	
Adjustments										
Stock-based comp	7	8	9	11	13	15	19	22	23	2016-24
Non-operating, non-cash (gains) / losses on securities	-	-	(7)	(3)	(6)	(12)	6	1	(3)	Total
Adjusted Net Income	**26**	**20**	**33**	**42**	**47**	**79**	**85**	**97**	**120**	**551**
Relevant Cash Flow Figures										
Acquisitions	(1)	(0)	(1)	(3)	(1)	(3)	(7)	(0)	(3)	2016-24
Dividends	-	-	-	-	-	-	-	-	(7)	Total
Stock Repurchases	(4)	(5)	(9)	(18)	(31)	(50)	(59)	(62)	(62)	
Total Shareholder Return	**(4)**	**(5)**	**(9)**	**(18)**	**(31)**	**(50)**	**(59)**	**(62)**	**(70)**	**(308)**
Relevant Balances										
Cash & Equivalents	86	102	109	120	137	140	114	111	96	2016-24
Total Debt Balance	4	4	4	5	14	15	15	12	11	Change
Net Debt (Debt - Cash)	**(82)**	**(98)**	**(105)**	**(115)**	**(123)**	**(125)**	**(99)**	**(99)**	**(85)**	**(2)**

Source: Author's analysis based on Alphabet Inc. 10-K and annual report. Totals may not match due to rounding.

Shareholder Returns Fully Funded by Internally Generated Profits

The only thing I'll highlight about this table is that, unlike Disney and Verizon, Alphabet's net debt is shown as a negative value. But don't let this throw you off; this simply means the company has more cash than debt, and it doesn't change how we approach this part of the analysis.

What we're still interested in is whether that balance has changed over time. As with the previous examples, the goal is to determine whether Alphabet's shareholder returns have been indirectly funded by issuing more debt or, in this particular case, by drawing on cash that was already on the balance sheet before the period we're analyzing.

Luckily for us, in this case Alphabet's net debt—or, more accurately, its net cash—didn't really change over the 9-year period we're reviewing. So whatever happened with shareholder returns had to be independent of the company's debt activity or any cash that was already on hand.

To help clarify this, let me put it differently. If the company had relied on either debt or cash previously on hand, we would have seen a meaningful decline in the net cash balance. But since the change was minimal—just $2 billion—we can conclude that all shareholder returns during this period came exclusively from internally generated profits.

Alphabet's Reinvestments Deliver Powerful Results

Knowing we can ignore this part, let's now run through the rest of the numbers. Over the 9-year period, Alphabet generated roughly $551 billion in adjusted net income and used approximately 56% of those profits—around $308 billion—to return money to shareholders. This means the remaining 44% was retained and reinvested into the business.

With this in mind, let's now look at the results of this history of retention and reinvesting. With just a quick glance, it's obvious that the outcome is completely different from what we saw with Disney and Verizon.

During the 9 years reviewed—which really covers an 8-year time horizon—adjusted profits grew from $26 billion to $120 billion. That's nearly a fivefold increase and represents a 21% compounded annual growth rate. So clearly, compounding is taking place here, and the reinvestment results must be very strong.

Not All Growth Is Attributable, but the Pattern Is Clear

As I explained before, we can't necessarily attribute all of this cash flow growth to reinvestments. It's highly likely that Alphabet's cash flows would have grown to some extent even without them. But at the same time, it's also highly unlikely that this level of growth would have been possible without the investments made along the way. The more you understand the business and its history, the better you can judge what actually drove that growth. But even without deep knowledge of the business, there's a clear and consistent pattern of reinvestment success here.

Don't Forget, It's Never the Final Word

As always, this doesn't mean reinvestments will be successful in the future—that's where qualitative research comes in to help investors make that judgment. But the point is, if you believe this pattern is likely to continue, then it's reasonable to expect a very high reinvestment rate going forward. By contrast, even with excellent past performance, if you think this pattern won't continue or that future reinvestment opportunities will be smaller in scale, you should be cautious about expecting high reinvestment rates.

One Final Thought: Precision Is Overrated

At this point, some of you may be wondering why I've avoided trying to pin down a precise reinvestment rate—both for past performance and for expectations going forward. So, let me be explicit: I haven't done so because it would be a ridiculous endeavor. With so many moving parts involved, any attempt to be precise would be inaccurate at best and misleading at worst. It would be more of an intellectual exercise than a practical one.

In fact, I believe it's precisely this obsession with precision that has led finance—and valuation analysis in particular—down the wrong path. This is a perfect example of why it's better to be approximately right than precisely wrong.

The desire for exact answers is what led academics to embrace concepts like Beta, WACC, and other theoretical frameworks that, in the opinion of many investing greats like Warren Buffett and Charlie Munger, are essentially useless. And when you focus on tools that don't work, not only do you fail to reach your objectives, but you also lose sight of the tools that do.

So, to avoid falling into that trap, I haven't tried—and don't plan to try—to arrive at a precise reinvestment rate. Instead, I suggest you look at the broader picture and think about potential outcomes in terms of probability ranges.

With Verizon and Disney, for example, I might conclude that there's very little chance they'll achieve reinvestment rates above 5%. Based on their recent financial history, it seems more likely that their reinvestments are a necessity for avoiding declining cash flows rather than a luxury used to grow them.

Alphabet, by contrast, presents a very different scenario. In this case, I suspect that the likelihood of reinvested earnings yielding rates above 15% is quite high. I don't think the future rate will be as high as its recent performance might suggest, but I don't believe this conclusion is overly aggressive either. And this is the kind of ballpark assessment I aim for to help determine whether a deep dive is warranted—nothing more precise than that.

Conclusion: A Three-Step Framework for Evaluating Reinvestment

That said, to make this process easier for you, let me summarize what we've just covered in terms of how to analyze a company's historical financial performance. In simple terms, you really just have to focus on three things:

First, evaluate how much of the company's adjusted profits have been retained and reinvested over time. As you do this, keep in mind that if net debt has increased or if net cash has declined during the period being analyzed, it means that any shareholder returns weren't funded exclusively by internally generated profits. You'll need to subtract the portion that was funded by newly issued debt or cash that was already on the balance sheet.

Second, assess the impact of those reinvestments by examining whether cash flows have grown over time. If the company retained and reinvested a significant portion of earnings and cash flows didn't grow, something is off and the reinvestment rate might even be negative. On the other hand, if cash flows have grown meaningfully, that's likely a sign that the reinvestments are bearing fruit. How much fruit depends on three things: how much of the earnings were reinvested, the rate at which cash flows grew, and the extent to which you believe that growth was actually caused by the reinvestments rather than by momentum the business would have had anyway.

Third and finally, you need to study the business closely to determine whether the past performance might reflect the future or whether the future is likely to look different, and why. Once you've done this, you can arrive at ballpark conclusions like the ones I just gave. You won't get to a perfect number, but you'll have something far more useful: a grounded and thoughtful perspective.

CHAPTER 11 SUMMARY AND TAKEAWAYS (OPTIONAL READING)

- Because ROE has real limitations, this chapter introduces a complementary way to assess reinvestment effectiveness.
- This second approach is based on analyzing a company's historical financial performance and studying the impact of retaining profits over time.
- To better understand it, it's critical to first appreciate how reinvesting works in the much simpler context of bonds.
- Specifically, we looked at what happens when investing in a $100,000 bond that pays a 10% annual coupon. Even more importantly, we examined what happens to our stream of cumulative coupon payments if each time a coupon is received, it's reinvested in successive bonds that also pay a 10% coupon.
- I referred to the breakdown of this exercise as the "reinvestment chain," and studying its dynamics can lead to simple yet invaluable insights.
- The first major lesson is that cash flows should always grow over time when reinvesting is truly generating successful results.
- With businesses, this may not happen in a straight line, but sooner or later, cash flows should rise—or else compounding is clearly not taking place.
- If cash flows are not growing despite reinvestments, there are only two possible explanations: either the reinvestments are not bearing fruit, or they are—but their impact is being offset by declining profits from the pre-existing business.
- Regardless of the reason, the implication is that if the company decides to return all earnings to investors, its cash flows will likely wither away.
- Another major insight from the theoretical bond reinvestment chain is that investors can't assume a company is a "growth" company simply because its cash flows are growing.

- Our hypothetical exercise clearly shows that cash flows can grow from reinvesting and compounding, even if the underlying investments themselves have flat cash flows.
- The original bond in our reinvestment chain isn't really a "growth bond," because if its coupons were used for consumption rather than reinvesting, the stream of cash flows would no longer grow.
- So be careful not to assume a company is a "growth company" simply because its cash flows are increasing.
- More importantly, don't base your valuation on the cash flows that include the results of reinvesting. Instead, think about the cash flows as the business currently stands, and then evaluate the impact of reinvestment separately. Otherwise, you risk double-counting growth.
- The final critical lesson focuses on the relationship between cash flow growth and the reinvestment rate.
- For growth that stems exclusively from reinvestments, the growth rate of cash flows is equivalent to the annual returns those reinvestments are generating.
- With businesses, we can never reach a definitive conclusion since it's difficult to fully separate reinvestment-driven growth from growth that would have occurred independently.
- That said, understanding this mathematical relationship can help us gauge whether reinvestments are bearing fruit—and to what extent.
- Be careful, however, not to equate the cash flow growth rate with the reinvestment rate. For the two to be equal, not only would all growth need to be explained exclusively by reinvestments, but the resulting incremental cash flows would also need to be sustained for 30+ years.
- Furthermore, don't forget that many businesses don't retain 100% of their cash flows. In these cases, the relationship between cash flow growth and underlying reinvestment returns is even harder to apply.
- With these lessons in mind, we looked at two real-world examples—Disney and Verizon—where successful reinvesting wasn't taking

place, and another example—Alphabet—where compounding was clearly working its magic.

- Examining these examples was particularly insightful because, among other things, they showed that ROE doesn't always lead to the right conclusion.
- ROE is a blend of how efficiently a company deployed capital in its early years and how efficiently it's doing so today.
- As a result, it can mask the true picture of more recent business performance. This was the case with Disney and Verizon, both of which had decent ROEs but haven't reinvested successfully in the past decade.
- These examples also laid the groundwork for understanding how to put the theoretical lessons into practice. In this regard, the chapter highlighted three necessary steps for determining whether a company is effectively compounding.
- The first step is to determine the extent to which cash flows—or adjusted profits—have been retained. In doing so, any shareholder returns funded by newly issued debt or previously held cash should be excluded from the analysis.
- The second step is to examine the impact of those earnings retentions and their respective reinvestments. If cash flows don't grow, then successful reinvesting isn't occurring. But if they do grow, it's likely a sign that they are—though this still depends on the context of the business.
- Because we can't simply extrapolate past performance into the future, the third and final step is to study the business closely and assess whether its recent performance is likely to continue.
- As a final thought, I emphasized that it's practically impossible to determine the reinvestment rate with precision.
- And because I don't believe time should be spent chasing unnecessary precision—especially when it isn't useful—I don't attempt to calculate the exact reinvestment rate in any specific case. Instead, I suggest focusing on the broader picture and thinking in terms of probability ranges.

CHAPTER 12

IS PROPER REINVESTING TAKING PLACE?

PART 3 — SHARE REPURCHASES

So far in our discussions, we've been focusing on reinvestment results from capital deployed into internal initiatives or acquisitions. And without a doubt, these investments are almost always the most important driver of reinvestment outcomes over time. However, they're not the only options a company has for putting its earned money to work—nor are they the only ones that can have a material impact. Publicly traded companies can also choose to use their internally generated cash flow to buy back their own shares on the open market. This activity is also referred to as share or stock repurchases.

Shareholder Returns or Reinvestment? The Dual Nature of Buybacks
At first glance, this may not seem like a reinvestment, since share repurchases are often categorized as a form of shareholder return. And conceptually, they are—buying back shares does return capital to investors in some form. I even categorized them this way in the examples we just discussed. However, as I'll show in just a moment, they are, at their core, an investment decision. When a company buys back its own shares, it is effectively investing in itself.

Given this, we can't evaluate a company's reinvestment rate without also considering its stock repurchase decisions. If management and the board approach buybacks wisely, they can meaningfully enhance the reinvestment rate. Conversely, if done poorly, buybacks can significantly drag it down. In fact, even if a company's other reinvestments are highly successful, ineffective repurchase decisions can undermine the overall reinvestment return.

The Mechanics Behind Stock Repurchases

Keeping this in mind, let me explain in more detail what stock repurchases are and how they work. In essence, when a company buys its own stock on the open market, it's simply reducing the number of shares available to the public. As a result, the ownership percentage of shareholders who didn't sell increases.

As a quick example, imagine a company that currently has 100,000 shares outstanding. Suppose you own 9,000 of those shares, meaning you hold a 9% ownership stake. Anytime the company pays a dividend, you'd receive 9% of the total payout.

Now, imagine the company uses its cash to buy back 10,000 shares on the open market. This reduces the total number of outstanding shares from 100,000 to 90,000. Assuming you didn't sell any of your 9,000 shares, your ownership stake would automatically increase from 9% to 10%.

It's simple math: before, you owned 9,000 out of 100,000 shares—9%. Now, you own 9,000 out of 90,000—10%. As a result, going forward, you'd be entitled to 10% of any dividends paid, instead of the original 9%.

Buybacks vs. Dividends: Two Paths to the Same Outcome

What I'm hoping you understand—and something I believe most people don't fully realize—is what all this math actually implies. In practical terms, share repurchases have the same effect on investors as if the company had paid them a dividend, and they then used that dividend to buy more shares on the open market. In other words, from the investor's perspective, using dividends to purchase additional shares of the same company has the same economic outcome as the company simply repurchasing its own shares instead of paying a dividend.

Step One: Increasing Ownership Through a Dividend-Funded Buyout

To illustrate this, let's walk through a simple example involving a private business owned by five people, each holding 20,000 shares. In total, there are 100,000 shares, so each owner holds a 20% stake in the company.

Now imagine that one of them—John—no longer wants to be an owner and asks the others to buy him out. After some thought, he proposes that if he receives this year's profits—which totaled $1 million—he's willing to sell his shares to the other four on a proportionate basis.

His thinking is straightforward: the company is sitting on $1 million in cash from this year's profits, and they typically declare a dividend equal to those profits shortly after year-end. So his proposal is that the company declare the dividend, he collects his $200,000 (his 20% share), and the remaining four owners use their own $200,000 dividend to buy John's shares. So John would be receiving $200,000 from his share of the dividend plus $800,000 from the other owners—a total of $1 million.

If they move forward with this plan, each of the four would purchase one-fourth of John's shares—5,000 shares each. After the transaction, the total number of shares outstanding would remain at 100,000, but each remaining owner would now hold 25,000 shares: their original 20,000 plus 5,000 acquired from John. That gives each of them a 25% ownership stake.

They discuss it and all agree—it's a fair proposal, and frankly, they're surprised John is willing to sell at such a low price. From their perspective, it's an attractive deal.

Assuming profits remain at $1 million per year, their annual dividend would increase from $200,000 to $250,000. In other words, they'd be investing $200,000 today—essentially by forgoing this year's dividend—in exchange for an additional $50,000 annually going forward. Since none of them needed the cash right now, they were happy to reinvest in the business for a larger future payout.

Step Two: Achieving the Same Outcome Through a Share Repurchase

Having agreed, they reach out to a lawyer to help draft the necessary share transfer agreements. But after reviewing everything, the lawyer proposes a much simpler solution. Instead of paying the dividend and executing four separate purchase agreements, why not have the company itself buy John's shares?

The group is a little confused, so the lawyer explains: there are essentially two goals they're trying to achieve through a dividend-funded buyout:

1. For John to receive $1 million in exchange for his 20,000 shares; and
2. For each of the remaining shareholders to increase their ownership from 20% to 25%.

While it's true that several interim steps are involved, these two outcomes are ultimately what John's proposal is designed to achieve. And because a company repurchase would accomplish both objectives with far less paperwork, it's simply a better approach.

Here's how it would work: the company uses the $1 million in cash to repurchase John's 20,000 shares. That reduces total shares outstanding from 100,000 to 80,000. With the remaining four still holding 20,000 shares each, they now each own 25% of the business. John gets his $1 million, and the rest end up with a larger stake, just as they would have if they had each bought the shares individually. And just like in the dividend scenario, assuming profits stay at $1 million, each would now receive $250,000 in annual dividends going forward.

Comparing the Two Paths to the Same Outcome

For a clearer comparison of the alternative scenarios, please refer to the table on the next page.

DIVIDEND-FUNDED BUYOUT	SHARE REPURCHASE
John receives a total of $1 million—$200,000 from his 20% share of the dividend plus $800,000 from selling his 20,000 shares to the other owners.	John receives a total of $1 million directly from the company by repurchasing his shares.
Shares outstanding remain at 100,000.	Shares outstanding fall to 80,000.
By purchasing one-fourth of John's shares, each remaining owner increases their number of shares to 25,000.	Each owner retains ownership of only 20,000 shares.
Each remaining owner increases their ownership stake from 20% to 25%—since 25,000 shares divided by 100,000 total shares equals 25%.	Each remaining owner increases their ownership stake from 20% to 25%—since 20,000 shares divided by 80,000 total shares equals 25%.

What Buybacks Really Mean for Investors

With this example, hopefully you can understand and appreciate what repurchases actually do. They essentially force investors who retain their shares to reinvest profits into the business. And this is really important to understand and appreciate for the following reasons.

Repurchases Must Be Judged Like Any Investment

Share repurchases are subject to the same considerations as any other investment. Whether a repurchase is a good decision depends entirely on the same factors that determine whether any outside investor is making a smart decision by purchasing the company's stock.

Just like any investor deciding whether to buy shares, the company must evaluate whether the stock is fairly valued, undervalued, or overvalued before executing a repurchase. If the stock is overvalued for you as an investor, it will be overvalued for the company repurchasing the shares on your behalf. The opposite is true when the stock is undervalued.

Repurchases Are Directly Tied to the Reinvestment Rate

Stock repurchases are intricately linked with the reinvestment rate. Remember, the reinvestment rate is essentially the compounded rate of return of any reinvestments made. And we've established that repurchasing shares is basically the same as investing in them, so whatever return those shares produce will be the reinvestment rate for that portion of capital.

Internal Investments Usually Offer Higher Returns

With few exceptions—such as when a company's stock is extremely cheap—internally generated initiatives will typically lead to a higher reinvestment rate than share repurchases. Think about it: when a company buys back its own shares, it's paying market prices. And those prices usually reflect the market's expectations, which, even if not always accurate, often incorporate a company's positive attributes.

Because of this, strong businesses almost always trade at a significant premium to their accounting equity. In some cases, market valuations can exceed accounting equity by 10 times or more. And since accounting equity represents the total capital injected or retained in the business, paying a premium to that amount means the return from share repurchases will almost always be lower than the return from reinvesting directly into the business.

Given this reality, in a perfect world we'd want companies that can reinvest all their profits directly into internal initiatives. Of course, most publicly traded companies are past the stage where they can reinvest all of their earnings. But the key takeaway is this: even if you find a great company with a high return on equity, the reinvestment rate will likely fall far short of that ROE if most of the profits are being used to repurchase shares.

Moving On: Why Buyback Discipline Is Non-Negotiable

I can't emphasize how important all these considerations are. It's why I said that even if a company does well with internal initiatives and acquisitions, all of that can be offset by poor share repurchase decisions. If the management team is willing to buy back stock regardless of price, that's not going to be fruitful. You want management teams that understand everything we've been discussing and, as a result, only repurchase shares when they're undervalued or, at worst, when they're fairly valued.

If you see a company that's doing really well operationally but trades at a very expensive valuation and management is still aggressively repurchasing shares, stay away. There's no point in owning a great business if all the profits are being used for poor capital allocation decisions.

Other Considerations Matter, But Investment Logic Must Prevail

All this being said, I don't want to be overly simplistic. In many cases, there are tax advantages to doing share repurchases instead of paying out dividends. And I'm not suggesting that these considerations—or any others like them—should be ignored. A management team should always make decisions based on the full range of factors that affect shareholder value.

However, be very cautious when you hear management teams justify repurchases based on reasons that aren't grounded in sound investment logic. As we've seen, repurchasing shares is essentially an investment in the company itself. And in many cases, management teams don't fully understand this. They engage in buybacks for reasons that have little or nothing to do with the value of the stock.

A Closer Look at Why Many Buybacks Go Wrong

One could reasonably expect most management teams to understand the impact of repurchases and act accordingly. After all, nothing I've explained here is rocket science and how repurchases work is relatively well known. And yet, I can't tell you how common it is for management teams to engage in buybacks for all the wrong reasons.

I don't want to go too far off-topic, since this falls a bit outside the main focus of the book, but just to give you some perspective, let me go over a few of the most common examples.

Using Buybacks to Boost EPS

Aiming to boost earnings per share (EPS) is one of the most commonly cited reasons management teams give for engaging in share repurchases. As the name suggests, earnings per share simply measures how much of a company's earnings are attributable to each individual share. It's calculated by dividing total accounting earnings by the number of shares outstanding. And, since stock repurchases reduce the number of shares outstanding, EPS automatically increases when shares are bought back.

But buying back shares for this reason can easily lead to overpaying. That's because EPS will increase no matter what price the company pays for its shares. It's true that buying shares at a lower price increases EPS more, since the same amount of money buys more shares. But even at high prices, EPS still goes up. This makes it easy for management to be less careful with price and more focused on just making EPS look better.

Now, you might wonder why a company would focus on EPS in the first place. In some cases, it's because management compensation is tied to EPS, giving them a direct incentive to boost it. Other times, short-term investors may be pressuring management to increase EPS with the hope that it will lift the stock price. Whatever the reason, I can almost guarantee that the people making these decisions—or pushing for them—don't truly understand what we've just gone over.

Using Buybacks to Influence the Stock Price

Another misguided motivation for share repurchases is the attempt to influence the stock price—both directly and indirectly. As you can imagine, investors are not the only players in the market with a short-term focus on the stock price.

Many management teams also fall prey to the temptation of focusing on short-term stock prices. After all, they're human and the short-term pressure that Wall Street exerts on them can be very difficult to overcome. In fact, I believe it's rare to find a management team that is truly and exclusively focused on maximizing long-term value. Consequently, many companies tend to use stock repurchases in the hopes of keeping the stock price as high as possible.

The idea is that a stock's price reflects what buyers and sellers are willing to agree on. And, all else equal, the more buyers there are bidding at a given time, the higher the price tends to be. So when companies use their cash to purchase shares, they're adding to the pool of buyers pushing the stock price up.

Of course, a company repurchasing shares isn't the only player in the market. So, buying shares doesn't guarantee the price will rise. But the reality is that the stock price will likely be higher than it otherwise would have been if the company weren't in the market buying its own shares.

In addition to this, there's also a psychological aspect to share repurchases that can influence the stock price. It's not a perfect signal, but many market participants may see a company buying back its shares as a positive sign.

They might believe the company is doing it because management thinks the stock is undervalued, even if that's not actually the case. Others may simply take comfort in knowing the company is consistently in the market buying shares, which can help support the stock price. As a result, share repurchases can attract more buyers, and that extra demand can further push the stock price up.

So, not surprisingly, if management is focused on short-term price movements, buying back shares—regardless of price—can seem like a good idea. But for long-term holders, repurchases only make sense when the stock is fairly valued or, ideally, undervalued. If you see that management's decision to repurchase shares is driven by short-term thinking, you'd do best to stay away.

Moving On: Final Thoughts on the Role of Buybacks

To conclude, the key takeaway from this section is that share repurchases can be a significant contributor to what the reinvestment rate turns out to be. In fact, the reinvestment rate for any earnings used to repurchase shares will be equivalent to the returns those shares produce. As a result, repurchases can be very detrimental in the long run if they're made when the stock is more than fairly valued. Conversely, they can be very beneficial if management understands this reality and chooses to buy back stock only when it's undervalued.

That said, even when repurchases are done appropriately, they may not be the best use of capital if the company still has attractive internal opportunities. But if those internal opportunities are questionable, well-executed repurchases can help boost returns over time. So pay very close attention to how management thinks about share repurchases. If they don't have the right capital allocation mindset, it almost doesn't matter how good the business is.

CHAPTER 12 SUMMARY AND TAKEAWAYS (OPTIONAL READING)

- While reinvestment results from internal initiatives or acquisitions tend to be the most important drivers of reinvestment outcomes, they're not the only activities that can have a material impact on reinvestment rates.
- Publicly traded companies can also choose to use their earnings to purchase their own shares on the open market—an activity referred to as share or stock repurchases.
- At first glance, repurchases may not seem like a reinvestment since they're also a form of shareholder return.
- However, as the chapter later unfolds, buying back shares is essentially the equivalent of investing in the company itself.
- From a mechanical standpoint, buying back shares reduces the number of shares outstanding and, as a result, increases the ownership stake of the remaining shareholders.
- Technicalities aside, the important thing to understand is the practical implication of this activity.
- In short, repurchasing shares has the same economic outcome for investors as receiving dividends and then using those dividends to purchase more shares on the open market.
- To visualize this, we discussed an example involving a private business with five owners, one of whom—John—wanted to exit the business and proposed selling his shares to the others.
- In the example, we saw that John would be completely indifferent between 1) being bought out by the others through a dividend-financed transaction and 2) selling his shares to the company via a stock repurchase.
- In both cases, John would receive the same amount of money—which comes from the company's profits—and the remaining owners would increase their ownership stake by the same amount.

- The implication of this reality is that share repurchases should be evaluated in the same way as any other investment.
- In other words, whether a repurchase is a good decision depends entirely on the same factors that determine whether any outside investor is making a smart decision by purchasing the company's stock.
- Just like any outside investor, the company must evaluate whether the stock is fairly valued, undervalued, or overvalued before executing a repurchase.
- Repurchases are directly tied to the reinvestment rate—so much so that the reinvestment rate for the portion of earnings directed toward this activity will be equal to whatever returns those repurchased shares produce.
- Consequently, if shares are repurchased when they are fairly valued—or, even better, undervalued—repurchases can meaningfully enhance the reinvestment rate.
- Conversely, if repurchases are made when a company's stock is overvalued, the reinvestment results will be poor—even if the underlying business is fundamentally strong.
- This reality also means that, unless a company's shares are extremely cheap, internally generated initiatives will typically lead to a higher reinvestment rate than share repurchases.
- Great businesses almost always trade at a premium to their accounting equity. And because accounting equity represents the total capital put to work in the business, any premium paid on top of that will result in inferior reinvestment outcomes.
- Given the importance of having the right capital allocation mindset, one would think management teams fully understand and appreciate these principles.
- Sadly, however, many management teams engage in buybacks for all the wrong reasons.

- Two common misguided motivations are the attempt to boost EPS or to influence the stock price directly—by becoming another buyer supporting the stock—or indirectly—by signaling others to join the pool of buyers.
- In both cases, attention is diverted away from whether the stock is actually undervalued or, at the very least, fairly valued—and as we know, that should be at the core of the investment decision.

CHAPTER 13

CONCLUSION

SUMMARIZING WALL STREET'S MOST SIGNIFICANT BLIND SPOTS

As I promised in the introduction of the book, I'll soon reveal my favorite stock and the rationale behind it. Before I do, though, I want to take a brief moment to conclude this main portion of the book with a summary of the most important points. Specifically, I want to highlight the key insights we've discussed because these are the very blind spots I set out to uncover from the start. In other words, this chapter brings together the key ideas and takeaways covered in the book.

To start with, let's talk about the discount rate and its use in discounting future cash flows. The main blind spot here is that many people don't fully understand what it actually represents. Academics and investment professionals are so accustomed to deriving it through rigid, formulaic calculations that they've unfortunately lost sight of its meaning.

In short, the discount rate is simply a version of the return. So, rather than deriving it through a formula, you just need to determine your desired return and apply that rate to discount the expected future cash flows. You can approach it this way because the value produced by the discounted cash flows essentially tells you how much you would need to pay today in order to achieve that desired return.

Of course, you can't just pick a return out of thin air. You need to consider the risk that your expectations for future cash flows might be wrong, as well as your opportunity cost. The higher the risk, and the better the returns offered by alternative investments, the higher your desired return should be—and, therefore, the higher the discount rate.

Understanding these basic principles behind the discount rate will help you make better, more common-sense decisions. But even with a proper understanding of what the discount rate is, using it to discount future cash flows has one major flaw. And this brings us to the most important blind spot I've highlighted throughout the book.

When discounting cash flows, the discount rate is only equivalent to your actual return if—and only if—any interim cash flows are reinvested at a rate equal to the discount rate. Otherwise, even if your expectations of future cash flows turn out to be correct, your actual return could end up being significantly lower or higher. More specifically, if the reinvestment rate of each interim cash flow is lower than the discount rate, the actual return from paying the discounted value will be lower. Conversely, if the reinvestment rate is higher, the return you generate will be higher as well.

The importance of this cannot be overstated: it means that the discounted cash flow method is incomplete. If you try to value a business using it, you're essentially missing half the picture—and in fact, you're missing the most important half. How interim cash flows are put to work is the single biggest driver of long-term returns. This holds true even for high-growth businesses. And yet, it's a variable that traditional valuation methods completely ignore.

Given this reality, rather than discounting future cash flows, my suggestion is to always approach valuation efforts through inverse analysis. As I hope you'd agree by now, the inverse valuation method is far more intuitive and practical. Most importantly, though, it places proper focus on the reinvestment rate which has traditionally been overlooked.

Additionally, by conducting an inverse analysis and focusing on the reinvestment rate, we can uncover many other hidden insights. For example, we know that after a certain point in time, future cash flows have very little impact on overall returns. In the case of mature businesses with limited growth prospects, a life expectancy of roughly 25 to 35 years is typically enough to achieve our desired returns—assuming, of course, an adequate reinvestment rate for the cash flows produced during that period.

Beyond those initial decades, cash flows generated contribute less and less to returns, simply because the earlier cash flows have already undergone years of compounding. In other words, any cash flows expected 30 or more years down the line will have far less impact than the early cash flows that have been compounding for decades.

For high-growth businesses with high valuations—meaning low cash flow yields—we might need a life expectancy closer to 40 years. This is precisely because the initial cash flows are relatively small and need more time to compound meaningfully. In other words, those early, smaller cash flows take longer to grow enough to completely overshadow the return contribution of cash flows expected in 40+ years. This is, in fact, one of the key dangers of investing in low cash flow yielding companies. If the expected growth doesn't materialize, you'll never earn a good return.

With the inverse analysis, it also becomes much clearer what buying undervalued companies actually means. It's not about finding the ones with the highest cash flow yield or lowest price-to-earnings ratio. Instead, it's about identifying businesses whose valuation hurdles are lower than what you reasonably expect will happen. If the combination of required growth and reinvestment rate is undemanding, the company is likely undervalued. On the other hand, if those hurdles are extremely demanding, then even a great business can be overpriced.

Knowing this, you realize that a high-growth company with tremendous potential isn't necessarily a better investment than a mature company with little or no growth ahead. What ultimately matters is what you're paying relative to what the valuation demands. The best investment will always be the one with the most modest expectations baked into the price relative to its actual potential.

Another blind spot that's easier to spot with this valuation approach relates to what growth actually means and how compounding really works. A company is a growth company when it's expected to grow cash flows even without reinvesting over time. If cash flows are growing because the company is reinvesting, that's compounding—not growth from the business itself.

If growth comes from reinvesting, then those cash flows can't be paid out to shareholders. Calling this growth is like labeling a bond a "growth bond" just because reinvesting its coupons leads to higher cumulative payouts over time. Not only does this make little sense, but it can also lead to double-counting growth.

Furthermore, if investors don't learn to separate growth from existing operations and growth from reinvesting, they might miss another important blind spot. More specifically, they may overlook the fact that if profits are being retained and reinvested, then an increase in cash flows should be expected over time. As just mentioned, this wouldn't technically be growth from the business itself, but cash flows need to increase when reinvestment is happening. If they don't, it means reinvesting hasn't been successful and real compounding isn't taking place.

The inverse approach and its focus on the reinvestment rate also helps put into perspective the importance of good capital allocation decisions. Both companies and investors need to understand that, in a perfect world, the best use of capital is when the company can invest in internally generated initiatives with strong return on equity prospects. In the absence of these opportunities, companies may consider acquisitions, but they must be aware that acquisitions almost always come at a high price.

Acquisitions are typically made at a premium relative to the capital required to build the underlying operation. And that premium means the reinvestment results from acquisitions are likely to be lower than what the company has achieved historically. So, when thinking about the reinvestment rate, be cautious if you expect reinvestment returns to come primarily from acquisitions.

Finally, investors must never forget the importance of sound decisions around stock repurchases. This practice is essentially the company choosing to invest in itself. And just like it would be for any outside investor considering buying the stock, the success of this decision depends entirely on the purchase price.

Stock repurchases made at overvalued prices can completely offset the good underlying economics of a business. So make sure you understand how the management team thinks about repurchases. And don't forget, even if repurchases are executed properly, the reinvestment rate from this investment will almost certainly not be as high as that of good investments within the business.

That said, I truly hope I've been able to offer a unique and fresh perspective on valuations and, by extension, value investing. As I acknowledged at the start, I know time is increasingly scarce for most of us, so I genuinely hope you've found our time together worthwhile.

CHAPTER 14

CASE STUDY

MY FAVORITE STOCK FOR THE DECADES TO COME

Throughout the book I've worked hard to include plenty of examples to help clarify the theoretical concepts I laid out. And from my perspective, those examples should be more than enough to help you understand the valuation framework and key ideas we discussed. So, truth be told, I'm not sharing my favorite stock pick to deepen your understanding of the valuation framework.

The Broader Valuation Framework Is Not Enough

I'm sharing my favorite stock because I want to make one thing clear: even if you apply the principles from this book correctly, that alone isn't nearly enough to make sound investment decisions. Interpreting financial statements and using them to theoretically value a business is the easy part. In our case, arriving at a set of valuation hurdles based on a given stock price isn't all that difficult.

What's hard is doing the qualitative research that helps determine whether those hurdles can reasonably be overcome. That's why I want to walk you through my thought process for one company—to give you more perspective. For practical reasons, I won't cover every detail of my investment thesis, but I'll go over the most important points so you get a solid sense of what a fellow value investor focuses on.

For full disclosure, this case study reflects my independent analysis based on publicly available information, company disclosures, and in-depth research into the cross-border payments industry. And just to be clear, none of this is investment advice.

My Currently Favorite Stock: Wise

Based on its current valuation and the broader universe of investment alternatives, my favorite company at the time of this writing is Wise. Conveniently, its ticker symbol on the London Stock Exchange (LSE) is also WISE. The company is headquartered in the United Kingdom.

Wise at a Glance

So, what does Wise do? At a superficial level, it could be described as a kind of digital bank. Both individuals and businesses can use Wise to hold and transfer money, as well as spend through debit cards. As a digital platform, Wise doesn't operate any physical branches. Instead, customers manage all activity through an online portal or mobile app, and if they need support, they can access assistance through various phone or online customer service channels.

Now, even though Wise's service offerings overlap with those of digital banks, the company is not technically a bank. It doesn't hold any banking licenses and, as a result, it can't offer loans or traditional banking products like credit cards. In fact, customer funds are not actually held by Wise itself; they're custodied by partner banks. This underlying reality, though, is imperceptible to customers. They simply see their balances reflected in the app and likely assume that Wise is the deposit holder.

Wise's Mission: Money Without Borders

Wise is unique in that its core focus is making it seamless to transfer or spend money globally. In fact, the company's overarching mission is to offer money without borders.

With a Wise account, users can hold and transfer money in over 50 currencies. For about 10 of those currencies, customers can even receive local bank details, enabling them to get paid as if they had a domestic account. For instance, a European customer can have a U.S. bank account through Wise, making it easy for someone in the U.S. to send him dollars as if he banked locally.

Due to regulatory limitations, not all features are available to everyone. In some countries, only individuals can open accounts, not businesses. In others, customers might not be able to obtain local bank details or may be restricted to sending money cross-border by linking a local bank account.

Still, Wise is active in 160 countries in some form, and with few exceptions, most developed markets and major emerging economies have access to nearly the full suite of services.

From Real-World Utility to Global Reach

To give you some perspective, here are a few examples of who Wise is ideally suited for. The platform is especially helpful for parents sending their kids to study abroad and needing to cover tuition or living expenses in a different currency. It's also a great solution for companies that hire freelancers in other countries and need to pay them in their local currencies. The reverse is true as well. If you're a freelancer based in an emerging economy and your clients can only pay you in dollars, you can receive the payment in your Wise USD account and then convert it into your local currency for spending—all within the platform.

The use cases are nearly endless, as Wise is useful to anyone who needs to hold, transfer, or spend money across multiple currencies. Not surprisingly, as of this writing, Wise serves nearly 16 million customers and facilitates close to $190 billion in cross-border transactions each year. It also holds around $25 billion in customer funds.

To give you a sense of how globally diversified the business is, roughly 30% of its revenue comes from Europe, 20% from the UK, another 20% from North America, 20% from Asia-Pacific, and the remaining 10% from the rest of the world.

Wise's Infrastructure at a Glance

Wise can move all this money across the world thanks to the proprietary infrastructure it has built over the past 14 years since its founding. The company has secured more than 70 licenses in dozens of countries and has integrated with over 90 banks worldwide. In eight countries—or regions, in the case of the European Union—it has even been granted direct access to central bank payment and settlement systems.

Now, how this infrastructure works is even more important than its scale and complexity. What this integrated network essentially enables is for Wise to minimize the amount of money that actually crosses borders when transfers are made. And this is a massive advantage because it allows Wise to process transfers more quickly and at a significantly lower cost.

Understanding SWIFT and the Correspondent Banking Model

Let me explain what I actually mean when I say that Wise can minimize money from actually crossing borders. To do so, though, it helps to first understand how the conventional international banking system works.

Typically, when a customer in one country wants to send money in one currency to someone in another country using a different currency, the money moves across borders. This transfer happens through a chain of international and local banks that are connected to one another indirectly.

Imagine a Japanese Company X that wants to use its yen to pay a US Company Y in dollars. In all likelihood, Company X's Japanese bank isn't directly connected to Company Y's US bank, so a direct transfer wouldn't be possible. However, through the SWIFT network (Society for Worldwide Interbank Financial Telecommunications), the Japanese bank can connect indirectly.

In simple terms, here's how it works: the Japanese bank holds an account with an intermediary bank that is connected to the US banking system. When Company X tells its bank to make the transfer, the Japanese bank sends that instruction to the intermediary bank via SWIFT. The intermediary then uses the funds it holds on behalf of the Japanese bank to send money to Company Y's US bank account. These intermediary banks are usually large institutions and are commonly known as correspondent banks.

The following bullet points provide a clearer breakdown of the example.

- Japanese Company X wants to send USD to US Company Y.
- Company X's Japanese bank is not directly connected to the U.S. banking system, so it can't execute the transfer on its own.

- However, the Japanese bank holds funds at a U.S. bank, known as its correspondent bank.
- The Japanese bank instructs its correspondent bank via SWIFT to send USD to Company Y.
- The correspondent bank sends the funds, reduces the balance held on behalf of the Japanese bank, and in turn, the Japanese bank reduces Company X's account balance.
- The end result: Company Y receives the funds, and Company X's balance is reduced—the transfer is complete.

What If Transfer Requests Spanned the Entire Globe?

I just used the example of a Japanese bank wanting to transfer customer funds to a US bank. In reality, though, the Japanese bank may have customers who want to transfer money to Europe, the UK, and other regions as well. To facilitate these transfers, the Japanese bank would need to establish additional correspondent relationships. That means it would need to hold accounts with European correspondent banks for euro transfers, UK correspondent banks for transfers in pounds, and so on.

Now, aside from the most prominent countries, the Japanese bank is unlikely to have direct correspondent relationships with banks all over the world—it would simply be too costly and complex. However, there is an alternative that allows the bank to reach nearly all countries without needing a direct relationship for each. The Japanese bank can instead hold accounts with correspondent banks that, in turn, have their own accounts with other correspondent banks in different countries.

Understanding Transfers Involving Multiple Correspondent Banks

As an example, imagine Company X wanted to transfer money from Japan to Guatemala to pay a vendor. The Japanese bank likely wouldn't have a direct correspondent relationship with a Guatemalan bank. However, its correspondent bank in the US might have such a relationship. In this case, the Japanese bank could instruct its US correspondent, which would then instruct its Guatemalan correspondent to pay Company X's vendor.

The Guatemalan bank would complete the payment and reduce the balance the US bank holds with it. In turn, the US bank would reduce the balance the Japanese bank holds with it. Finally, the Japanese bank would deduct the amount from Customer X's account. In the end, Customer X's balance at the Japanese bank has decreased, while the vendor's balance at its Guatemalan bank has increased by the same amount—exactly the intended outcome.

The bullet points below provide a clearer breakdown of the example.

- Japanese Company X wants to send money to a Guatemalan vendor.
- Company X's Japanese bank is not directly connected to the Guatemalan banking system, nor does it have a correspondent banking relationship with a Guatemalan bank.
- However, its U.S. correspondent bank does have a correspondent relationship with a Guatemalan bank.
- So, the Japanese bank instructs its U.S. correspondent bank, which in turn instructs its Guatemalan correspondent bank to make the transfer.
- All transfer instructions are sent through the SWIFT messaging ecosystem.
- Upon receiving the transfer request, the Guatemalan bank sends the funds to the Guatemalan vendor's account.
- In doing so, the Guatemalan bank reduces the balance held by the U.S. bank, which then reduces the balance of the Japanese bank—and finally, the Japanese bank reduces Company X's balance.
- The end result: the vendor is paid, and Company X's balance is reduced—the transfer is complete.

The Final Stage: Currency Conversion

Regardless of whether there's one or multiple intermediaries involved, at some point one of the banks in the chain has to convert the sender's currency into the recipient's. In most cases, this currency conversion is handled by one of the intermediary banks, as they are typically large institutions with the necessary foreign exchange capabilities.

This process either involves buying currencies in the foreign exchange market or maintaining reserves in multiple currencies to manage incoming and outgoing flows. Either way, it adds costs for the converting bank, which then passes those costs along as fees in the international transfer.

Wrapping Up: Layers of Complexity and Their Implications

As you can imagine, given the number of operations and intermediaries involved in conventional international transfers, the underlying mechanics can become quite complicated. More importantly for our purposes, balances are transferred across borders, moving from bank to bank through a network of institutions holding funds with one another. Not surprisingly, this leads to costs for each bank in the chain, which ultimately results in higher fees for both the sender and the recipient.

Back to Wise: A Different Infrastructure Entirely

This is where Wise comes in and disrupts the international money transfer market with a completely new and independent infrastructure. And it works almost in the opposite way as the correspondent banking infrastructure, which communicates through the SWIFT network.

Rather than having banks around the world connect to a centralized network, Wise is going to each country and joining each local payment system to create its own network of payment rails. And the important thing to reiterate here is that, with Wise, money doesn't need to cross borders—at least not for most transactions in its network.

The Mechanics of Wise's Infrastructure

How does Wise actually do this? Well, it's precisely because the company has a presence in most countries that it can match or net transfer requests at the local level.

Let's use the UK and the US as an example. At any given time, Wise has customers in both directions: UK senders who want to send dollars to the U.S. and U.S. senders who want to send pounds to the UK. We'll call these Route 1 and Route 2, respectively.

Since there are requests flowing in both directions, Wise can use the pounds from UK senders in Route 1 to pay the UK recipients in Route 2—meaning the money never leaves the UK. At the same time, it can use the dollars from US senders in Route 2 to pay the US recipients in Route 1—again, without the money ever crossing borders. This is all made possible through Wise's direct integration with each country's local payment systems.

The bullet points below provide a clearer breakdown of the example.

- Route 1 — Wise has UK customers with pounds (GBP) who want to send dollars (USD) to recipients in the U.S.
- Route 2 — Wise has U.S. customers with dollars (USD) who want to send pounds (GBP) to recipients in the UK.
- When UK customers from Route 1 request transfers, Wise doesn't purchase USD to send to the U.S. recipients.
- Similarly, when U.S. customers from Route 2 request transfers, Wise doesn't purchase GBP to send to the UK recipients.
- Instead, Wise matches—or nets—transfer requests from Route 1 with those from Route 2.
- On one side, Wise takes GBP from Route 1 and sends them locally to the UK recipients in Route 2. In other words, Wise uses GBP from its UK customers to fulfill transfers to UK recipients requested by U.S. customers.
- On the other side, Wise takes USD from Route 2 and sends them locally to the U.S. recipients in Route 1. In other words, Wise uses USD from its U.S. customers to fulfill transfers to U.S. recipients requested by UK customers.
- In short, customers from Route 1 send to recipients from Route 2, and customers from Route 2 send to recipients from Route 1.

Wise's Treasury: Solving for Flow Imbalances

In truth, transfer requests from Wise customers will never perfectly offset each other. In other words, there may be more requests in Route 1 than in Route 2. To cover these gaps, Wise relies on its unique treasury management capabilities. It maintains liquidity reserves in dozens of currencies, and these reserves are held in local liquidity pools specifically to avoid money from crossing borders.

This treasury management infrastructure is extremely powerful because it was built to be global from the start. As such, the company can monitor global payment flows and manage its liquidity needs in real time, 24/7, ensuring it can always meet customer demands. Not surprisingly, Wise uses big data analytics to forecast demand accurately, and it does so effectively thanks to the sheer volume of transactions it handles. These forecasting capabilities help limit local liquidity shortages across countries and regions.

Cutting Out the Middlemen: Wise's Cost Advantage

Wise's infrastructure offers a tremendous number of advantages over the SWIFT network built on correspondent banking. To start with, it eliminates the need for intermediaries or correspondent banks.

It's true that Wise does partner with banks at the local level—but not to help intermediate international transfers. From the local bank's perspective, Wise simply uses them to hold deposits and initiate local transfers. In many ways, Wise is just another customer to them.

The key point is that removing intermediaries reduces the number of players charging fees in an international transaction. In the correspondent banking model, each bank isn't charging fees just because—they have to, because maintaining their infrastructure is expensive. At the very least, they need to charge enough to cover those costs. So by cutting out intermediaries, Wise's infrastructure dramatically reduces costs—and it can pass those savings on to customers.

There's another cost-related advantage, and it also stems from cutting out another middleman. Thanks to the netting or matching mechanism in Wise's infrastructure, the need for actual foreign exchange—FX—purchases is significantly reduced. Wise only needs to buy FX to cover volume gaps between payment flows in each route, or more accurately, each payment rail. Using our earlier example, this happens when Route 1 requests are larger than Route 2 requests.

Minimizing FX purchases reduces costs because buying foreign currency in the market always comes at a price—even if it can be done very cheaply at scale, as is the case with Wise. Because every FX transaction involves at least one external party, it inevitably comes with fees—no matter how efficient the execution.

As a result of both these cost advantages, Wise can offer international transfers at a cost substantially lower than traditional banks. Exactly how much lower depends on the specific route and its characteristics, but Wise estimates it can be up to 9 times cheaper than a traditional bank.

Wise's Speed

Another very important advantage is that Wise can offer international transfers that are just as fast as local transfers. This is partly because there are no intermediaries involved, which reduces the number of checks and steps required. But more importantly, it's because the money isn't actually crossing borders. Think about it—if the money stays within the country or region, why should it take longer than a local transfer? In fact, 65% of Wise transfers are completed instantly, and 95% are completed within 24 hours. That's an incredible achievement.

Breaking Down Wise's Business Model

Now that you understand what powers Wise, let's talk about its business model—or more concretely, how it makes money. There are essentially three main revenue sources.

The first is that Wise charges a fee for every cross-border transaction it processes. This fee is significantly lower than what banks charge and, for most currencies, it's also the most competitive among fintech peers.

Wise applies a percentage fee on each transaction, which varies by currency pair, but currently averages around 0.53%. Importantly, Wise doesn't charge any exchange rate mark-ups or hidden spreads. It prides itself on being extremely transparent. The sender knows upfront exactly how much the transfer will cost, with no hidden fees at any point.

The second revenue stream comes from fees charged when customers use their Wise debit card. There are two types of fees involved here. The first applies when customers spend money in a currency they don't hold in their Wise account. For example, a customer might have US dollars in their account but use their card at a restaurant in the UK that charges in pounds. In this case, Wise charges the same fee as it does for cross-border transfers. This fee is significantly lower than the foreign exchange fees charged by most other debit card providers. It can be lower precisely because of Wise's infrastructure, which allows it to use its local liquidity pools to pay merchants directly in their local currency, avoiding traditional FX costs.

The second type of debit card fee is the standard interchange fee paid by merchants when a customer uses a debit card. This fee varies by country and type of transaction, but Wise doesn't disclose its specific rate. However, based on industry norms it's likely close to the typical 0.3% of the transaction value.

The third and final revenue source is the interest income Wise earns on customer funds. As mentioned earlier, Wise is not a bank, so it can't lend out its customers' money. However, it is generally allowed to invest those funds in very safe, short-term instruments such as government treasury bonds.

Even though Wise is entitled to retain all of this interest income, it chooses to share a significant portion with its customers. Its strategy is to keep the entire first 1% of interest yield, and then retain just 20% of any yield above that. The remaining 80% is passed along to the customer.

Now, there are two things worth pointing out about this interest income. First, because interest rates can fluctuate significantly, this revenue source can be quite volatile. Recently, rising interest rates have helped drive this income to record levels. But if we return to the near-zero interest rate environment that lasted for about a decade, this source of income could quickly dry up.

Second, due to regulatory limitations, Wise is currently unable to share the full 80% it intends to pass along to customers. As these regulatory hurdles are resolved, a portion of the interest income Wise currently retains will decrease.

The company is very self-aware of both of these realities. As a result, it prefers to measure its progress by excluding any interest income above the first 1% yield on assets. The goal is to evaluate profits based on what is more likely to be recurring. Technically, rates could fall below 1%, so even that first percentage point isn't guaranteed.

Still, it's reasonable to assume that, in most economic environments, short-term interest rates will stay above this level. I don't want to get ahead of myself, but to be conservative, I also try to evaluate the company's cash flow yield excluding any interest income above this 1% threshold.

Wise's Three Business Segments

In terms of business segments, Wise has three. The first is Wise for individuals, offering its suite of services to people from all walks of life. The second is Wise for business, which provides a very similar offering but tailored specifically for small and medium-sized businesses.

These two segments could almost be viewed as one, given how similar they are. The business version includes additional features—like support for multiple user profiles under one account—to accommodate business needs, but at their core, both operate in much the same way.

The third business segment, however, is quite unique—and I'd even go so far as to call it the elephant in the room. I haven't mentioned it until now because it's harder to fully appreciate without the background I've already provided. This segment is called Wise Platform, and it's focused on enabling other banks and fintechs to use Wise's infrastructure to power their international payment needs.

Wise Platform's Reach

To give you some perspective on Wise Platform, more than 100 financial institutions are currently leveraging it in some way for their international payment needs. For example, Morgan Stanley recently announced a partnership with Wise to enhance its international transfer capabilities for corporate clients.

Another major global bank, Standard Chartered, also joined Wise Platform to enable its cross-border payment service, SC Remit, to send money in 21 currencies using Wise's infrastructure. Other notable banks using Wise include Bank Mandiri—Indonesia's largest bank—and Shinhan Bank—one of South Korea's oldest and largest national banks.

From the fintech side, Nubank—one of South America's largest digital banks—is now using Wise's infrastructure to offer international banking services to its premium customers. In this case, Nubank has gone beyond transfers and relies on Wise to provide multi-currency accounts and debit cards, allowing customers to spend, convert, and manage money internationally with the same ease as Wise's own users. Other notable fintechs tapping into Wise's global payment infrastructure include Monzo, N26, and Mox, just to name a few.

As you can imagine, the technicalities around how these institutions connect to Wise's infrastructure are complex. But in practical terms, connecting to Wise Platform means these financial institutions can offer international money services directly through their own apps or platforms. Even though the institutions' customers may not realize it, much of the backend is handled entirely by Wise.

An Example of Wise Platform in Action – Nubank

To give you a rough idea of how this works, let's walk through a simple example. Just as a quick disclosure, however, this example is something I've put together myself based on my understanding of everything I've read about Wise Platform and its infrastructure.

While I've verified with publicly disclosed information many of the details, some aspects of the example involve me connecting dots from various sources. While I'm personally confident it's accurate in all material respects, I haven't received any kind of validation from Wise or any industry expert.

That said, imagine a Nubank customer—Customer A—wants to send money from Brazil to a friend in the US. He logs into his Nubank app, chooses to send Brazilian reals (BRL), enters the recipient's details, and confirms the transfer. Behind the scenes, because Nubank is connected to Wise, the app immediately notifies Wise to send the equivalent amount in US dollars to the recipient.

Thanks to its dollar liquidity pool in the US, Wise can instantly send the USD from its local reserves—so the money never actually crosses borders. The recipient receives the funds just as fast as they would with a domestic transfer.

Then, within a few days, Nubank settles the transaction by transferring the BRL to Wise. In fact, given that Wise is now directly connected to the Brazilian payment system, settlement in Nubank's case likely happens even faster.

Either way, the transfer happens at the real mid-market exchange rate at the time the customer initiates it, since Wise doesn't apply any mark-up or spread. But Wise does charge Nubank a fee. And Nubank can decide whether to charge its customer a fee on top of that as well. In most cases, the partner does charge a fee and applies a mark-up relative to Wise's original fee.

Platform vs. App: Maintaining Pricing Discipline

Importantly, Wise's fee is based on the same rate it charges customers who use its own app. This is done to maintain internal discipline. If Wise charged a different rate, it would no longer be indifferent about where transaction volume is coming from.

Additionally, charging more to platform customers could dissuade them from using Wise's infrastructure, while charging less could make Wise's own app less competitive. And Wise wants to avoid either of these outcomes because, as we'll discuss further shortly, Wise's app services and Wise Platform complement each other extremely well.

Platform Partners: Millions of Indirect Users

All this being said, Wise Platform opens up a world of opportunities and possibilities for Wise. While it takes time and money to integrate financial institutions into Wise's infrastructure, each platform partner often brings with it millions of underlying customers.

Earlier, I mentioned that Wise has around 16 million customers—and that's true, but it only includes direct users. Nobody can say for sure how many customers Wise has when including those who use its services indirectly through a platform partner. But I'd be shocked if it's not substantially more than 16 million.

And the other beauty of this is that Wise doesn't need to service those indirect customers. It's able to monetize them without bearing the cost of customer service. That can result in significant cost savings and provide meaningful economies of scale.

Let's Not Forget: The Moat is Critical

As we'll see in more detail shortly, Wise is growing both revenue and profitability at a very rapid pace. But as I've emphasized many times throughout the book, it's never wise to assume that past performance guarantees future results.

As I explained when discussing what I called the "Zoom path", success attracts capital and competition. And unless there are barriers that limit others' ability to compete effectively, a company's growth and profitability will eventually come to a halt. These barriers can take many shapes and forms, but at the end of the day, they are simply strong and sustainable competitive advantages. Value investors often refer to them as moats.

As we'll also see shortly, Wise's current valuation isn't overly demanding when it comes to the hurdles that need to be met for it to be justified. Still, it does require growth to continue for quite some time. Additionally, it's just as important that once growth slows and the company reaches maturity, it can sustain those mature cash flows for decades to come.

Because of these reasons, it's incredibly important that we try to understand what will allow Wise to achieve these hurdles, even as its success continues to attract significant competition. In other words, we need to identify the competitive advantages that will prevent competitors from slowing Wise's momentum over the coming decades. Without those barriers in place, the hurdles implied by its current valuation may not be met—even if they don't appear overwhelmingly demanding at first glance.

Avoiding Temptation: Let's Focus on the Real Threat

Before I lay out what I believe those moats are, let me emphasize one important point. I try to avoid the temptation of comparing Wise's cross-border capabilities with those of traditional banks.

Many analyses out there attempt to justify Wise's investment case by doing exactly that. But I personally think this is a mistake, because it's unlikely that existing banks pose a real threat to Wise. Anyone with even a basic understanding of the subject can see that banks simply aren't built to compete with a company like Wise.

The real threat to Wise comes from other fintech players—both existing and future—that will, in one way or another, try to mimic or improve upon what Wise has done. That's why the competitive advantages I'll highlight focus on why I believe no one, not just banks, will be able to dethrone Wise.

All that said, the following represent Wise's competitive advantages or barriers against competitors. Just note that, because some of the moats are somewhat lengthy, I've bolded the first sentence of certain opening paragraphs to signal a shift in topic and highlight key points.

A Sustained Cost Advantage with a Complementary Pricing Strategy

While transfer speed, convenience, and transparency matter in cross-border payments, what Wise customers value most is how cheap cross-currency transfers are. So, even though Wise is the fastest and arguably the most transparent and convenient player out there, what matters most to me is whether they'll be able to retain their low-cost provider status.

In short, I'm confident they will maintain this low-cost status over time—not just because Wise continues to make its infrastructure increasingly cost

efficient, but because it proactively lowers its fees as these infrastructure costs come down.

Earlier I mentioned that Wise's average fee for cross-border transfers is 0.53%. What I didn't mention is that just two years ago, this same fee averaged 0.67%, and five years ago it was around 0.75%. This ongoing price reduction is a deliberate strategy by the company. In fact, management describes it as a cost-plus strategy: they apply a relatively consistent mark-up to their per-transfer cost. So, as their costs go down, the fee they charge customers also goes down.

It doesn't happen in a straight line, as they only reduce fees when they're confident any cost savings achieved are sustainable—avoiding the need to raise prices later. But over time, the company has been remarkably consistent in applying this strategy. In the short term, it may seem like the wrong decision since Wise could likely retain its customers for a while even with the higher fees. And by keeping fees higher, the company's short-term profitability would be much stronger.

But I love this strategy because it makes it extremely difficult for competitors to outcompete Wise. And it's for this reason that the company—rightfully so, in my opinion—refers to these fee reductions as an investment. It's sacrificing short-term profits, essentially deploying capital like any other investment, in exchange for more customers, higher volume and ultimately higher profits in the future. And this is exactly what has happened in the past. Despite the above-mentioned fee reductions, the company's profitability has continued to rise dramatically over time.

Now, the most important point I want to highlight is that precisely because management's strategy is to reduce fees as costs come down, Wise will remain the cheapest provider as long as it maintains the lowest cost structure. So the key question for us becomes whether Wise can continue to keep its costs lower than anyone else.

I believe Wise will be the lowest-cost player for many reasons, but without a doubt, the most important is that it's extremely difficult to achieve two-way flows without relying on intermediaries. Recall from my explanation of Wise's infrastructure that the company can net or match flows across different routes, allowing money to stay within borders. But in order to achieve this kind of netting, there must be consistent flows in both directions.

In our UK-US example, Wise had UK customers looking to send dollars from pounds, and US customers looking to send pounds from dollars. If Wise only had customers from one of those countries, it wouldn't have been able to match flows between the two routes.

So the biggest barrier for any existing or potential competitor is achieving two-way flows—meaning they need to acquire customers all over the world. Without that global presence, they'll need to rely on one or more third parties—essentially introducing intermediaries. And just like with the SWIFT network of correspondent banks, intermediaries take a cut, adding to the cost of cross-border transfers.

Now, there are ways other fintechs have found to make things more efficient than traditional correspondent banking. But I've never come across anything as lean and unique as what Wise has built. And after countless hours of research and deliberation, I personally can't think of a more efficient infrastructure than one that avoids intermediaries and one that avoids money actually crossing borders altogether.

The closest I've seen to what Wise has is the process that Dlocal—a Uruguay-based fintech—has implemented with some of its financial institution partners that specialize in remittances. In this setup, these remittance businesses facilitate cross-border transfers to Latin American countries through Dlocal. As I'll explain in a moment, there is netting involved, which makes the transfers efficient and relatively low-cost. However, since both the remittance company and Dlocal take a cut of each transaction, it's unlikely to be as cost-effective as Wise.

In very simple terms, Dlocal is a payment processor for large global corporations like Uber, Netflix, and many others. When an Uber customer pays for a ride in Brazil, for instance, that payment is processed by Dlocal, and the customer's Brazilian bank sends the payment in BRL to Dlocal. Naturally, Uber eventually wants those BRLs converted to dollars and transferred back to its headquarters in the US.

This is where Dlocal's remittance partners come in. These remittance players have many customers in the US who want to send money back home to family in Brazil. In other words, these customers have dollars and want to convert them to BRL to send that currency to recipients in Brazil.

But because these remittance players are integrated with Dlocal, rather than converting the dollars to BRL and moving money across borders, they simply send the dollars to Dlocal. Dlocal then routes those dollars to Uber and uses the BRL it already holds in Brazil—on behalf of Uber—to send to the intended recipient from the remittance partner's customer.

So, just like with Wise, the BRL is never converted to USD and no money crosses borders. A form of matching or netting of payment flows is taking place. However, while this solution is innovative and efficient, it still falls short of what Wise offers. There are still multiple players involved, not only adding layers of fees but also increasing operational complexity.

My point with this example is that, even with clever integrations like Dlocal's, they will never be more efficient than a setup where only one player is involved. And the only way to have just one player involved is by having access to payment flows in both directions for each currency pair or payment rail. That's the only way to transfer money without it crossing borders and without needing intermediaries.

This is exactly what Wise has achieved—at least for the most important currency pairs—and it's steadily working toward doing the same for the remaining ones. These two-way flows are extremely difficult to build and represent a massive barrier for any current or future competitors.

Even if someone could obtain all the licenses and local payment integrations Wise has—which is already a remarkable feat—just imagine the time and resources it would take to acquire customers across the globe. And even then, to outcompete Wise, that competitor would need to operate at a comparable scale to Wise. But Wise already has a major head start and shows no signs of slowing down.

Setting aside how difficult it is to achieve, there are other reasons why meaningful two-way flows are unlikely for other players. Take remittance businesses, for example. By the nature of their business model, their flows tend to go in only one direction—typically from developed to developing economies. As a result, companies like Remitly will never be able to achieve the kind of two-way flows needed to enable netting without intermediaries.

Even when you consider large digital banks with a meaningful international presence—such as Revolut and Nubank—achieving two-way flows remains very difficult. In Wise's case, people are drawn to it specifically for cross-border transfers. Thanks to its unique positioning and focus, the customers it attracts over time are those with international payment needs. As a result, as Wise's customer base grows, its cross-border volume grows as well—and with it, its two-way flows expand too.

By contrast, the typical Revolut or Nubank customer is more local in nature and primarily uses their services for domestic banking needs. Sure, a decent portion appreciates that they offer cross-border capabilities, but that's not the main reason they're using them.

Additionally, these digital banks simply won't achieve the same level of customer flows in each country. Revolut might be extremely successful in Europe and the UK, but will it really become the largest digital bank in the US or Brazil? Both countries already have their own digital banking champions, making competition fierce. So, as Revolut expands internationally, it's unlikely to generate the same volume of transfer requests from European customers sending money to the US as it will from US customers sending money to Europe.

Just think about it—unlike Wise, their focus is spread across multiple products like credit cards, loans, and other banking services, all of which need to be tailored for each market. Customer preferences and regulatory requirements vary greatly between countries, and it's hard to imagine any one digital bank achieving equal success in every geography.

So even if Revolut manages to generate two-way flows between the US and the UK, they would likely be far more limited than what Wise can achieve. Customer demand on one side of an international route will almost always outweigh demand on the other, limiting any opportunity for netting or matching payment flows.

The other players worth noting are those that build cross-border infrastructure and, to put it simply, rent it out. This includes companies like Currencycloud and, to a lesser extent, Dlocal, as in the example we discussed earlier.

Take Currencycloud, for instance—it's largely thanks to this company that Revolut is able to facilitate cross-border transactions. Revolut isn't connected to all local payment systems or even to the SWIFT network in most payment rails like Wise is. Instead, it often relies on Currencycloud's infrastructure.

Maybe the best way to view Currencycloud is as a version of Wise Platform. Just as Wise Platform enables Monzo or Nubank to make international transfers, Currencycloud enables Revolut to do so—at least to a large extent.

But Currencycloud—and, to my knowledge, most other infrastructure players—don't really have any flows of their own. They offer the connections and routes through which payments can move, but it's up to their clients to generate any flows. In other words, Revolut might be able to move money like a local in various countries thanks to its integration with Currencycloud, but unless it actually holds money in those countries, it won't be able to make transfers.

So, with the exception of setups like the one we discussed with Dlocal, these infrastructure players won't help their clients achieve two-way flows. And even when they do, there's still an intermediary involved. As a result, it's very unlikely that their customers—like Revolut—will ever be as cost-efficient as Wise for cross-border transfers.

Given this reality, my bet is that Wise will retain its lowest-cost status for cross-border transfers for decades to come. Just as it has reduced cost over time in the past, it will continue to do so with more effectiveness than any other player. And because it plans to pass these savings on to customers over time, Wise's competitive advantage and leadership position seem pretty bulletproof to me.

The Synergistic Moat: App and Platform Feed Each Other

In addition to its innate ability to generate two-way flows, Wise also benefits from strong synergies across its business segments. In particular, Wise Platform gains a lot from the Wise app—its direct-to-consumer service—and the reverse is also true.

This is important to highlight because, to my knowledge, Wise is the only player in the space that offers both a direct-to-consumer platform and infrastructure-as-a-service at a large scale. While Currencycloud, Thunes, Abbeycross, Dlocal, and many others offer some form of infrastructure-as-a-service, they don't have a direct-to-consumer platform. Conversely, while Revolut, Nubank, Remitly, and several others offer a direct-to-consumer platform, they don't have an infrastructure business. In other words, they don't commercially license any meaningful part of their infrastructure to third parties. In fact, most of these players rely heavily on infrastructure providers in one way or another.

There are some exceptions to this, like Airwallex and Nium, but they operate at a much smaller scale—Airwallex, for example, only offers a direct-to-consumer platform for business customers, not individuals. Even so, Airwallex is probably the player most similar to Wise in this regard, but it falls short because, although it licenses out its infrastructure, its cross-border capabilities still rely on intermediaries.

The company claims to have built its own infrastructure, and in the sense that it doesn't rely heavily on just one or two infrastructure providers, that may be accurate. However, it still depends on third-party providers for key payout functions in several markets, including Latin America. Connecting the dots from my research, for example, I have strong reasons to believe Airwallex uses Dlocal for many of its Latin American payout needs.

Anyway, I don't want to digress too much. The point is that very few players—if any—offer this dual model at the scale and depth that Wise does. And Wise benefits from this setup in many synergistic ways that would be extremely difficult to replicate.

In other words, having the direct-to-consumer business makes Wise Platform more competitive than any other infrastructure provider out there, and at the same time, Wise Platform makes the direct-to-consumer business materially stronger as well. In fact, it's thanks to the direct-to-consumer business that Wise was originally able to generate meaningful two-way flows. And it's these two-way flows that allow Wise to offer a better experience to Wise Platform customers. They enable Wise to maintain local liquidity pools in most regions around the world at significant scale. And these liquidity pools are what allow Wise to process transfers on behalf of its Wise Platform partners before settlement even takes place.

In the Nubank example we discussed, Wise was able to transfer USD immediately after receiving the request from Nubank—which ultimately came from Nubank's customer—because it already held USD in the US. It didn't need Nubank's incoming BRL equivalent to complete the transfer. And the reason Wise had those USD in place was due to the funds it receives and holds through its direct-to-consumer business.

So without this business segment, this value-add to Wise Platform customers wouldn't be possible. And as we discussed, this is something most infrastructure players don't have. That said, the reverse is also now true. Wise Platform contributes to growing two-way flows, which in turn improves the direct-to-consumer business in a virtuous cycle.

To understand this more clearly, let's consider Shinhan Bank, a large South Korean bank that uses Wise Platform. I don't know this for a fact, but let's assume Wise's direct-to-consumer app doesn't have many South Korean users. In that case, Wise may not be receiving much WON—South Korea's currency. So, when it needs to make a payout in WON, it might have to purchase it in the FX market to complete the transfer.

But with Shinhan Bank as a Wise Platform partner, Wise might start receiving WON from settlement flows triggered by Shinhan's customers. For example, a Shinhan customer might want to convert WON to USD to send money to a friend in the US. The customer places the request via Shinhan, who then passes the USD payout request to Wise. Wise completes the USD transfer using its liquidity pool in the US. While it may not receive the corresponding WON from Shinhan that same day, it will get it within a few days during the settlement process.

These incoming WON flows from Shinhan's settlements can then be used by Wise to complete outbound transfers to South Korea. In other words, when a US customer—or any Wise user globally—wants to send money to a South Korean recipient in WON, Wise may be able to fulfill that request using the local currency inflows from its Shinhan Bank partnership, reducing reliance on FX markets.

The following bullet points provide a clearer breakdown of the example.

- In a normal scenario, Wise receives WON inflows when its South Korean app users send money abroad and fund those transfers in their local currency.
- Because this example assumes Wise has few South Korean app users, it doesn't generate significant WON inflows from its direct-to-consumer service.
- Consequently, if a U.S. customer—or any customer outside South Korea—requests to transfer WON to South Korea, Wise wouldn't have sufficient incoming WON flows to match that payout need.
- However, thanks to Wise Platform's partnership with Shinhan Bank, it receives WON inflows that can be used to fulfill the required payouts.
- Essentially, Shinhan's customers place foreign currency transfer

requests, which Wise fulfills in the payout currency in exchange for receiving the WON equivalent—plus its fee, of course.

The way to view this synergy from a more holistic perspective is that any effort that increases transfer volumes across a wider geographic reach naturally expands the two-way flows Wise has across more and more currency pair routes. Wise Platform plays a key role in this dynamic, feeding the virtuous cycle of growing two-way flows, which in turn allows Wise to eliminate intermediaries and minimize the need for money to cross borders. This reduces Wise's overall transfer costs, which helps attract more direct users. And the more direct users Wise has, the greater the value it can provide to Wise Platform customers—and so the cycle continues.

Given the importance of two-way flows, this is without a doubt the most critical synergy between the two business segments. But there are many other synergies, and while I'll refrain from listing them all for practicality, let me focus on another important one.

Wise's direct-to-consumer business provides validation for Wise Platform customers, helping the company make a stronger case than other infrastructure players. Beyond that, many of the insights and learnings gained from the consumer side are passed on to Wise Platform customers, adding further value.

For example, Wise has invested considerable time and resources in optimizing its app to make the user experience for cross-border transfers as smooth and intuitive as possible. It shares these best practices with its Wise Platform partners—something most infrastructure providers simply can't do because they lack direct experience with end users.

So when evaluating Wise's sustainable competitive advantage, this synergistic relationship between the two business segments stands out as a powerful barrier to entry. If replicating Wise's success in just one segment is already a significant challenge, imagine how much harder it would be for a competitor to build both segments and recreate this level of synergy.

Additional Barriers Worth Noting

As if the competitive advantages discussed thus far weren't enough, Wise benefits from several additional barriers to entry. In fact, because these are easier to grasp and explain, they're the ones most commonly cited by investment analysts. And to be fair, that makes sense—while they may be less critical than what we've already explored, each of them still represents a meaningful barrier on its own. And to avoid overextending myself, let me just briefly go over them.

Regulatory Reach and Deep Local Integrations

Wise currently holds around 70 licenses globally, has more than 90 integrations and partnerships with domestic banks, and—most importantly—has secured 8 direct connections to local payment networks. Obtaining this level of access takes significant effort, resources, and most crucially, time. And even with time, these licenses and integrations aren't simply handed out. In many jurisdictions, regulators are selective and demand the highest operational and compliance standards.

One standout example is Japan, where Wise became the first non-bank to be approved for direct access to Zengin, the country's domestic payment network. It took Wise years to secure this approval, and it would be extremely difficult for any competitor to achieve the same level of access.

Even if they eventually do, it will likely be years behind Wise—giving Wise the chance to capture market share in the meantime. And market share brings higher volume, which drives more two-way flows, fueling the powerful virtuous cycle that's very difficult to match.

This is just one example, but there are many others that highlight how far ahead Wise is in terms of regulatory reach. Each of these hurdles is difficult on its own—overcoming them collectively is a massive challenge for any competitor.

Wise's regulatory depth simply cannot be overstated. As of today, 46% of Wise's transactions occur on payment rails where it has direct connections. Specifically, these direct local integrations extend to the UK, Hungary, the European Union, Singapore, the Philippines, Australia, Brazil, and Japan.

Collectively, these countries or regions represent a population of roughly 1 billion people. And what this essentially means is that, through Wise, anyone can send money to recipients in these locations without any friction from any third parties. While local banking partners are still involved for account and settlement purposes, there are no intermediaries in the transfer path itself—resulting in faster and cheaper payments.

Scale-Driven Network Effects

As we discussed, having two-way flows across multiple global routes is critical to Wise's success. But it's not just about having two-way flows—it's about having them at a significant scale to maintain liquidity pools large enough to meet transfer demands from both direct users and Wise Platform customers. And this scale stems from a virtuous cycle that feeds itself and is extremely hard to replicate. As Wise processes more volume, it lowers its costs. As costs go down, it reduces fees. Lower fees attract more users, which in turn increases flows—and the cycle continues.

A Strategy That Deters Competition

Wise's clear cost advantage, coupled with its publicly stated strategy to reduce fees as it lowers costs, deters competition. Just think about it—who in their right mind would want to compete with Wise knowing they can only win by building a lower-cost infrastructure?

It would be a different story if Wise used its cost advantage to charge market rates and simply enjoy higher profit margins. In that case, a competitor might try to undercut Wise on fees, even with thin margins. But because Wise consistently reduces fees in line with cost reductions, any competitor trying to win on price would likely need to operate at a loss.

To make matters worse, the existence of Wise Platform removes much of the incentive to compete directly. If you're a bank, what makes more sense: tapping into Wise's infrastructure for your international payments or trying to build your own to compete?

Sure, to make money on international transfers, banks still need to add a mark-up to Wise's fees, which means they won't be the top choice for customers who frequently transact internationally. But do they really have a better alternative? Wise still makes them more competitive than relying on the traditional correspondent banking system.

Moving On: Laying the Groundwork for Valuation Analysis

Now that we know what Wise is and what its competitive advantages are, let's turn to the valuation analysis. To start, let's look at the company's most relevant financial information on the next page. Since Wise only went public in 2021, I can't show data prior to 2020—but six years should be more than enough to reach an appropriate conclusion.

Also, to avoid any confusion, note that Wise's fiscal year ends on March 31 rather than December 31 as is typical. So, for example, fiscal year 2025 represents the 12-month period from April 1, 2024, to March 31, 2025.

Relevant Financial Data for Wise Plc (Fiscal Year Ends March 31)							
GBP (£) in millions	2020	2021	2022	2023	2024	2025	
Relevant Income Statement Profitability Figures							
Fee Revenue	303	421	560	846	1,052	1,212	
Net Interest Income	-	-	(3)	118	360	433	
Total Revenue	**303**	**421**	**557**	**964**	**1,412**	**1,645**	
Net Income / Profits	15	31	33	114	355	417	
Adjustments							2020-25
Stock-based comp	24	37	43	58	73	59	Total
Adjusted Net Income	**39**	**68**	**75**	**172**	**427**	**476**	**1,257**
Relevant Cash Flow Figures							
Acquisitions	-	-	-	-	-	-	
Dividends	-	-	-	-	-	-	2020-25
Stock Repurchases	-	-	-	(10)	(70)	(71)	Total
Total Shareholder Return	**-**	**-**	**-**	**(10)**	**(70)**	**(71)**	**(151)**
Liquidity and Debt							
Corporate Cash	155	286	358	671	1,061	1,430	2020-25
Total Debt Balance	49	79	79	250	203	99	Change
Net Debt (Debt - Cash)	**(106)**	**(208)**	**(279)**	**(421)**	**(858)**	**(1,331)**	**(1,225)**

Source: Author's analysis based on Wise plc annual reports and interim filings. Totals may not match due to rounding.

Interpreting Wise's Financials

The first thing to note is that the company's cash flows—as represented by adjusted net income—have grown quite significantly over the analyzed period. While growth has leveled off somewhat, the compounded annual growth rate over the past five years is roughly 65%. In total, Wise has generated £1.26 billion in profitability between 2020 and 2025.

While Wise hasn't returned much money to shareholders—meaning it has retained most of its cash flows—it hasn't actually needed to reinvest any of it to achieve that growth. If you look at the company's net debt—or more accurately, its net cash—the balance grew from £106 million to £1.33 billion. Remember, don't get confused by the negative net debt figures shown above. Just as we discussed with Alphabet, the negative net debt numbers simply indicate that cash exceeds debt.

So, its net cash position increased by roughly £1.23 billion, which is nearly the same as the total cash profits it generated. In other words, while Wise retained its earnings, it didn't need to deploy much of them to support its growth. This tells you how capital-efficient the business model is. It requires very little incremental capital to keep growing, and so we can truly call Wise a growth business. It's not growing as a result of reinvesting and compounding but rather from its own business momentum.

Not surprisingly, Wise's unadjusted return on equity is around 35%. But this figure actually understates the return the company is generating relative to the capital that's truly been put to work in the business. If we remove its net cash balance from the company's equity, the return on equity becomes extraordinarily high—roughly 860%.

With all this in mind, let's now look at the hurdles Wise must overcome for its valuation to be justified. And because it's clearly a growth company, we'll use the standard growth sensitivity table we discussed in prior chapters. But before we do, let's look at the company's valuation and related metrics.

Adjusting for Cash in Valuation

At the time of this writing, Wise's market value is around £10.5 billion. However, the more appropriate valuation we need to base our inverse analysis on should exclude the company's net cash balance. I hadn't emphasized this adjustment in earlier examples for practical reasons and because it didn't materially impact those cases. But here, Wise's net cash balance accounts for nearly 13% of its market value, so it's significant enough that we can't ignore it.

When we do our inverse analysis, we're essentially asking how much cash the company needs to generate in the future for an investor to achieve a particular return—10% in our case. But if the company already holds a certain amount of cash, the burden on future cash generation is reduced. After all, that cash is already available today and can be used either for reinvestment or for distributions to shareholders. By already being on the company's balance sheet, the investor has effectively earned it the moment they buy into the company. So, not excluding that cash would unfairly inflate the amount the investor needs to earn from future performance.

That said, the valuation from which we need to determine our hurdles should really be £9.17 billion—£10.5 billion minus £1.33 billion in net cash.

Adjusting for Non-Recurring Interest Income

In theory, we should divide this valuation figure by the company's adjusted profits—since these serve as our proxy for cash flows—to arrive at a price-to-cash flow ratio. We would take £9.17 billion divided by £0.48 billion, which results in a roughly 19x price-to-cash flow ratio. The problem with this, however, is that much of the £0.48 billion in cash flow stems from interest income on customer funds, which is unlikely to be recurring over the long term.

As we discussed when reviewing Wise's business model, the company only intends to retain the first 1% of interest yield from customer funds, plus a small share—20%—of any excess. And in 2025, the actual yield retained was significantly higher than that 1%. In fact, approximately £0.28 billion of the company's profits came from net interest income above the 1% threshold. So, to be conservative, I don't believe this portion should be included in adjusted net income.

However, we can't just subtract the full £0.28 billion because the £0.48 billion includes a higher tax burden that comes along with this income. If we assume this interest income won't exist in the future, we should also assume that the tax cost associated with it will disappear as well. In other words, we need to adjust for the lower tax burden that would result from not having this interest income. Using the company's effective tax rate of 26% in 2025, the appropriate subtraction to apply would only be £0.21 billion.

So we subtract £0.21 billion from £0.48 billion, which gives us roughly £0.27 billion. This figure represents the portion of profits we can expect to grow on a more recurring basis, making it the more appropriate profit base to use.

Dividing the £9.17 billion valuation by this £0.27 billion, we arrive at a more conservative price-to-cash flow ratio of approximately 34x.

Where Wise Stands on Our Growth Hurdle Table

Now that we have our valuation, let's look at where Wise falls on our required growth sensitivity table. See the next page for easy reference. As always, I've highlighted the row that most closely matches Wise's current valuation.

Growth Required to achieve 10% Return assuming 10% Reinvestment Rate

P / CF	CF / P	\multicolumn{8}{c}{Length of Growth Period (Years)}
		5.0	7.5	10.0	12.5	15.0	17.5	20.0	25.0
200x	0.5%	83%	58%	41%	35%	29%	27%	24%	21%
100x	1.0%	59%	42%	31%	27%	23%	21%	19%	17%
67x	1.5%	46%	33%	25%	22%	19%	17%	16%	14%
50x	2.0%	37%	28%	21%	18%	16%	15%	14%	12%
40x	2.5%	31%	23%	18%	16%	14%	13%	12%	11%
33x	3.0%	26%	20%	15%	14%	12%	11%	11%	10%
29x	3.5%	21%	17%	13%	12%	11%	10%	9%	9%
25x	4.0%	18%	14%	11%	10%	9%	9%	8%	8%
22x	4.5%	15%	12%	10%	9%	8%	8%	7%	7%
20x	5.0%	12%	10%	8%	8%	7%	7%	6%	6%

As a reminder, the highlighted percentages essentially show the annual cash flow growth Wise would need to deliver under different growth period assumptions for an investor to achieve a 10% compounded return.

If we believe Wise only has 5 years of growth left before maturing, it would need to grow 26% annually during that time. If the growth period is 7.5 years, the required annual growth drops to 20%. For 10 years, it's 15%, and so on. In all these scenarios, the assumption is that once the company matures, its cash flows will grow at a consistent 3% rate for the remainder of our 40-year time horizon.

Assessing Wise's Market Share and Growth Potential

With this said, let's think about how long Wise can remain in a high-growth phase. In its fiscal year-end presentation dated June 5, 2025, Wise cited research from Edgar, Dunn & Company estimating that the total annual volume of cross-border transfers is around £32 trillion. This breaks down into £3 trillion transferred by individuals, £14 trillion by small and medium-sized businesses, and £15 trillion by large enterprises. Based on Wise's current annualized transfer volume of roughly £160 billion, the company holds only about 0.5% of total market share.

Because I don't want to fall into the trap of being precisely wrong, I won't even attempt to estimate the exact market share Wise will eventually capture. But no matter how you look at it, the company is barely scratching the surface and is clearly still in the early stages. Given the competitive advantages we discussed, I see no reason why Wise couldn't eventually capture 10% or even 20% of the total market—perhaps even more, depending on how the industry evolves.

To my knowledge, management hasn't publicly projected how much share they expect to gain either, but they frequently emphasize that they're just getting started and often speak about being on the path to moving trillions. And I fully agree.

So, because Wise could eventually move 20 to 40 times the volume it does today, I believe it easily has at least 15 years of growth ahead. In fact, I wouldn't be surprised if it ends up being 20 to 30 years. I truly view Wise as analogous to where Visa and Mastercard were 30 years ago—both of which continue to show solid growth even today.

A Conservative Scenario: What If Growth Lasts Just 15 Years?

To add another layer of caution, let's assume Wise reaches maturity 15 years from now. In that conservative scenario, its cash flows would need to grow at an annual rate of around 12% over that period. I do expect 1%–2% dilution over time, so—as we've discussed at length—this would raise the required growth rate to roughly 13%–14%.

While growth may not happen in a straight line, as no business grows perfectly linearly, this still feels like a very undemanding hurdle given Wise's current position and the strength of its competitive advantages.

Other Revenue Streams Add a Layer of Conservatism

Now, bear in mind that I've only discussed the company's addressable market in the context of just one of its revenue streams—fees from cross-border transfers. But remember, Wise also earns fees from debit card usage and generates interest income, both of which are also likely to grow meaningfully over time. On top of that, even though it's hard to predict, there's a good chance that Wise will identify new monetization avenues in the future.

The company had no debit card revenue 6–7 years ago and earned no interest income even just 4 years ago. I'm not saying we should count on future revenue streams that don't yet exist. They may never materialize. But the fact that it wouldn't be unusual if they did adds yet another layer of conservatism to my expectations.

A Conservative Case with Strong Upside Potential

So even using a conservative price-to-cash flow ratio, a similarly conservative growth period assumption, and ignoring parts of Wise's current and potential addressable market, the required growth to achieve a 10% compounded return remains very undemanding.

This creates a meaningful margin of safety. Even if the company doesn't grow as much or for as long as I believe it can, there's still a strong chance I'll achieve that 10% return. And if my expectations are right, the return could end up being significantly higher.

Reinvestment Rate: The One Assumption That Is Only Mildly Conservative

We can't forget that our sensitivity table is conservative in yet another way. Specifically, always keep in mind that it assumes a 10% reinvestment rate. And, based on the company's return on equity, one could argue that this is excessively conservative. And if that's the case, then yet another layer of margin of safety is built into our overall conclusion that the current valuation is undemanding.

That said, I'd caution against jumping to this conclusion too quickly. Wise's business model is so capital efficient that it likely won't have many opportunities to reinvest its profits internally. Don't get me wrong—it will definitely reinvest in the form of forgone profits through fee reductions, as we discussed, and likely also through increased marketing spend. But both of these investments are already accounted for in the adjusted profit figures we're using in our analysis.

What Wise is unlikely to be able to do is reinvest a meaningful portion of what's available in excess of these profit-reducing investments—that is, after those types of investments have already been made.

In that sense, it's in a similar situation to what we discussed with Palantir. It's great that Wise is a growth company, but it's not ideal that the growing cash flows can't be easily reinvested in internally generated initiatives.

Instead, most of those profits will likely be distributed to shareholders via dividends—effectively passing the reinvestment burden to the investor—or used for share repurchases. And even if management proves to approach buybacks responsibly—certainly what I expect—those repurchases will still likely be done at a premium. So while the 10% reinvestment rate assumption in our sensitivity table might seem overly conservative at first glance, I'd consider it only mildly so.

This is also why I haven't—and won't—apply the first approach for valuing high-growth businesses that we discussed in Chapter 8. In other words, I won't be using the sensitivity table that explores different reinvestment rate scenarios. I simply don't see the need to explore the impact of higher reinvestment rates when I don't consider those scenarios to be conservative for Wise.

Besides, the margin of safety already seems large enough using the second approach—the one we just applied—that adding the first would feel like overkill. As we've discussed, in most situations I recommend using both approaches, but in this particular case, it just isn't necessary.

Wrapping Up: Why Wise Tops My List

So to conclude, based on the current universe of investment opportunities available to me, Wise is my favorite investment at the time of this writing. Despite the unfortunate reality that a large portion of its cash flows likely won't be reinvested in internally generated initiatives, the hurdles implied by its current valuation remain very undemanding. I believe this is largely due to the sheer size of its total addressable market and the strength of the competitive advantages we've discussed.

At this stage, I'm simply grateful that the market hasn't yet fully recognized what Wise truly is or what makes it so unique. In all likelihood, it still sees Wise as just another fintech or digital bank—and because that space is highly competitive, the company's value is being unfairly discounted out of fear.

Of course, I can only speculate as to why the market doesn't see what I see. But regardless of the reason, I truly hope this walkthrough has shown you that valuing a business goes far beyond valuation theory. That theory is certainly a necessary foundation—and I hope I've given you the right framework and tools in this book—but successful investing requires much more than that. You have to dig deep into the business itself, and I hope this case study has helped provide a clear and useful example of how that should be done.

Made in the USA
Monee, IL
02 August 2025